REMEMBER ME TO TOM

EDWINA DAKIN WILLIAMS

As told to LUCY FREEMAN

Remember Me To Tom

G. P. Putnam's Sons   NEW YORK

© *1963 BY EDWINA DAKIN WILLIAMS, WALTER
DAKIN WILLIAMS, and LUCY FREEMAN*

The poem on page 18 is from *In the Winter of Cities,* © 1956
by Tennessee Williams; the paragraph on page 78 is from
"The Resemblance Between a Violin Case and a Coffin,"
published in the book *Hard Candy,* copyright 1954 by
Tennessee Williams; the lines on page 147 are from *The
Glass Menagerie,* copyright 1945 by Tennessee Williams; the
excerpt on pages 253-254 are from "The Past, Present, and
Perhaps"—Introduction to *Orpheus Descending & Battle of
Angels,* © 1958 by Tennessee Williams. All reprinted by
permission of New Directions, Publishers.

The three "Sonnets for the Spring," pages 76-77, were published by the Wednesday Club in *An Anthology of Honor
Poems,* 1950.

Library of Congress Catalog Card Number: 63-7760

MANUFACTURED IN THE UNITED STATES OF AMERICA

Second Impression

To "Grand"

Contents

Illustrations will be found following p. 128.

REMEMBER ME TO TOM

1.

"Diggin' to de Debbil"

IT was just before curtain time at the opening of *The Night of the Iguana*. I was sitting in the fourth row center with Mr. Lewin Wright Croft, father-in-law of my younger son Dakin.

Mr. Croft was getting great delight out of attending his first Broadway premiere and being introduced to some of Tom's friends, including Helen Hayes, Lillian Gish and Carson McCullers, who came over to wish us well.

"Where's Tom?" I asked Dakin, who was sitting near us with Joyce, his wife.

"He's pacing up and down somewhere," said Dakin.

I hadn't seen Tom all evening. I know he is always nervous opening night, the desperate hours during which he finds out if he has reached the hearts of drama critics and public. He suffers over the premiere of each play as though it were the first.

Mr. Croft and I talked together excitedly until we were *"sh-shhed"* by those around us as the lights slowly dimmed. The audience at Tom's plays demands silence, as though it wishes a complete break between the world of worn plush seats and first-night finery and the world of magic about to unfold before its eyes.

We watched Tom cast another dramatic spell as he led us eloquently into the lives of four lonely people at the Costa Verde Hotel near Acapulco—a sensual widowed landlady, a ninety-seven-year-old poet, his spinster granddaughter, and a minister barred from the pulpit for sexual misbehavior. Not as violent as some of Tom's other plays, to me *Iguana* was gripping and one of the most poetic.

When the curtain fell I looked around the theatre but still no Tom. I did not see him that night or the next day before I returned to Clayton. But I did not worry because I read the reviews and knew *Iguana* was safely launched, as indeed it proved to be, winning the coveted New York Drama Critics' Circle Award a few months later.

As I left New York, a city I visit only for Tom's openings, I found myself thinking of the torment he must have suffered the night before and all those first nights that mean life or death to a playwright, first nights that for Tom had not always ended in triumph but which finally exploded in fame and fortune.

The fame stems from the creation of characters now part of America's fantasy. Shocking and controversial though they may be, Tom's people breathe life. Catharine Holly in *Suddenly Last Summer,* threatened with lobotomy, the death of the mind, so she will not reveal the truth about her cousin who was torn apart and then eaten alive by the starving children he sexually exploited. Chance Wayne in *Sweet Bird of Youth,* castrated by the jealous father of a girl to whom he had given a venereal disease. Valentine Xavier, the young wanderer of *Orpheus Descending,* who seeks to escape loneliness through love only to be burned alive by a blowtorch. Blanche DuBois in *A Streetcar Named Desire,* raped by her brother-in-law before she goes insane. Elena and her brother, who indulge in a love affair, then die, in *The Purification,* a play produced off-Broadway and on television.

12

Murder, cannibalism, castration, madness, incest, rape, adultery, nymphomania, homosexuality. There exists no savage act about which my son has not written. Yet, his plays are filled with beauty. And they offer truth, truth that many of us do not like to face.

A local drama critic, Myles Standish of the St. Louis *Post Dispatch*, called me up after I had seen a preview of the movie version of *Suddenly Last Summer*.

"What do you think of your son's new play, Mrs. Williams?" he asked. "Were you shocked?"

"Was I supposed to be?" I replied.

Even if I had been, I would not have admitted it.

Brooks Atkinson is one critic who gets Tom's message. He once wrote that Tom possessed "a terrifying knowledge of the secrets of the mind." Another time he said Tom was "a poetic writer who could look through the polite surfaces of life into the pain that froze the hearts of lonely people." And again, "Mr. Williams has made art out of malignance and maleficence."

What do people expect Tom to write—inane comedy? As the plane jetted through the darkness toward St. Louis after the opening of *Iguana*, I recalled a day when he was about two years old and we were living with my parents in Columbus, Mississippi. Our home was the rectory which sat in the shadow of massive, elegant St. Paul's Church where Father was minister.

It was a hot summer day and I looked out of the window to make sure Tom was all right as he played in a yard dotted with rocks. There he was, with his little spade, digging madly away amidst the rocks. Perspiration dripped down his chubby face and his little golden curls clung damp to his head.

"What are you doing, Tom?" I called out, wondering why all this great labor under the hot sun.

"I'm diggin' to de debbil," he explained as he doggedly shoveled out another spadeful of dirt.

Ozzie, his colored nurse, had probably been telling him stories in which the devil starred, and Tom, no doubt, had asked where the devil lived. Ozzie, thereupon, told him in the middle of the

13

earth where it was dark and deep and Tom set out, the first chance he had, to find the devil's lair.

You might say Tom went on "diggin' to de debbil" the rest of his life, trying to discover where the devil lives inside all of us. Through his searching words, he turned the tragedy in his life to art. He once said he wrote to escape madness. His sister, Rose, was not as fortunate, for she became forever lost in mental illness, not strong enough to combat the horror she felt threatening her life.

As the plane whirred on, its motors drummed me into a reverie of other places, other premieres. There was the heartbreak of *Battle of Angels*, Tom's first important play, which closed after a tumultuous tryout in Boston where it was described as "dirty" and the City Council censored certain scenes. Then there was what I call "the night of the miracle" at the Civic Theatre in Chicago when *The Glass Menagerie* opened, an icy, gale-swept night that nearly hurled us into Lake Michigan as we fought our way on foot to the theatre but which, instead, blew Tom right to Broadway.

This was Tom's first triumph and it came at a moment he desperately needed it. He had struggled through years of misery, both within himself and in his work. If ever a man deserves praise for a dauntless attack on life, it is Tom. He allowed nothing to defeat him, not a destructive father, not crippling illness, not failure of a first play.

I have always kept quiet about the early years for my children's sake. But because so many misunderstand both Tom and me, I feel it's time to tell the truth, that the truth is not amiss. I couldn't hurt Rose any more, for she lives in a world where she remembers only the good things. Tom and Dakin are so successful in their own right, nothing could harm them.

Rehashing old memories is not pleasant, especially for me because I have always liked to forget the unpleasant. But if one is going to write an autobiography, not fiction, one has to permit memories, buried because they were painful, to rise to the surface. I have done the best I could to tell the truth as I saw it. The truth of our lives can only emerge as tribute to Tom.

14

2.

"Home Is Where You Hang Your Childhood"

WHERE did it start with Tom, this search into the soul, this preoccupation with poetry and primitive feeling? He was exceptionally observant as a child. Other children would pick a flower, then carelessly throw it away, but Tom would stand peering into the heart of the flower as though trying to discover the secret of its life.

One of my favorite photographs, enlarged and hanging on the wall of my bedroom, shows Tom when he was about a year and a half, with his back to the camera, wearing a blue playsuit, his golden ringlets curling about his head. He clutches in his hand a blue morning glory as he studies it intently.

As a baby, even, he seemed to be carefully observing the world and drawing his own private conclusions. One evening when I was all dressed up and going out, Tom, then barely able to talk, asked his grandmother, "Is my mother a lung lady?"

15

My mother, who could speak his language, replied, "No, she's not a young lady."

"Well, if she's not a lung lady, she must be a dwarf lady," he said. I am not very tall.

As Tom grew older, this propensity for studying people increased. We would be walking along the street when suddenly he would stop and stare at someone, as though transfixed. Rose would come home from a walk with him and plead, "Mother, you've got to do something about Tom. He stopped on the street today to look at a lady and then he laughed out loud." Something about the woman must have struck Tom as absurd, for he would always laugh at the ludicrous. Later he learned to control the laughter, but not the intent gaze.

Tom (I think of him as Tom and speak of him as Tom, except to those who know him only as Tennessee) was probably born with his eyes open wide at a world that fascinated him, although I have no way of proving this. But I can prove, contrary to every story I have ever seen published about his birth, that it did not take place in the rectory of St. Paul's Church in Columbus, Mississippi, but in a hospital built by my doctor. We barely made it to that little hospital on Palm Sunday morning, March 26, 1911.

I had been living with my mother and father since the birth of my first child, Rose, two years before. My husband, Cornelius Coffin Williams, called C. C. by his friends and business associates, had lost his position with the telephone company as manager of several small exchanges in Gulfport, Mississippi, where we lived when we were first married. He never told me why and I didn't inquire too closely.

My husband started a new kind of work for him, selling men's clothing on the road, which meant a lot of traveling. He considered my parents' house as headquarters, visiting us about every two weeks. Thus, Tom's earliest home was the rectory, the rocky yard in the rear, his first playground.

When Tom was born, Rose resented the new baby heartily, as natural with every child on earth. At first she wouldn't come any nearer to me than the bedroom door; she would just stand there and stare at me reproachfully as though to say, "How could you do this to me?"

My father would try to comfort her. He would say, "Rose, I hear you've got a new little baby brother."

"Ess," she'd admit regretfully.

"What'll you take for him?" asked Father. "Will you take a pony for him?"

She brightened up. "Ess. I take a pony."

Cornelius, too, tried to reassure her. He would tell her, "We don't think much of that new baby, do we? He's not good for much," and her long, auburn curls would fly up and down in agreement.

She would turn to her grandfather and say, "Let's shoo him away, Grandfads," a name of endearment she used always with him. Mother was "Grand" to all my children.

Rose would raise her Teddy bear and threaten, "I'll make my bear turn somersaults at him." When wound up, the bear would spin in the air and Rose would scream in fright. She was hoping the terrifying, twisting Teddy bear would scare Tom to death and thus she would be rid of the unwelcome little monster.

But as they grew up, the two became exceedingly close, drawn together by many bonds. Rose is supposed to be the model for Laura, the pathetically shy sister of *The Glass Menagerie.* Perhaps she was; only Tom knows how much of Laura is Rose and how much his imaginative portrait of a sister he never knew. But, unlike Laura, Rose was never a shy child, for she was the ringleader in games, and very spirited; perhaps too spirited at times as far as her father was concerned.

Rose resembled a little queen in her beauty of face, framed by curls that glinted bronze, hair so curly she never needed a permanent, nor did she have one until she was committed to a mental hospital and they frizzed her hair all up because they claimed going to the beauty shop was good for her morale. I cried when I saw what they had done to her lovely hair. She had blue eyes, as did our whole family. Tom's were much bluer as a boy; they seem more gray now.

Rose was always faster than Tom in acquiring knowledge in

the little classes I conducted at home. Sometimes we would hear her scream and Tom would be pulling her hair angrily and saying, "She's too proud of herself." He wrote a poem about his feelings years later.

> My sister was quicker at every-
> thing than I.
> At five she could say the multipli-
> cation tables
> with barely a pause for breath,
> while I was employed
> With frames of colored beads in
> Kindy Garden.

That "Kindy Garden" proved quite an experience for both Tom and me. He was only three years old, younger than most of the other children when I took him to a kindergarten in Nashville, where we lived for a while. He enjoyed himself sculpting in clay, usually forming elephants, as long as I stayed with him. The moment I left the room, he would throw himself on the floor and scream, refusing to stop despite all bribery. I had to sit next to him the entire time; fortunately the session lasted only half a day.

I had always enjoyed reading for my own pleasure and I read a lot to Rose and Tom, first fairy tales and all the children's books, then Shakespeare, Dickens, Thackeray and even magazines of the day. Tom especially liked the *Literary Digest,* whose name he could not pronounce—he called it the "Little-ary Digest." He would also command me to read from what he called "The Commershiakel Appeal," committing verbal mayhem on the title of this Memphis newspaper.

Even when he was little he didn't like his name, so I'm not surprised he later changed it. One evening I was reading nursery rhymes (they must have included "Tom, Tom, the Piper's Son," "Little Tommy Tucker" and "Little Tommy Tittlemouse") when I noticed my son sitting with his underlip stuck out, a characteristic pose when annoyed.

"What's wrong, Tom?" I asked.

"Evvy'body's named Tom," he said aggrievedly. The name had no distinction to him, even then.

When I was busy helping Father with church activities, singing in the choir or serving at ice cream festivals to raise money, Ozzie would play with the children as if she were one of them. Tom absorbed many of his early ideas from Ozzie, I am sure. In her own style, she would reel off stories which sounded very much like the tales of Joel Chandler Harris' hero, Uncle Remus, although she could not read or write and I wondered where she had learned of Br'er Rabbit and Tar Baby.

I came across a scrap of paper on which Tom as a young man had written a few sentences about his early life.

> Before I was eight my life was completely unshadowed by fear. I lived in a small Mississippi town. My mother and my sister and I lived with our grandparents while my father travelled around the state, selling clothing to men. My sister and I were gloriously happy. We sailed paper boats in wash-tubs of water, cut lovely colored paper-dolls out of huge mail-order catalogs, kept two white rabbits under the back porch, baked mud pies in the sun upon the front walk, climbed up and slid down the big wood pile, collected from neighboring alleys and trash-piles bits of colored glass that were diamonds and rubies and sapphires and emeralds. And in the evenings, when the white moonlight streamed over our bed, before we were asleep, our Negro nurse Ozzie, as warm and black as a moonless Mississippi night, would lean above our bed, telling in a low, rich voice her amazing tales about foxes and bears and rabbits and wolves that behaved like human beings.

Tom has recalled that Ozzie would often tell stories that frightened him. "We would sit under the trees while she read us some ghost stories and made up others," he remembers. "And then I would go home at nap time and make up more stories while I was going to sleep." This was when Ozzie took Rose and Tom to Centennial Park in Nashville, after I taught her to read and write.

19

For a while I thought Tom would end by talking like Ozzie, who spoke with a plantation dialect. We would hear her reminding him at mealtimes, carrying out my instructions that the children chew their food thoroughly, "Chaw, honey, chaw!" As she gave him a bath, he would chase little celluloid fishes around the tub, calling out excitedly, "I kotch him, Ozzie. See? I kotch him." I was afraid that child was never going to speak proper English.

But eventually he gave up imitating her, just as he gave up playing with dolls. Santa Claus had been in the habit of leaving Tom a doll every Christmas, just as he did Rose, placing it in the corner of the room set aside for Tom's gifts. When he was four, he became interested in a little girl in the neighborhood, and Christmas morning of that year, he walked over and said seriously, "Santa Claus made a mistake, Mother. He left a doll in my corner." He hated to relinquish that doll. As he reluctantly handed it to me, he turned his head away.

In addition to listening to stories, Tom also liked to tell them. When the band of small boys and girls who usually filled our back yard tired of racing around, Tom would entertain them by making up tales as they gathered around him to rest on the benches.

We went away one summer to a resort in North Carolina because of Mother's health, when Tom was three. To amuse ourselves, we would sit on the floor in front of the fire at night and tell stories. One evening, a woman turned to Tom and said, "Now it's your turn to tell a story."

To my surprise, for Tom was quite shy and would often hide behind my skirts when someone tried to talk to him, he started off on a story of getting lost in the woods where he was chased by one wild animal after another. Suddenly he stopped. He closed his eyes and said, "It's getting scarier and scarier. It's just getting so scary, I'm scared myself."

Tom adored his grandfather. He was always running along at Father's heels when he paid calls on sick parishioners, part of his duties. I would watch out the window as they walked away from the rectory, my father who, although not tall, gave the impression of height because he carried himself so erectly, and the little boy trying to keep up with him, proud that his grandfather would allow him to be company.

I always thought of Tom as a small pitcher with big ears; he would sit perfectly quiet never saying a word, listening with every sinew. I don't imagine he missed a trick on these calls. He has said, "I remember my grandfather's visits to deathbeds." I don't think many of Father's parishioners actually died, although Tom may have imagined they were dying, or one death may have stood for many in his mind.

Tom has recalled a lady named Laura Young they visited, who, he said, loved him and he, in turn, adored her. But there was something wrong with her, "there was a shadow upon her," and for that reason, they called on her more than anyone else. Then, one day they stopped going there and Tom says he learned the lady was dead. She was the inspiration for the heroine in his first professionally produced play, *Battle of Angels,* according to Tom.

To Tom, as to all children, seeing an adult die would have been a fearful experience. To Rose, it would have been unbearable. Rose always dramatized everything that happened to her; a friend of mine from Columbus would love to visit us just to listen to Rose's tall tales.

One day she and Rose were talking confidentially in our back yard when Rose suddenly announced, "I have to go in now because my grandmother makes me do all the hard work."

Chuckling at the idea of this beautiful six-year-old forced into slave labor by the minister's wife, my friend asked, "What does she make you do?"

"She makes me wash and iron all of my grandfather's shirts," said Rose. This was, of course, a complete yarn, for she wasn't allowed near washing board or iron. This overdramatization of details, this distortion of reality, was to prove disastrous to Rose in later life.

Rose always caught every illness Tom had and, believe me, that meant every one listed in the medical books. But they reacted very differently to sickness. The doctor would ask Tom

21

how he felt and, no matter how ill he might be, Tom would say, "I'm fine, Doctor."

But Rose, always the actress, would groan, "I'm dying, Doctor! Do something. I'm dying!"

One time she embarrassed me slightly at a party where there was a long delay in the serving of refreshments. "But Mother, where's the party?" she kept asking. She refused to take part in the games. Finally, to my relief, the ice cream and cake were hauled in, and Rose exclaimed exultantly, "Oh, *there's* the party!" Then she was willing to play games.

There was great difference in their dispositions. Rose showed plenty of temper and temperament while Tom was usually quiet and calm and still is, in spite of the violence in his plays. I think his salvation was that he could express in words the conflicts he saw and felt around him.

Very seldom did Tom do anything dramatic. He indulged himself once when he was about three. We were expecting a first visit from Aunt Ella, one of Cornelius' two sisters, who lived in Knoxville. She had never seen Tom but had heard much about her first and only nephew, particularly his golden curls and particularly an especially provocative one that fell in a ringlet over his forehead. We had been talking at great length about her impending visit and how much she would enjoy seeing her little golden-haired nephew for the first time.

Tom evidently had been brooding about that cowlick and decided the new aunt was not going to make a fuss over it if he could help it. He waited for his moment of action. It came when Ozzie, who was giving him a bath just before Aunt Ella's arrival, left the room to get a towel. Tom jumped out of the tub, ran into the bedroom, seized a pair of scissors from the bureau and whacked off the offending curl.

The first three years of Tom's life we lived in Columbus, then moved to Nashville for about a year where Father became rector of the Church of the Advent. Tom remembers picking little yellow flowers in Centennial Park, and crying when I left him at kindergarten. He also recalls a violent thunderstorm that tore the awning off the porch.

22

I remember that thunderstorm, too. Ozzie and I raced around the house trying to make it safe against the storm. I knew Tom was deathly afraid of thunder and lightning and so, when I saw him running back and forth from the yard into the house, all the while talking to himself, I stopped for a moment and listened.

He was pleading, "Please, God. Wait. Just wait a minute, God, until I get all my toys in."

When we left Nashville, we lived for a few months in Canton, then moved to Clarksdale, Mississippi, a plantation region eighty miles south of Memphis, where Father became rector of St. George's Church. He was to remain there thirteen years, a record for Father who did not believe in staying with any one parish too long. He had a reputation for building up run-down parishes and the bishop would often ask him to take over parishes in a sorry state and strengthen them. Under Father, the Episcopalians began to thrive in the community.

Clarksdale was quite different in spirit from Columbus, Tom's earliest home. Columbus considered itself far more cultured and sophisticated than the newer, more rural town of Clarksdale, looking down its nose at the younger settlement across the state.

Clarksdale became the scene of near-tragedy for Tom. When he was five years old, he almost died, as many children actually did in those days of epidemics which doctors did not know how to fight. There were no drugs, few hospitals, and a scarcity of pediatricians.

Tom came down with diphtheria. Today he would have been taken to a hospital, but then all we could do was to care for him as best we could at home. I slept with him for nine nights, following the doctor's direction to keep his throat packed in ice, changing the ice all night, so he would not choke to death. On the ninth day I looked down his throat and noticed that his tonsils, which had become enlarged by the illness, had completely disappeared.

I called the doctor in a panic. He came over, examined Tom

23

and said he must have swallowed the tonsils. I have spoken to several doctors who say this could have happened, that some reaction of the diphtheria might have loosened the tonsils, and no matter how unscientific this may sound, I have always believed it.

When his fever returned to normal, I allowed Tom to get up. Then I noticed that, instead of walking, he would sit on a little stool and push himself around the room to reach his toys. There was evidently something wrong with his legs. Again I called the doctor. He said the diphtheria had affected Tom's kidneys and paralyzed his legs; he called it Bright's disease. It was my thought that perhaps the poison from the infected tonsils had damaged Tom's system.

For the better part of two years Tom could not use his legs. He was unable to play outdoors with the other children. We invented all sorts of indoor games and I'd make up stories which I hoped held enough adventure to be interesting. It was sad to see this handsome, husky little fellow suddenly stricken helpless, unable to walk across the room.

Tom had always been a very active child. Mothers would come to the house complaining he had beaten up their sons, little boys twice his size. He did not strike girls, although he might chase them into a patch of cockleburs as he did little Mary Louise, whose mother marched her over indignantly to show me her daughter's long tresses tangled into a web by cockleburs.

That disease was a fearful thing. It took all the belligerency out of Tom. I bought him a toy called an Irish Mail which permitted him to steer himself around the room without putting pressure on his legs. Gradually his legs became stronger and by the end of the two years he could use them, after learning how all over again. I would watch as he painfully practiced walking up and down the sidewalk outside our house.

For the two years of his illness Tom was thrown back on his own resources, for he could not play with other children. But at least he had lived, unlike the little boy down the street who died because he was not kept on the correct diet during the diphtheria attack. The doctor said I had saved Tom's life by

24

giving him my entire attention during those critical first nine days. During this time Mother looked after Rose who, of course, had followed her brother and caught diphtheria, only very mildly.

Cornelius was not around a lot those years, when he turned from selling men's clothing to selling shoes. He never paid much attention to the children, anyhow; my father was more like a father to them. One summer, when we vacationed in Tennessee, I did not see my husband at all. Occasionally, he would pick me up at the rectory and we would drive off in his car for the weekend. I remember the ancient Ford, in which he carried his shoe samples, spinning around in one circle of mud after another in this macadamless world of Mississippi mud roads.

The important people in Tom's early life were his grandparents, his sister, Ozzie and myself. Ozzie, incidentally, disappeared forever one day when Tom was six. He has said she left because he hurt her feelings by calling her a "nigger," but I doubt this is true. Tom loved Ozzie and I'm sure she felt his love. I think the truth, rather, is that she came to some harm.

Each summer Ozzie would visit her family who lived on a plantation. The fall that Tom caught diphtheria, she did not return to us (perhaps he blames his illness for her departure) and we wondered what had happened for we knew she was very attached to us. She had come to us clad in rags and we clothed her, gave her a good salary, taught her to read and write. It was not like Ozzie to leave without a reason.

Mother finally wrote to her, asking what had happened. Several months later Ozzie appeared, eyes bloodshot, looking thin and acting very nervous. She told us that her brothers had forced her to work in the cotton fields.

"Did you come back after you got my letter?" Mother asked.

"I didn't get a letter," she said. "I came back on my own."

The following fall she did not return at all. I think she met with foul play at the hands of her brutal brothers, for she had looked deathly ill when she showed up the year before. Whatever Ozzie's fate, she can feel, if she is alive, that she exerted

25

some influence on Tom's life because he was so devoted to her, his little mind devouring the stories she would tell.

Just as Tom was recovering from his illness, Cornelius was promoted. He was made sales manager for the Friedman-Shelby branch of the International Shoe Company. This meant he no longer would sell shoes on the road but would have an important desk job. It also meant we had to move to St. Louis, the branch headquarters.

It meant, too, that for the first time in our marriage, Cornelius and I would be setting up a home for the children. It was Tom who said, "Home is where you hang your childhood."

Tom once wrote of those early years:

> My grandfather was a clergyman. It was really he that supported us, although my father must have made good money on the road. My grandfather was a kind man. He was soft spoken and gentle. Somehow he created about the whole house an atmosphere of sweetness and light. Every one in the house seemed to be under his spell. It was a spell of perfect peace. There were no angry scenes, no hard words spoken. Even Ozzie, a few generations out of the jungle, had succumbed to the spell. She never lost patience with us when we teased her in a childish way. Not even when we imitated the children next door and called her, with unwitting cruelty, a big black nigger!
>
> Only on those occasional week-ends when my father visited the house were things different. Then the spell of perfect peace was broken. A loud voice was heard, and heavy footsteps. Doors were slammed. Furniture was kicked and banged ...
>
> Often the voice of my father was jovial or boisterous. But sometimes it was harsh. And sometimes it sounded like thunder.
>
> He was a big man. Beside the slight, gentle figure of my grandfather, he looked awfully big. And it was not a benign bigness. You wanted to shrink away from it, to hide yourself.

Nevertheless, until the time we moved to St. Louis, I believe his childhood was a fairly happy one.

26

3.

"Nine Years in Limbo"

WE arrived in St. Louis in the heat of July and St. Louis in summer can be as torrid as the tropics. I left Rose with my parents while I looked for a place to live. It was wartime, 1918, and the city was bulging at its housing seams. I, too, was bulging slightly, carrying my third child.

The first thing that happened to me, auspicious start, was to come down with the mumps which Tom generously gave me. We stayed at a fashionable boardinghouse until I recovered. Then I searched the newspapers for advertisements of apartments near my husband's place of business. There just weren't any available.

After a few days I found one advertisement stipulating that whoever rented the apartment also had to buy the furniture. That suited me, for the thought of shopping for furniture in that heat sent terror through my soul.

I walked into the advertised apartment on the ground floor of a building on Westminster Place, then one of the most exclusive residential districts in the city. A young man was sitting dejectedly in the midst of fine furniture and the wreck of a marriage. He explained his wife and he were separating and he wished to get rid of furniture and lease. I liked his taste and bought the furnishings. I still have the chaise longue and an old clock in my bedroom.

We now had a home. This was the apartment Tom supposedly used as a model for *The Glass Menagerie*. It was a gloomy place, that I admit, for it was so dark we had to leave the lights on most of the day, but it was no tenement. Rose's bedroom boasted white furniture, and I added pink curtains. No doubt, to an eight-year-old boy suddenly cut off from the spaciousness of a house and garden, the apartment loomed grim. It was long and narrow, six rooms and a bath, and Tom said he was allotted the worst room, a tiny bedroom off a side hall, but at least he had a room of his own.

He has recalled the sight of bloody remains of cats in the alley outside Rose's window but I never saw any cat corpses lying about. There were the usual dog-and-cat fights but they generally ended in a tie. Memory can be a false thing, especially when you look back at childhood, for sometimes you see only what you want to see, remembering what you wished, rather than what happened.

After we were in St. Louis five months, Dakin was born. I nursed him, as I did all the children, for as long as I could. At the end of two or three months, I would have trouble giving milk and then would supplement the nursing with bottles until gradually I stopped the nursing entirely.

Following Dakin's birth, I came down with influenza which developed into tuberculosis. Cornelius had to go West at this time for the shoe company so they decided to send me along, too, to recuperate, and Mother came to St. Louis to take care of the children while I was away.

A large city is not hospitable to newcomers, unlike a village or town. Rose and Tom did not like St. Louis from the moment they set foot in it. As the minister's grandchildren, they enjoyed the run of Columbus, Nashville, Canton and Clarksdale, but here they were transplanted to the turmoil of a city where no one knew or cared who they were. They had lost old childhood friends and it was difficult to find new ones. They grew even closer, allies in an alien world.

Rose's reaction to her new little brother was quite different from that to her first one. Now a young lady of ten, she was ecstatic over Dakin, whom she has always adored. And Tom shared this devotion.

Children, however, can be very cruel to each other, especially to strangers. The boys at the Eugene Field Public School made fun of Tom's Southern accent and manners. They taunted him as "sissy" because he would not take part in their games—I am sure he never told them that less than a year before, his legs had been paralyzed and he could not even walk, much less run.

After we had been in St. Louis only a short time, one afternoon Tom came home with his ankles black and blue.

"What happened, Tom?" I asked, examining the bruises.

He explained he had been sitting on a bench watching while other boys played a game, and as each boy walked by the bench, he would give Tom a kick on the ankle.

It was not only children who resented him. One day he walked into the house and announced, "I'm not going back to school, Mother."

"Why, Tom?" I asked.

He had been slow in answering a question, perhaps not understanding a Northern accent, and the teacher had remarked scornfully, "Anybody can tell you're from the South—you're as slow as January molasses."

"I'm not going back, Mother," Tom repeated with emphasis.

"You certainly *are* going back," I said, with just as much emphasis.

I knew he must return to school, unhappy though he might be. He had to learn to accept a certain amount of cruelty from a world where all that is different from the self is regarded with ridicule and contempt.

Tom has said of this time in his life, "I was scared to death of everyone on earth and particularly of public school boys and public school teachers and public school principals, most of all. That name, public school, kept stabbing at my guts till I wanted, as old as I was, to sit down and cry."

Even Sunday school became a terror for the two children. I sent them weekly to the Presbyterian Church by bus, giving them money for the offering. One Sunday I felt something amiss when they returned, and asked what had happened.

"Nothing," they said.

I pressed the point. They admitted they had not been attending Sunday school, that they proceeded no further than the steps of the church where they sat munching chocolate bars, bought with the collection money, waiting until school was dismissed, when they would board the bus homeward.

"Why didn't you want to go to Sunday school?" I asked Rose. Since she was the elder, she had the greater responsibility.

"The girls snobbed me," she explained.

They had asked how many cars her father owned and sniffed at the answer "one." They turned further disdainful when, in reply to where she lived, she named an apartment building, not a house in the suburbs. The last straw toppled when they asked what school she attended and she mentioned a public school, not a private school like the ones to which they went.

Social status in St. Louis depended on how much money you possessed. This was not true of the Mississippi and Tennessee towns where we had lived. There you could have very little money and still hold a superior place in the community, for who you were and who your family were was all that mattered. The line was quite impassable; you were either born to the purple or you were not. Which, of course, was rather unfair if you didn't happen to inherit the proper social niche. But most people in those days seemed to take their station in life as a matter of course.

My husband, accustomed to Knoxville society and the paying of constant social visits, would come home and ask, "Well, has anybody been to call on you today?"

"No," I'd say.

"Not a soul in the apartment?" he'd ask in surprise.

Life for me, as well as the children, changed radically. For one thing, I had to learn how to cook for the first time in my life. The seven years we had lived with my parents, I was not allowed in the kitchen for we always had excellent cooks and I was perfectly content to give them the stove as domain. But Cornelius would have been unhappy to arrive home after a grueling day's work and not find a hearty meal on the table. At first it took the entire day to prepare dinner but I eventually learned how to be more efficient.

My husband went to work very early, so I would arise at six o'clock to cook a big breakfast for him. I have had friends who have bragged that their husbands brought them coffee in bed, believing it proof of devotion, but I could never understand the poor man's not only starting out the day making his own breakfast but also handing his bedded wife a cup of coffee on his way out the door.

Southern women may have been spoiled but they were taught to keep a good house. Their husbands never came home to a slatternly wife or surroundings. Northern men, I think, sometimes expect too much of their wives, demanding that they keep house and earn a living. Southern men seem a little embarrassed to let their wives work, and therefore, the women have more time to spend taking care of the house and themselves. No matter how difficult the drudgery all day, I always took a bath in the evening and changed to a dainty dress for dinner, as did Rose.

Because I was learning to cook and cope with household chores, all of which took quite a bit of doing for me, I had little time to give Dakin, certainly none to entertain him, so he entertained himself. He would totter into the kitchen carrying heavy books and seat himself on the floor, getting down to serious business. One book contained pictures of the flags of the nations of the world and Dakin would point to the flags, one by one, and ask me to tell him the name of the country each represented. I would then see him studying the flags and digesting such names

31

as "Czechoslovakia" and "Yugoslavia." He quickly learned them all.

Dakin always loved to see flowers grow, as do I. In one apartment, the landlady gave him the rights to a patch of land in a back yard choked with ashes. You wouldn't believe a weed would survive that ashy wasteland but Dakin soon had every imaginable flower blooming, even persuading a watermelon vine to thrive.

As they learn, children seem to pick up the most obscene words adults utter, catching the tone of voice, I believe, rather than the word itself. One of the two times I ever heard Cornelius swear occurred on a Sunday afternoon when we were driving around looking for a house to rent. The red lights went against Cornelius about six times in succession and as he braked on the sixth one he let out one big "damn." I ignored it. But to Dakin, this was an exciting new word.

The next day I saw Dakin playing outside with a little boy who had just moved into the apartment and whose mother had dressed him to the hilt to impress the other little boys. In turn, Dakin wanted to impress the newcomer. He did so by emitting a perfect volley of "damns," showing off his new word in great pride. It wasn't long before I saw the boy's mother dash out and haul her resplendent son out of range of Dakin's damns.

Those first years in St. Louis were hard on us. We could not afford to buy a house in an exclusive neighborhood so we kept trying to find roomier apartments, and houses for rent. We made nine moves in St. Louis—they say three moves is equal to a fire—before I bought the home where I now live on Wydown Boulevard in Clayton, a few houses beyond the city line, just west of Forest Park.

In one apartment Tom said we slept on everything but the kitchen table, which was practically true. Rose slept on a folding bed in the living room and Tom on one in the dining room. Although I tried to get out of there as quickly as possible because such close quarters makes it difficult for people to get along, we had to remain almost two years. This is what happens when a city becomes too crowded.

Tom has called his nine years in St. Louis "nine years in limbo." Yet it was not all limbo. I remember the many times he would come home from school and sit down at the piano and sing at the top of his voice. My mother, who had taught piano and voice professionally, tried to convince all three children of the beauty of music, even for a time teaching them herself. Looking at a picture of my mother, a queenly woman who, in this photograph however, appears stern and forbidding, Rose once commented, "That's exactly how Grand looks when she gives me a music lesson." Later, Mother paid for Rose's voice and violin lessons, which came to naught.

Tom also enjoyed reading, for he spent endless hours when he wasn't studying, in the library. He was always bringing home books. One afternoon he walked in with a copy of *Lady Chatterley's Lover*. I picked it up for a look—Tom said I had a veritable genius for opening always to the most lurid pages of a book—and was shocked by the candor of the love scenes.

I promptly marched Tom and book to the library, where I gave the librarian a piece of my mind. "The idea of allowing a fifteen-year-old boy to read this!" I told her.

I didn't like the book or D. H. Lawrence as a person. From what I read about him, he had a vile disposition. His wife seemed devoted to him and so did other women, but I didn't admire anything I heard about his character or how he treated his wife, who deserted her husband and children for him. The one play of Tom's I have not read or seen is *I Rise in Flame, Cried the Phoenix,* his poetic version of Lawrence's last few hours on earth.

Tom seems to have a psychological hangover which prevents his coming home. He would much prefer I visit him. I feel it's not the cold spirit of St. Louis, however, that repels him but memories of our home life that lie at the root of his distress. True, his reception at school and the strangeness and discomfort of city life could not have endeared him to St. Louis. But even more important, he could not help but become locked in the vise of anger that slowly gripped our house.

Every marriage holds some measure of disillusionment which, if it can be weathered, means the marriage survives. I imagine it is a matter of the degree of disillusionment and its impact. My disillusionment was deep and when it came I felt stunned.

Before we arrived in St. Louis I saw only the charming, gallant, cheerful side of Cornelius. For a while he tried to keep the Mr. Hyde from me. But he could hardly hold secret his excessive drinking, not when he would come home emitting fumes of alcohol and in a cross and ugly mood.

My husband was an earnest worker and loyal to his company. My sons have inherited some of his best qualities—honesty, perseverance, integrity. He worked very hard but he also wanted to play very hard. He was a man's man and liked long poker games and drinking bouts. I didn't object to a poker game that ended at a reasonable hour but not one that lasted the weekend.

At first he brought his company to the house, but because of the drinking and the late hours and the rough way they would sometimes talk in front of the children, I asked if he wouldn't take his games elsewhere. He started going to his club or hotels for the weekend, often staggering home Sunday with a hangover, moaning, "The old Studebaker knew the way back."

The children may have heard me remonstrate about his drinking at times but I was afraid he'd lose his job and then where would we be? I didn't have to worry, though, for as drunk as he might become, my husband was always ready for work on Monday. He would never let his drinking interfere with being at his desk on time.

I don't think he liked the new job in St. Louis. He was really a salesman at heart, with a love of the open road and the human contact between customer and salesman. Now he was tied down not only to the routine of family life, new to him, but also to a desk. He probably felt a deep dislike for the tremendous pressures he had to exert on the salesmen and the ruthless hiring and firing necessary to keep up sales. He had a fondness for the lonely salesman of the road, and suddenly found himself tyrant to the salesman. I think perhaps he hated himself for what he had to do each day and when he came home at night

34

took out his self-hate on us, for we symbolized confinement of another sort. Also, because of us, he had to take this higher-paying job, one he didn't really want or like.

He was a very restless man as I found out early in our marriage when we lived in Gulfport before the children were born. He would always want to be out doing something, although he also liked to be read to; one way to keep him home at night was to read aloud a good novel.

He could see out of only one eye because he had lost sight in the other at the age of five when he fell from a second-story window onto a brick pavement. He did not complain about his vision. He was a slow and careful driver and never got into a serious accident as far as I know. But he never read very much after I stopped reading aloud. His whole life seemed to be shoes —that's all he discussed when company came to the house. I never knew so much could be said on the subject of shoes! But perhaps that is natural when you work for the largest shoe company in the world.

It soon became apparent Cornelius had a quick temper. He was not the kind of man who liked to be questioned about where he had been or what he had been doing, so I learned not to ask. You never knew what made him angry—it was like walking on eggs every minute of the day and night. The most trivial act might spin him into a tantrum and after it was spent, he would sit on the couch and glare, when he wasn't stretched out on it snoring, recovering from a hangover.

He took no joy in the children, seeming to consider them just a nuisance, as though he wished they had never been born. All but Dakin; he and Dakin would listen for hours to the ball game on the radio. Because Rose and Tom did not care for baseball, they were a total loss.

Cornelius loved two breathing things: Dakin and the dog in the house. One time it was a little Boston bulldog Cornelius bought after a poker game. He took Dakin with him to the game, said, "Sit right here, Dakin, until I win enough to buy a dog."

This turned out to be Jiggs, who lived to the grand old age

35

of twelve. If he hadn't been such a greedy dog he would have lived longer. Not content with what I fed him, he found a bone that perforated his intestines. Cornelius rushed him to the veterinarian but couldn't save him. My husband made more fuss over Jiggs than over any member of the family; he only summoned the doctor when he or Jiggs felt sick.

One time I left St. Louis to visit my parents and when I returned, the place looked torn up; evidently Cornelius had thrown a wild party. I found both him and Jiggs ill, Jiggs lying mournfully in one corner of the room and Cornelius stretched out on the sofa groaning, "It was a draw who would pass out first before you got here—me or Jiggs."

The day Jiggs died, I saw Cornelius cry, something he never did. In his room he pasted on the wall a cartoon of a wire-haired terrier with the caption: *A friend's a friend who knows your faults and doesn't give a damn.* When we lived in Columbus with my parents, he gave me a wire-haired terrier named Neal as a present. The dog didn't particularly appeal to me or my parents because he would carry home dead rats and drop them on the rectory doorstep.

Dakin went out more emotionally to his father than did Tom, but then Dakin, always seeming wise beyond his years, was a smiling child. He has told me he got along with his father because he was not afraid of him and felt his father liked him. Dakin also believes that, as a child, he had a less jolting life than Rose or Tom. In his words, "I never knew anything *but* turmoil, while they at first enjoyed a serenity between my parents. The shock, when they moved to St. Louis and suddenly saw Mother and Father plunged into fights, must have been devastating."

I felt pity for Cornelius, more than anything else. He had everything to make life happy and successful. He held the esteem of his business associates, which I took care not to destroy, no matter how deeply he hurt us. I don't think you could have found three more promising children. I was doing my full duty in making a comfortable home. I felt sorry to see him ruining his own life as well as that of his family but then some are hell-bent on destruction, to use a direct expression, without any apparent rhyme or reason, and Cornelius seemed one.

Much of his wrath centered on money. He resented every penny he gave us. Money was rarely mentioned by my parents as I grew up and it was uncomfortable for me now to quibble over each cent. The bickering made my life and the children's pretty miserable. Cornelius always bought the best clothes for himself but never seemed to care whether we had enough. Once Dakin had to go to bed while my mother, who was visiting us, mended his only suit. Cornelius never wanted to buy Tom shoes even though he could get them wholesale. In any discussion of money, the one word, "No," covered everything for him.

Yet he spent money lavishly as he gambled on weekend poker sprees, usually at the Westborough Country Club, with his favorite crony, a man eventually fired from the International Shoe Company for drunkenness who then shot himself.

Dakin reassures me I have not exaggerated about Cornelius' penuriousness as far as his family was concerned. Dakin remembers that the family fights usually reached their peak during the end of the month when bills arrived and during the weekend drinking sprees. There would be a good-sized row as Cornelius fumed over the bills and I battled for grocery money.

Cornelius made what was considered a good salary during the depression days, about $7,500 a year. Yet I had to fight to get money to eat.

The second and final time I heard Cornelius swear was one Saturday when I discovered I did not have enough money to buy food for the weekend.

"Cornelius, I need money for food," I said.

He threw down the princely sum of $6 on the kitchen table and said, "There, take it and go to hell!"

One time he stopped all of my charge accounts, a foolish thing to do, for I was never extravagant. He then doled out money for every small expense.

He was parsimonious in one way, crazily extravagant in another. Once we owned three dining room sets. The one which we had been using, of Queen Anne style, I had bought from

37

the young man who rented us our first apartment. We were moving to a larger apartment and Cornelius decided we needed a new set. He noticed in the newspaper that a wealthy family was advertising the sale of furniture at a sacrifice because they were forced to move East.

"Here's a chance for that dining room set," he said.

"Why do we need another dining room set?" I asked. "If anything, we need a bedroom set." The new apartment had an extra bedroom.

He and one of his friends went to the mansion to look at the sacrificial furniture. He came home to announce he had purchased an elegant dining room set. He returned to the mansion a few days later with another friend who needed furniture, only to discover to his dismay that the dining room was still full of furniture—the set he bought had been replaced by another. This was all a scheme devised by a furniture company to promote sales. Cornelius felt he had been gypped but the new set was on its way to our home so there was nothing he could do. When it arrived, I put my first dining room set in the large kitchen, where the children enjoyed eating, and the new one in the dining room.

A few months later I was in bed, suffering from one of the painful attacks I had over the years, when Cornelius informed me that two of our friends were moving to a larger home and wanted to sell their furniture. He said, "Well, you've been wanting a bedroom set and here's a chance to get one." He was in an expansive mood that day.

Away he went, and I sat up in bed consoling myself that at last I would have a bedroom set that matched. I had a dresser of one kind of wood, a bed of another, a table of a third.

My husband returned in a few hours in very good humor. "Edwina, what do you think?" he said jovially. "They sold me their dining room set. It's a beauty."

If I hadn't been in bed, I would have fainted. "Do you know how many dining room sets we have?" I asked feebly.

"And you know that grandfather's clock?" he went on.

38

"I hope you didn't buy that!" I protested. "We have no hall to stand it in."

We now owned three dining room sets, a mammoth grandfather's clock and no bedroom set. Cornelius eventually was able to sell the set on which he had felt cheated, to one of his salesmen. I am still using the third set, of very handsome mahogany, in my dining room. Fortunately, our living room was large and could comfortably hold the grandfather's clock.

This was one of Cornelius' moments of largesse. But most of the time, life with him held either spoken or unspoken terror. In my mind, my husband became "the man of wrath," a phrase I remembered from a book, *Elizabeth and Her German Garden*, about a woman who married a German with a terrible temper. There seemed nothing I could do to please my man of wrath, much as I tried.

Friction between Cornelius and Tom existed from the start, with Cornelius even unconsciously putting it into words when he tried to reassure Rose upon the birth of her first baby brother: "He's no good, is he?" All through Tom's life, that seemed to be his father's feeling about him. Because Tom preferred to read, or write, or go to the movies rather than play baseball, his father contemptuously called him "Miss Nancy." Cornelius proved little better than the boys at school who taunted Tom with cries of "sissy."

I suppose if I had been like the woman of today, I would have left my husband after the first few years. The Episcopal Church is strict, though, about divorce. And if I had left him, there would have been no Rose, or Tom, or Dakin. So I just stood by and took it. I wanted my children to feel there was one parent in whom they could have faith.

Thus, while the callousness of city life may have been partially responsible, I think the widening breach between his parents, and his father's attitude toward him, gave the feeling of loneliness and agony to Tom's boyhood. It made every experience seem a crisis, for when there is too much anger in a home, everything becomes life or death to a child.

39

Tom once wrote a few lines that seem to tell of his hunger for a father who would be compassionate.

> I walk the path that
> leads me straight
> Beyond the town's bustling
> > estate—
> Till in some silent, secret wood
> I find that perfect fatherhood
> Where all is known and understood.

On the other hand, in a poem he wrote about me, I suspect his tone lies somewhere between amusement and fond exasperation.

LOOK BOTH WAYS CROSSING STREETS

> Every school day of the year
> I used unfailingly to hear
>
> My mother's anxious voice repeat,
> "Now, Tom, look both ways crossing streets!"
>
> With perfect filial subjection
> I would glance in each direction,
>
> Ere with conscientious feet
> I braved the hazards of the street.
>
> By virtue of this cautious habit
> I grew to be a model Babbitt,
>
> With a wifey and a kiddie,
> And a home just out of city.
>
> Lots of shrewd wit beneath my hat,
> Behind my belt, a little fat.
>
> Oddly, beneath this deep contentment,
> Now and then, with dull resentment—
>
> With a weary, baffled sigh—
> I hear my heart enquiring why

Every school day of the year
Mother's voice I used to hear

With such acute concern repeat,
"Now, Tom, look both ways crossing streets!"

Tom's youth does explain, I feel, his deep interest in and sympathy with people trapped in emotional tragedy, like Blanche in *Streetcar* and Brick in *Cat*. I am sure Tom felt at his wit's end many a time, hemmed in by disaster, just like the characters he created. What saved Tom, perhaps, was his humor, always a part of him. Rose never possessed a sense of humor and she could not save herself.

4.

"... My Place of Retreat,
My Cave, My Refuge"

A<small>T</small> an early age Tom started to write and seemed to be writing much of the time. Writing was his talent. When he was eleven, I decided to buy him a typewriter, thinking it would make the writing easier. The only ambition I ever had for my children was that they do what they wanted.

I saved $10 out of household money and bought him a typewriter I found in a secondhand store. It was large and clumsy and sounded like a thrashing machine but Tom was delighted with it. I could hear him hitting the keys for hours. He has said of acquiring the typewriter, "I forgot to write longhand after that." I suggested he take a course in typing in the spring of 1929 after he was graduated from high school in mid-term, the month of January. I thought he might become more efficient if he gave up trial-and-error typing and learned the professional way.

His first short story was written when he was twelve, according to him inspired by a picture of Tennyson's the Lady of Shallot floating in a trance downriver. In a collection of Tom's writings that I have saved, I came across what I believe are two of his earliest published poems. They appeared in his junior high school newspaper in 1925, written when he was fourteen and in the ninth grade, as the signature attests.

NATURE'S THANKSGIVING

The Bob-White is whirring
And beating, and throbbing;
The wood-brook is singing
And happily sobbing;
The carnival leaves
In resplendent descent,
Fall in a glory o'er merry content.
The wood has all colored,
And flaunting in pride,
Is swaying and laughing
Before they subside
To the sleep—
And the dark—
Of the winter.

THOS. WILLIAMS, 9TH GR.

OLD THINGS

In the silence of the garret,
'Midst rusted things of long ago.
Aloft from the clamor of life below,
Old things—sallowed and hallowed,
Grayed in the gloom;
Things from the old life
In the dusk of their tomb.
This is the place for him and his dreams,
His old gray head bowed over the remnants
Of days that are dead.
The silver candelabrum blazes anew,
And the tapestry blooms to a brighter hue.

43

> The melodeon chimes,
> A faint caprice,
> And the whole world dims to a softened
> peace.
> Eyes gently shine through
> The dusk of years,
> Old faces he sees,
> Old voices he hears,
> Amidst the rusted things of long ago.
>
> THOMAS WILLIAMS, 9TH GR.

This was the year 1925, when I took the children to a summer resort in Tennessee where we rented a house in Elkmont, a small resort on a mountain that slopes up to the Great Smokies. The Scopes trial was then in progress, creating a sensation. We had more than a perfunctory interest in it, for the presiding judge, the late John T. Raulston, who died eight years ago, was married to my mother's sister.

Clarence Darrow was staying in Elkmont, not far from us, walking around in galluses, not even wearing a coat for dinner, which startled some of us Southerners. But we admired his wit and erudition. He certainly wiped up the earth with silver-tongued Bryan, as he took the heart out of him. I have heard that one of the plays on which Tom is working has to do with the Scopes trial. Tom never lets me read his plays, or tells me about them, until they are produced.

For several years I had not been well and before we left for Elkmont, I fainted one day trying to get lunch. We lived on the top floor of a two-family house with a flat roof which made it uncomfortably hot. I had been taking Dakin back and forth to school three times a day, in addition to caring for the household.

I was ill during most of Tom's high school days, first undergoing five minor operations and then a major one. I also had a miscarriage two years after Dakin's birth. Mother would always help out when needed. Rose would telephone and plead, "Grand, come quick. Mother's sick," and her grandmother would board the next train for St. Louis.

Many were the times I dragged myself out of bed to fix

dinner, for I believed that even though feelings were strained between my husband and myself, I should cook for him, although he would have preferred a thick steak every night to the menus I so frugally planned. In spite of the pain, I made a point of being cheerful, for no man wants to come home to a sick and complaining wife.

After the major operation, I lingered between life and death for five days. Even Mother was not allowed to see me. The doctor warned, "Just a breath would take her away." Tom sent a letter to my father at this time:

> DEAR GRANDFATHER,
>
> Being of thrifty Quaker lineage, it is opposed to my nature to throw away this good piece of paper simply because it has the remnant of a french lesson on its back—and so I'm utilizing it for this letter, with apology.
>
> As Grand has informed you, Mother got through her very serious operation quite well according to the reports we have received. We haven't seen her yet. The doctor said that it would be dangerous for us to visit her as she had to be kept absolutely quiet. We feel now that she has survived the operation and these first two days, she will surely get through allright.
>
> The morning of the operation was certainly an anxious one for us. We waited two hours while she was on the operating table.

The rest of the letter has been lost. I do remember, though, while I was recuperating at home a friend brought over a graceful blue vase filled with cosmos and Tom just stood there, drinking in the beauty of vase and flowers. Then he disappeared and a few minutes later I heard the typewriter clacking away as he wrote a poem, "Cosmos in a Vase," one of his loveliest. It was published some years later under the title "After a Visit," in the magazine *Voices* and then in the *Literary Digest:*

> The petals of the cosmos
> Are fallen to the vase;
> And evening is denial
> Of all that morning was. . . .

The smell of tea and lemon,
And an angle of a chair
Remain your only signature
Against the darkening air.

Tom kept writing during his last years in high school, sending out poems and short stories to magazines, hoping to earn spending money since his father gave him so little. He would enter all kinds of contests, even one on why Pillsbury flour was the best of all. He didn't know anything about flour, since he always avoided the kitchen like the plague. But that did not stop him from describing it in such seductive terms as "silky soft."

A month after he reached his sixteenth birthday, he received his first writing prize (it is fantastic how many things have happened to Tom just around his birth date). The prize was awarded by the magazine *Smart Set*. I have kept the letter he received telling of this momentous occasion.

APRIL 8, 1927.

MR. THOS. LANIER WILLIAMS
6254 ENRIGHT AVENUE
ST. LOUIS, MISSOURI

MY DEAR MR. WILLIAMS:
Enclosed herewith you will find check No. 7040 in the amount of $5.00, representing the Third Prize in the Contest entitled "Can a Good Wife Be a Good Sport?"

Your interest as a reader of SMART SET is greatly appreciated and we trust you will continue to support the Magazine. Mr. Lengel [William C. Lengel, then Editor] sends his best wishes and congratulations with this letter.

Try again, won't you?

Very truly yours
M. McINTOSH
Secretary to Mr. Lengel

Tom's contribution appeared in the May, 1927, *Smart Set*, in an issue with such other self-revelations as "Hunted Lovers,"

46

a "Self-Told Romance of the Wild North," and "Forgive Me My Trespasses," the "Life Story of a Girl with a Siren Heart." Out of twelve winners in the letter-writing contest, he was the only male. In introducing the prizewinners, the article started off: "She can not. That is the verdict of hundreds of *Smart Set* readers who answered the question, 'Can a Good Wife Be a Good Sport?' "

The magazine printed Tom's letter in full, saying, "Thomas Lanier Williams, of St. Louis, Mo., gave a rather dreary picture of the man's side of the problem and won the third prize. He writes:

> Can a woman after marriage maintain the same attitude towards other men as she held before marriage? Can she drink, smoke, and pet with them? Can she do those things which are necessary to good sportsmanship, as the term is generally applied to a girl? Those are questions of really great pertinence to modern married life.
>
> In recounting my own unhappy marital experiences, perhaps I can present convincing answers.
>
> Bernice was an unusually attractive girl, decidedly the flapper type. She had the gift of a quick tongue and a ready wit. I met her and fell in love with her in our mutual place of employment—a wholesale house on Washington Ave. I proposed to her across a glass-topped cafeteria table. However if a girl can accept you under such conditions as prevail in a cheap cafeteria without the stimulus of moonlight, moonshine, or music, it would seem that her love was strong.
>
> About a month after our marriage, I obtained a position as traveling salesman, for the same firm in which I had previously been employed as a clerk.
>
> We had rented a very pleasant little efficiency apartment and it seemed to me at first that my future was to be one of domestic bliss.
>
> Bernice had been a popular girl, so she was naturally dissatisfied to sit at home "darning socks," as she described it. I did not at all object that she should go out reasonably

47

often, or that she should retain her old friends—men as well as women. I reasoned that gradually she would slow down.

However the expected symptoms of slowing down did not appear. In fact, by our second year of marriage, her speed had noticeably increased. Her life seemed, almost, to be one continual stream of dates.

One week, after our third wedding anniversary, I completed my sales tour much sooner than usual. On entering our apartment after giving the customary signal, so that she would not be frightened, I found that she was not there. It was twelve o'clock—midnight. I decided that she must have been lonely and gone to spend the night with a girl friend. I went to bed but my worry concerning her prevented me from sleeping.

It was almost daylight when I heard her key turn in the lock. I was about to rise to greet her, when I saw, through the partially open door between the bedroom and hall, that she was accompanied by a young man. She looked cautiously around the parlor. I had placed my suit-case under the bed, and there were no evidences of my return. She then permitted the man to throw his arms around her and kiss her. I was astonished and furious at this. When the man had left, I presented myself. She almost fainted when she saw me.

We were divorced a year later. As I remember, "being a good sport" was exactly how she defined her actions. Being a good sport was drinking, smoking, and petting—staying up all night with the boys at cabarets—not sitting at home "darning socks."

No, I don't think that a wife can be that kind of a "good sport."

Shortly after Tom received his prize, I noticed he kept coming into the house through the back door instead of the front as he usually did, looking anxiously into the living room before he would enter. I am sure he feared the magazine would send someone to the house to check up and discover this supposedly sophisticated divorced prizewinner was sixteen and had never even proposed to a woman.

Tom did try again, as *Smart Set* suggested. His next step up the literary ladder came when *Weird Tales* sent him $35 for his first published short story. It was titled, "The Vengeance of Nitocris." Nitocris was an Egyptian queen placed on the throne by subjects who had slaughtered her brother, the previous ruler. Taking a paragraph from the histories of Herodotus, Tom spun a story around the way she avenged her brother's death. She ordered constructed on the banks of the Nile, a large underground chamber with concealed sluice gates. She then invited all the murderers to a banquet in the chamber and at the height of revelry, excused herself and opened the sluice gates. The waters of the Nile poured into the locked chamber and drowned all her brother's killers. Tom has said, only half in jest perhaps, that this story set the keynote for most of his work.

"Nitocris" made her appearance in the August, 1928, issue of this magazine of the "Bizarre and Unusual." Tom recalls that his grandfather and he were on their way to Europe when they picked up a copy of the magazine on a newsstand in Grand Central Railroad Station, New York, and discovered Tom's story in it.

His first paragraph read:

> Hushed were the streets of many-peopled Thebes. Those few who passed through them moved with the shadowy fleetness of bats near dawn, and bent their faces from the sky as if fearful of seeing what in their fancies might be hovering there. Weird, high-noted incantations of a wailing sound were audible through the barred doors. On corners groups of naked and bleeding priests cast themselves repeatedly and with loud cries upon the rough stones of the walks. Even dogs and cats and oxen seemed impressed by some strange menace and foreboding and cowered and slunk dejectedly. All Thebes was in dread. And indeed there was cause for their dread and for their wails of lamentation. A terrible sacrilege had been committed. In all the annals of Egypt none more monstrous was recorded.

49

The story ends on a note of tragedy after Nitocris has avenged her brother's death.

> When in the evening the queen arrived in the city, pale, silent, and obviously nervous, threatening crowds blocked the path of her chariot, demanding roughly an explanation of the disappearance of her guests. Haughtily she ignored them and lashed forward the horses of her chariot, pushing aside the tight mass of people. Well she knew, however, that her life would be doomed as soon as they confirmed their suspicions. She resolved to meet her inevitable death in a way that befitted one of her rank, not at the filthy hands of a mob.
>
> Therefore upon her entrance into the palace she ordered her slaves to fill instantly her boudoir with hot and smoking ashes. When this had been done, she went to the room, entered it, closed the door and locked it securely, and then flung herself down upon a couch in the center of the room. In a short time the scorching heat and the suffocating thick fumes of the smoke overpowered her. Only her beautiful dead body remained for the hands of the mob.

It struck me as amusing that just before Nitocris went up in smoke, Tom had won a $5 prize in a contest sponsored by the Citizens Smoke Abatement League whose slogan was SMOKE MUST GO. Tom had submitted an essay called "The Dragon," comparing the evil smoke to a dragon engulfing the city.

When Tom returned from his European trip with Father, he wrote a series of essays about the cities he had visited, including London and Venice, which were published in his school newspaper. Most travel pieces are dull but Tom's were eloquent and evocative.

Cornelius looked on Tom's writing as effeminate and a waste of time. His tirades were often directed against it. When the electric bill rose a dollar, he blamed this crime on Tom. "You're just spoiling him," he accused me. "He sits writing all night and runs up the light bill." Tom wore glasses and his father had a fit each time he broke them, which he did frequently. I would pay for new ones out of household money rather than risk another explosion.

Tom was graduated from high school in January, 1929, with a B average. That autumn he entered the University of Missouri at Columbia. In the scrapbooks of Tom's notices that I have saved over the years, there is a clipping from the university newspaper that reads:

SHY FRESHMAN WRITES
ROMANTIC LOVE TALES
FOR MANY MAGAZINES

At 17 years of age, Tom Williams of St. Louis, a freshman in the University, received $35 from the *Smart Set* magazine for an article on "The Type of Woman a Man Wants to Marry." Mr. Williams who has had stories accepted for the past two years (since he was sixteen) has had a number of stories published in *Weird Tales* and *Smart Set* magazines.

He likes to write love stories best and declares that he does not get his inspiration from actual experience but rather from reading a wide variety of authors. Louis Bromfield is his favorite author...

It bothers Mr. Williams to have anyone ask him questions about himself. He is little more than five feet tall. He has clean cut features and smooth brown hair. His eyes, which have a look that seems thousands of miles away, add to the unapproachable and reserved appearance which he presents. He is equally as reticent and shy as he appears and feels that his having stories published is nothing out of the ordinary...

He intends to enter the School of Journalism of the University and to be a journalist after his graduation from college.

This was October, 1929. Mother and Father were visiting us during that month and one day Mother and I decided to go downtown and buy a piano, even though it meant we both had to scrimp to pay for it. Mother had sold hers in Clarksdale and I wanted to get rid of my small upright and buy a larger one. "I'll pay half and you can pay half," Mother offered, since she played the piano whenever she visited us.

The Baldwin Company store was deserted except for Mother and me. I wondered why nobody was shopping for pianos, then thought perhaps the demand for pianos was not so large that a lot of customers would show up at once. We found a beautiful piano, gave a small sum as down payment and arranged to pay the rest on the installment plan.

At the dinner table that night we proudly told the men of our mammoth purchase. My husband looked at me hopelessly, then said in a sour voice, "I don't suppose you know the bottom dropped out of the stock market today."

Even knowing it was the day of the crash, Mother and I felt we could afford the piano. I sold the upright and each of us somehow squeezed out the regular installment payments. The piano still stands in my living room, Mother's picture as a bride of nineteen on the wall beside it, and a picture of Isabel, Cornelius' younger sister, on top of it.

One of the few letters Tom ever wrote to both his father and me is dated October, 1929. In legible handwriting, he told us exciting news.

> DEAR MOTHER AND DAD,
> I have some very big news for you in this letter. I have just pledged the Alpha Tau Omega. They invited me to supper last night and afterwards took me up to the council chamber where I was asked to join the Frat, and offered a pledge pin. I have never accepted anything with more alacrity. I have been over to the A.T.O. house several times and I liked the fellows there a great deal. They are just completing a new chapter house—one of the finest on the campus. I don't think I could have made a better Frat.
> They are very cordial and congenial. And they are not stereotyped, like the members of some frats. They don't

limit their membership to a single type of fellow. It is one of the oldest and largest national fraternities—was started in 1865, right after the Civil War, in Richmond, Va. Its purpose was to help cement the friendship of the North and South.

They recited the whole history to me last night.

As soon as I re-entered the parlor, wearing the pledge pin, the whole chapter swarmed around me with congratulations. I had never felt so important.

I think they will want me to move in as soon as the new house is opened. That will be near the end of next month. I have not broached the subject of moving out to Effie. Perhaps you could come up and negotiate with her, when the time comes.

From what I hear, living in a Frat is more expensive than boarding out. However, the social advantages of being a fraternity man are certainly great enough to warrant the extra expense. A non-frat man is practically "out of it" in Columbia, as I have found in the past month.

In business and social life after you are out of the University, belonging to a fraternity is still a very big asset.

A young man whom Mr. Morris, son of the shoe salesman, brought around to see me, is also being rushed by the A.T.O.

I expect I will have to go to parties and dances every week, as the pledges are always given lots of entertainment.

I am awfully sorry that Rose has had to go back to the hospital. I surely hope they finally succeed in curing her of her long trouble. Tell her that I want to have her up here as soon as she is able. Attractive sisters add much to one's prestige in a fraternity.

There are quite a number of older men—including some faculty members—in the Frat. The dean of men, Mr. Hechel, who teaches my citizenship course, is a member. There is no further news.

Lovingly,
Tom

"Effie," to whom he had not as yet broached the subject of moving out, was a maiden lady with whom Tom boarded. Cornelius was pleased to hear Tom had joined a fraternity; he would have thought his son's college career doomed if Tom had not become "one of the boys." But it must have been hard on Tom financially because his father gave him precious little allowance, if any. Mother and I would send him driblets when we could, from our household budget. Mother would sometimes do her own laundry so she could give the children an extra $5 for things they needed. I suggested, so Tom could save a little money, that he send his laundry home while at college, which he did.

In his letter, Tom referred to Rose's "long trouble." In the past few years something unknown and fearful had been taking place in the mind of our spirited, imaginative Rose. Her unhappiness seemed to start when her father took her out of All Saints College in Vicksburg, a junior college, not letting her finish her education. She was eighteen at the time. Originally her aunts wanted her to go to an exclusive girls' private school in Virginia but my father, who once had been asked to be dean of All Saints College, was able to get Rose a scholarship there. Naturally this impressed Cornelius, who wanted to send her to the least expensive place.

He became obsessed with the idea of removing Rose from college after he returned from a visit with his sisters in Knoxville, where he usually spent his summer vacation, never taking us, usually not leaving us enough money for a picture show. He returned home to announce, "Ella and I decided Rose should make her debut this fall in Knoxville instead of going back to school."

His family were members of the "400" in Knoxville. Although I never saw much of them, I felt close to Isabel and Ella, Cornelius' two sisters. They were so unlike him, you'd hardly think they were kin to him; they were of an affectionate nature. They loved our children, for they had none of their own. Isabel, Mrs. Isabel Sevier Williams Brownlow, was married to a man who owned a real estate firm, and Ella, who never married, operated a gift shop on her own.

Her aunts had always been very kind to Rose, inviting her to visit them on holidays. One time she attended a masquerade party

54

dressed as a Christmas tree. She wore a crown of stars on her head and a gown of green tarleton flounces covered with little tinkling glass ornaments, mostly animals. She brought the dress home with her from Knoxville and perhaps this is the inspiration of Laura's collection in *The Glass Menagerie*. As far as I know, Rose never owned glass animals other than the ones that dangled from her Christmas costume.

I agreed with Cornelius' suggestion that Rose leave college and make her debut, although I did not hold with debuts, as I once did. For most girls they are hardly the happy experience you're led to believe by the society columns. One of my friends claims, "A woman should be forty-five before she makes her debut," meaning she needs the wisdom of this age to cope with the disillusionment.

Cornelius thought Rose would meet some Prince Charming, marry him and thus remove herself as a financial burden from her father's shoulders. He was anxious enough for her to go to Knoxville but would not pay for the necessary clothes, and it was my mother who bought Rose her debut dresses.

The debut proved a fiasco from the first, as everything in Rose's life seemed destined to be. November arrived, the beginning of the social season, and Rose had her trunk all packed, her ticket bought, when a telegram came to the house with the news NINI DIED SUDDENLY. Nini, Aunt Isabel's mother-in-law and the ruling spirit of the family, had planned to give Rose her big party. Now the debut had to be postponed.

Because of the circumstance of mourning, her two aunts decided Rose should make an informal, quiet debut in a series of little parties, rather than coming out at one lavish affair. It was all rather a sad anticlimax and Rose came home exhausted. Although she attended a lot of parties, I don't think she enjoyed them. This was the time of prohibition and the boys all drank from hip flasks, which upset her. She told her aunts about the unhappy situation at home, how her father mistreated us, but they could not quite believe this of their beloved brother whom they had always spoiled. Rose had hoped they

55

would be moved to speak to Cornelius, for they were the only ones to whom he would ever listen.

After her dismal debut, Rose went to secretarial school to learn shorthand and typing so she could get a job and be self-supporting, but her heart obviously was not in this. She was always very secretive about her personal life yet I know she had several romances. One young man of whom she was very fond jilted her and she seemed devastated for a while.

She started to fight bitterly with her father whom, as a child, she adored. She had always been eager for his love. She would dance in front of him, her beautiful auburn hair flying out around her fragile face, and cry out excitedly, "Daddy, Daddy, see me dance!"

"Just like a moo cow," he would comment crossly. Cornelius was not one to show approval of anything Rose or Tom did. But she remained loyal to her father, writing in all her letters from school, "Daddy, I love you."

Rose was the one who saw my husband abuse me and she lived in fear of him herself. At first his abuse was only verbal. He would regularly order me out of the house once a month, enraged by some trivial occurrence, although I think he would have been astonished had I left. On the one hand he would insist I go, on the other he would snarl, "You needn't try to leave me, because I'll give away every cent I have rather than pay you alimony."

Once I asked him, "Why do you threaten me so, Cornelius?"

"Because I'm unhappy with you," he said.

"There's no point in your being unhappy here. Why don't you just pack your things and go to a hotel? I'll help you," I offered.

He threw some clothes into a valise and stalked out of the house. Rose burst into tears and sobbed on my shoulder, "Mother, he won't ever come back. What will we do?"

I wondered, too. If he left for good, how would I take care of the children? I was not fitted for any kind of work. My parents had no money to speak of.

But he stayed away only for the night. The next morning he

meekly walked in the front door with his suitcase. I said not a word.

Cornelius really started to frighten me, however, when he became very drunk and was not himself. One night, after he obviously had been drinking, he walked into the bathroom where I was standing and threatened angrily, "I'm going to kill you!"

I fled in terror into my bedroom and quickly locked the door. He pounded on it as he kept shouting, "Come out of there. I'm going to kill you!" He was almost six feet tall and very stocky, almost fat from all the drinking, and he broke down the door. It struck me and I fainted, mostly from fear.

Rose witnessed this fight and others. Her father was even abusive to her. One evening she wanted to invite a young man to the house but Cornelius refused to leave the living room so she could entertain her caller. He stayed stretched out on the sofa, listening to the radio, although he could have gone into his bedroom. She phoned the young man and told him not to come over. Then she walked into the living room and evidently said something her father considered saucy. He slapped her.

She burst into tears and ran out into the street. It was just about dusk and my mother, who happened to be visiting at the time, was returning home from the little neighborhood drugstore and saw Rose flying down an alley. She stopped her.

"Rose dear, what's the matter?" Mother asked anxiously. "Where are you going?"

"To find a policeman to come and lock up my father," she gasped. "He's crazy!"

Mother persuaded her to return home. Rose would not speak to her father for days.

She started to complain of severe pains in her stomach and to claim someone was trying to poison her. We thought it might be indigestion and sent her to Barnes Hospital for an examination. The doctors found nothing physically wrong and suggested she visit a psychiatrist.

She started going regularly to the psychiatrist, who made Cornelius give Rose an allowance. This was a sorry day for my husband—he not only had to pay for the psychiatrist, which must have tortured him, but give Rose an allowance in addition. The psychiatrist told Rose her trouble was sex, that she was too frightened of it, but I don't believe as Freud does, that sex is everything. I hold more with Jung and others.

Once Rose came home laughing after her session with the psychiatrist. "He asked me to tell him my dreams but I don't have any dreams," she said as though this were a huge joke.

Another time they were discussing violence and the psychiatrist told her violence was usually associated with the lower economic classes. Whereupon she said to him, "A common truck driver is more of a gentleman than my father."

For a while Rose seemed to feel better and decided to look for work. But before long, she retreated into apathy. She would stay home day after day and sit and stare into space. My parents, hoping a change would help, invited her to visit them in Memphis and she went for a while, then returned home as dejected as when she departed. This was not like Rose, for both she and Tom had always loved to visit their grandparents.

The psychiatrist thought a short stay in a private sanitarium might help so we sent Rose to one nearby. When she came home I decided to move. We were living on the top floor of a two-family house and I thought if we could rent a whole house in a quieter neighborhood, Rose might be happier. After we moved, she would sit in the yard watching the flowers and listening to the birds and gradually started to come back to herself.

A strange thing happened—life *is* sometimes stranger than fiction, even Tom's fiction. The man across the street, a widower, became attracted to Rose and made an engagement to take her for a ride in his car. But just before they were to meet on this first date, he broke down from overwork and was taken to a sanitarium, the same one Rose had just left. Then, the day he was to be released, he stepped in the path of a truck driving along the hospital grounds, and was killed. Shortly after, Rose, who once again became very depressed, entered the sanitarium for the second time.

She kept trying, between periods of depression, to find a job

58

but with little luck. Her fights with her father continued. One morning at four o'clock, I heard her go downstairs to let him in. He had pounded on the door, evidently having forgotten his key or unable to fit the key into the lock. I don't know what he said, but he must have been abusive, for she fled upstairs and I heard her moving furniture around her room to block the door, afraid he would break it down as he had broken mine.

The next day she packed and said she was moving out of the house. She walked into the living room where Cornelius was talking to a friend and coolly bid him good-bye. Tom, who was at home at the time, carried her suitcase to the car, and I followed. We drove around half the night trying to persuade her to return, and when she refused, we took her to the psychiatric ward of a general hospital, hoping she would be helped there.

I kept a diary which I later destroyed when I read it and realized the horror of the things happening in my daily life. But at the time, I had to write of my husband's brutality or I could not have endured it. Mother saw how he was treating me and after a visit she would go home and tell Father, "We can't leave Edwina in that terrible situation." Father would break down and cry.

Cornelius drank so much, I believe, because he was unhappy, not with me, but with his life in general. I am not so egotistical as to think I drove him to drink, for no one is powerful enough to force someone else to do anything he does not wish to do. We know, today, that the roots of such extreme behavior as alcoholism lie deep in an unhappy childhood. Cornelius drank long before he met me, starting as a young man in college, but that I did not know until years after I married him.

He usually hid a bottle of bourbon behind the bathtub and we would pretend not to notice it, allowing him this indulgence. As a result of Cornelius' example, Dakin says he formed a definite dislike of whiskey and has always been a very moderate drinker. He told me once, "This was the worst fault Dad had, in my opinion, and I tried to avoid him when he was drunk or heavily 'loaded.' " Tom was away at college much of the time the drinking was at its worst and I never heard him express an opinion about Cornelius' aptitude for alcohol. I think Cornelius was more concerned about Tom in this regard than vice versa, for it was in the fraternity at college that Tom took his first drinks.

Cornelius went to unbelievable lengths to destroy Tom's morale. Ever since he was twelve, Tom had known and liked a girl named Hazel Kramer, a year younger than he. By the time he reached his last year in high school, they had become very close. Tom would often take Hazel to the movies on money he earned from writing. Sometimes I would go with them, for it had reached the point where my husband didn't invite me any place; he had his men pals and could not be bothered with me, and I had long given up asking him to take me to a picture show.

Hazel was imbued with a joy of living, somewhat like Rose in her early years. One of the most wholesome girls I ever met, she was very fair of skin with a reddish tint to her hair. The friendship between her and Tom might have ripened into romance if Cornelius had not interfered because he didn't think Hazel good enough for Tom. Her parents were divorced and she lived with her grandfather, who worked in the sales department of the International Shoe Company, a job inferior to my husband's.

Hazel planned to go to the same college as Tom, for they did not want to be separated. When Cornelius learned of this, he hit the ceiling in fury. He said her presence at the University of Missouri would interfere with Tom's study. He handed down the ultimatum to her grandfather, that he would not allow Tom to attend the university if Hazel did. The grandfather, no doubt feeling his job in jeopardy, enrolled Hazel in the University of Wisconsin and thereafter, Hazel and Tom saw each other only during vacation.

If Tom had Hazel in mind when he wrote "The Field of Blue Children," one of his early short stories, I think he was drawing quite a bit on his imagination. This story tells of a young college student, a shy sensitive poet, who falls in love with a popular girl on the campus. She senses his loneliness and desire and goes

60

with him into a field of blue flowers which, in a poem, he described as the field of blue children. There they make love and when they part, each knows he is lost to the other. Years later, after she has married someone else, the young woman drives back to the field, haunted by memory.

While Tom cared for Hazel as a friend, I think the two enjoyed only a platonic relationship. Tom and I never discussed sex. When he became old enough to be told the facts of life, I took him to the family doctor just before he went to college, because I thought he had been shielded at home a good deal. The most difficult thing facing a parent is somehow to make sure his child knows the facts of life, although by the time most parents get around to this, the child usually does.

Tom's fury at his father for separating him from Hazel must have been titanic. But, as always, he said nothing, just quietly went off to the university. There he kept on writing, for the first time trying his hand at plays. A clipping from the college newspaper tells of one that won an award.

> The sixth selection was Thomas Lanier Williams' play, "Beauty Is the Word." This is a missionary play with an original and constructive idea, but the handling is too didactic and the dialog often too moralistic. Mr. Williams is the first freshman to win honorable mention in the Dramatic Arts Contest.

Tom attended the University of Missouri for three years, each year his marks becoming slightly lower although he never failed anything—except finally, R.O.T.C.

When he heard this, Cornelius became enraged. He had gone to military school as a boy and later enlisted in the Spanish-American War, in which he served as a lieutenant. Tom's failing R.O.T.C. was like a slap in the face to his father.

"I told you he's not doing any good in college," Cornelius stormed at me. "I'm going to take him out and put him to work."

This was the third year of the depression and Cornelius constantly felt the financial bottom dropping out of his world. The few stocks he owned had depreciated considerably, one plunging from 131 to 30.

I remember Dakin coming into the kitchen and saying with a laugh, "Did you know, Mother, that Dad was once a rich man? He said so. Before all his stocks went down."

I laughed, too. How could we have ever known, since we were never allowed to feel anything but pinched by pennies? I imagine my husband could have become rich if he had been wise enough to know when to invest money in the stock market. All the executives at the shoe company became millionaires overnight, buying stocks which they sold before the crash. They built handsome houses far out in the country, launched their daughters in society, and from then on, although they had been our friends, found no time for us.

Cornelius did not want to put out one more cent for Tom's education. He insisted Tom not return to the university for his final year. Tom wanted with all his heart to get a degree, to keep learning, to be able to write more effectively. I think he would have given anything to remain in college. But he did not defy his father. I can only guess what this must have cost him psychically.

Cornelius got him a job at $65 a month at the International Shoe Company. Tom entered a world of dusting shoes, typing out factory orders and hauling around packing cases stuffed with sample shoes, the world of his father.

5.

"A Season in Hell"

ONE afternoon I was riding home on the bus and, looking out the window, saw a young man struggling to cross a busy street carrying a box almost as long as a sofa.

Poor boy, I thought.

I looked more closely and it was my Tom! My heart had been in my throat for a supposed stranger only to find it my son staggering under a gigantic case full of sample shoes.

A sad letter arrived for Tom just after he went to work in the shoe company. Robert L. Ramsay, of the Department of English at the University of Missouri, wrote telling him, "Your absence from the University this year has been a matter for real regret to all of us who knew the excellent work you did here the last few years, especially in the field of creative writing."

He further explained, "This letter is concerned with the fine story 'Big Black' which you submitted in the Mahan Story Contest last year. I should like to see that story published some-where." He suggested Tom try sending it to the editors of St. Louis or Kansas City newspapers who "might like to run a series of our better student stories as a feature of the Sunday issue." I cannot recall whether Tom took his advice, but soon after he was awarded first prize in a contest for amateur writers sponsored by the St. Louis Writers Guild for his story, "Stella For Star."

The year was 1933 and Tom had started to think of himself as a serious writer in spite of spending twelve hours a day with shoes. That fall he wrote to his grandparents:

10/28/33

DEAR GRAND AND GRANDFATHER

As this is Sunday I know you will pardon my writing so short a letter. I just want you to know I am thinking about you and hoping you are both well. I believe Mother is sending you copies of a couple of eastern newspapers in which my poems were reprinted. It is nice to be getting a little recognition even without any money. It is as hard to get rich on poetry as fat on vinegar, you know.

I am going to night-school now at one of the high-schools, and am trying to get in a short-hand class, as Dad says if I become pretty good at it, it might be possible for me to get a stenographic job at the office with higher salary than I am now receiving.

Mother and Dakin are thinking about going to Memphis at Thanksgiving Time. But I am afraid that I wouldn't have time enough to make it. I only get Thursday off.

Rose and I are going to a costume dance tonight. Rose is going as a gold-digger.

With lots of love to you both,
TOM

Every evening when he came home from the shoe company, Tom would go to his room with black coffee and cigarettes and I would hear the typewriter clicking away late at night in the silent house. Some mornings when I walked in to wake him for work, I would find him sprawled fully dressed across the bed,

64

too tired to remove his clothes as he fell off to sleep at heaven knows what hour.

Tom has said of his writing, "I wrote not with any hope of making a living at it, but because I found no other means of expressing things that seemed to demand expression. There was never a moment when I did not find life to be immeasurably exciting to witness, however difficult it was to sustain." It was especially difficult in those days, I am sure. But no matter how tormenting, Tom *had* to keep writing, that I know, just as he now sits down at the typewriter every day at a set hour, as though he were a businessman going to work. This discipline, at least, he learned from his father.

I discovered it was not diplomatic to disturb Tom in any way while he worked. Once I had the temerity to offer food. His typewriter had been in action since early morning and I knew his only sustenance had been a cup of coffee, so I fixed a simple lunch, tiptoed upstairs and into his room. Quietly I placed the tray on a table, intending to say not a word and tiptoe out.

He looked up from the typewriter and glared at me. He said, "I *did* have an idea!"

I never tried it again. You would think I had interrupted some priceless gem of a story and perhaps I had. Anyhow, I was not going to risk disturbing his train of thought, whatever it might be.

There are scraps of Tom's writing in the house which I have no idea when he wrote, such as the following, handwritten on ruled paper, perhaps composed when he was at the shoe company. I think it an interesting description of what Tom may have been feeling and fantasying at the time.

> He was very much like the stalk of a withered flower.
> Therefore, to write an interesting biography of Geoffrey Wells, I must concern myself principally with that period of his life which came before his "Hour of Darkness."
> Rain fell upon the clay that day Geoffrey Wells was born. It fell heavily and continuously from a dark grey sky. It seemed to soak all color from the little Mississippi town; to envelop all things in its chill greyness.

Thunder rumbled at intervals throughout the day. But there was only one violent clap and it was this one that liberated Geoffrey Wells from his mother's womb, several hours earlier than was expected.

The woman's travail had been one of great pain. She was by nature high-strung and emotional. She had a great fear of pain. As her labor increased, she grew hysterical. The nurse and doctor attending, not daring to administer an anaesthetic so early, pleaded with her. . . .

Here it breaks off. The second fragment begins at a much later point in the story:

It is quite often in a mood of passionate rebellion against life that the creative artist produces his finest work. It was in such a mood that Geoffrey Wells sat down before his piano one evening in March. His fingers struck a rich and vehement chord; it was like the cry of a soul in torment. It was the cry which his lips could not utter but which he felt in his heart. He struck other chords, weaving them into a beautiful theme, that was vibrantly and majestically sorrowful. When finally he arose from the piano, he had composed a beautiful sonata, which he later titled, "The Hour of Darkness."

This sonata lifted him precipitously from obscurity to fame. He became known as the great composer of his day. He acquired considerable fortune of his own and he married a wealthy widow. However, he never produced another musical composition of much worth.

"The Hour of Darkness" had been the swan song of his genius.

There is very little left of a great artist after his genius has burnt out; very nearly as little as there is of a candle consumed by its flame. Of Geoffrey Wells there was nothing left, figuratively, but ashes, after he had composed his "Hour of Darkness."

That piece had been like a terrific volcanic eruption of his soul. It had cast up in one mighty heave all of the long-accumulated lava. It had left him cold and empty—flaccid and dull.

66

His few old acquaintances who continued to see him, after his sharp social elevation, were astonished at the change in him. His animation of spirit, which had made him so charming, particularly to women, was gone. And he had changed physically. His eyes had lost that striking brightness which had given his face such strong appeal. And his body, which had once been as graceful and well-knit as that of a hero of Grecian legend, had become paunchy and drooping.

At this time of his life, it must have been extremely hard for Tom to find energy to create at night after having to put so much of it into absolutely useless work during the day. Too, he must have been fighting deep anger at a father who forced him into what he called "a job designed for insanity...a living death." Another time he referred to his stint at the shoe company as "a season in hell."

He must have hated not only the work but the fact that, just as in high school, some of the young men made fun of his quiet manner and Southern accent, which he has never completely lost.

With the first money earned at the shoe company, Tom bought me a present. He ran home in great triumph with a painting under his arm. He had spent his whole week's wages on a framed copy of the "Mona Lisa." I scolded him for wasting his money on a luxury for me, rather than on necessities for himself. I didn't dare tell him I did not particularly like the "Mona Lisa," not sharing the enthusiasm of most people, because I thought her expression foxy-looking. Even when I saw the original in the Louvre, I still disliked her smile.

She hangs in my house, though, just as in the cellar sits an antique lyre Tom once bought with $5 that his grandmother sent him. Again, instead of purchasing something he needed, he rushed out to a store and hauled home this strange musical instrument. I doubt if he'd ever seen a lyre before and after a few attempts to play it, he gave up. Keeping company with the lyre in the cellar rests an old hand-cranked Victrola, another of the memories of music that haunt the house.

67

Tom purchased his first car with his earnings, paying $30 and buying it on time, at that, from a co-worker at the shoe company. He called it "Scatterboat" and the machine lived up to its name, for regularly it would fly to pieces. Tom would phone to ask if I couldn't persuade his father to come and collect the car wherever it had broken down. Cornelius would bluster a bit, but rather than see Tom's investment lying useless in the gutter, he would make an effort to find him and tow in the cantankerous car. Cornelius never liked to lend Tom his car and when he occasionally did, he would blame Tom for dents he himself had made. He never felt this way about Dakin, though, to whom he willingly gave the car if he did not need it.

As recreation from the shoe company and his writing, Tom would swim at the Westborough Country Club, to which his father belonged. I marvel that he ever learned to swim because when he was a boy, one summer at a resort on the Merrimac River, his father tried to teach him by throwing him into the river and Tom nearly drowned. Later I sent him to the Lorelei, a pool in St. Louis, where he learned to swim.

One day I was sitting in the garden, enjoying one of my rare moments of peace in St. Louis, when I looked up to see Tom stagger out of a car, handkerchief held to his mouth. As he took the handkerchief away, I nearly fainted. His mouth was one bloody mess.

He couldn't talk. The man who drove him home told me what had happened. Tom had walked out on the diving board at the club, jumped, and crashed into the edge of the cement pool. He knocked two front teeth out of his mouth and chipped off others. His father was somewhere on the golf course at the time.

Tom had been working in the shoe company for about two and a half years when he received word one day in February, 1935, that Hazel Kramer had married. He did not say much but I sensed he felt this intensely.

Tom recently told me his love for Hazel was, he supposed, "much the deepest love of my life." He said, "I still haven't the

68

faintest idea why my father opposed our attending the same university but then there was never any communication or understanding between us, since even being under the same roof with him was acutely uncomfortable to me. As I recall my reaction, it was desolation, not fury. I guess I had begun to regard Dad's edicts as being—as far as I was concerned—too incomprehensibly and incontestably Jovian to feel about them anything but what a dead-tired animal feels when it's whipped on further. Of course, under this hopeless nonresistance there must have been an unconscious rage, not just at Dad but my own cowardice and impotent submission. This I realize because as I have grown older I have discovered a big underground rebellion was there all along, just waiting for a way out."

The rebellion exploded in a way, about a month after Hazel's marriage, on a Sunday in March just before his twenty-fourth birthday. Tom and Rose went to Loew's State Theatre to see Leslie Howard in *The Scarlet Pimpernel*. Lost to Tom in one sense when she started to become a young lady, Rose always remained close to him even though it was no longer the wild intimacy of childhood where they shared each other's imaginative fantasies.

When they came out of the theatre after this movie of suspense and violence, Tom said to Rose, "Let's take a taxi home."

Rose was surprised, because they usually climbed on the bus, but she said nothing. As the taxi passed St. Luke's Episcopal Hospital, now Presbyterian, Tom turned to Rose and said, "I don't feel well. I think we should stop here."

"What's the matter?" asked Rose.

"I can hardly catch my breath and I feel numb," he said. He could not even walk but had to be carried from the taxi into the hospital. The old paralysis of his legs had returned.

Rose telephoned me to report Tom had had a stroke and was in the hospital. The doctor who examined him said he had collapsed from exhaustion and needed a rest. Tom was afraid he might have had a heart attack but the doctor assured him he had not.

69

Rose sailed magnificently through the crisis of Tom's attack. But that night at home, she broke.

She lost control of her senses, wandering from one room to another in a panic. She woke up her father screaming in terror, "You're going to be murdered! We're all going to be murdered!" It was as though Tom's slight breakdown had destroyed the slender thread by which she had been hanging on to a reality she could no longer grasp.

Even after that night of fear, she kept trying to find a job, as she had been doing on and off for eight years. She even managed to get one, taking care of an office for two doctors and a dentist. She sent out the bills, washed the bowls in the dentist's room, kept busy from early morning until late evening, proud she was able to hold a job. Then she lost it as the doctors told her they could not keep her because they thought the work too hard for her. It broke her heart; she cried for a week.

Tom came home from the hospital after a short stay. The shoe company sent him a month's salary which just about paid his hospital bill. That was the last money he ever received from the International Shoe Company.

I think his slight stroke, or whatever it might have been, was Tom's unconscious way of getting out of a job he hated, since he was unable to defy his father openly. People are fearfully and wonderfully made; what goes on in our mind is often unfathomable even to ourselves.

Tom spent that summer resting at his grandparents'. My father had retired as a minister and bought a small home in Memphis and, as it turned out, that visit of Tom's proved quite valuable to his literary life. While there, he became friends with Dorothy Shapiro, a young woman who lived near my parents. She was a member of a small summer theatre called Rose Arbor and she and Tom worked on a play which she persuaded the group to present. It was a comedy called *Cairo! Shanghai! Bombay!*, built around the adventures of two sailors on shore leave who pick up two girls.

This was Tom's first produced play. It was offered by the Garden Players on July 12, 1935. The program, which he sent me, listed the authors as "Bernice Dorothy Shapiro and Tom Williams."

During rehearsals, Tom wrote Dakin of some of his trials and tribulations.

JUNE 25, 1935

DEAR DAKIN:

Your letter arrived just this morning and was quite a sensation. Everything about it was exceedingly admired, penmanship, literary style, and most of all the news about your grades. Grand and Grandfather were beaming with pride. I don't know how I looked, but my complexion must have turned rather green, especially when you mentioned the honorary pin. What kind of pin was it, by the way?

You seem to have a very bad case of Urch-itis, even reading books for him during the summer. I should think you would find old Victoria pretty dull after Queen Bess and her various "thieves."

Summer is arriving at Memphis. It is just beginning to get comfortably warm. Miss Shapiro and I have fitted out a studio-solarium in our backyards and yesterday had lunch under the peach trees with a few other guests. As you know, we collaborated on a play that is going to be presented. I wrote the play and Miss Shapiro wrote the prologue and epilogue. It has been accepted by the Garden players and is now being rehearsed almost every night at the Shapiros'. The leading lady bawls her lines so loudly that she sounds like she is selling fish. I am intending to take a part in the first act, a street scene, in which all kinds of pedestrians cross the stage. I will probably be the blindman with the tin cup and dog. Not a very difficult part but quite sufficient for my dramatic capacities.

I am getting along quite well down here. I still have to rest a good deal but am feeling stronger. I'm sorry to hear Dad has been sick and hope he's now well. When you go to camp let us know what you're doing up there.

Grand and grandfather send their love to you and the rest of the family.

Lovingly,

TOM

71

He returned home that fall with a renewed interest in playwriting. When he saw the Garden Players acting his play, he found it surprisingly amusing, even laughing out loud with the audience, he has said, and decided right then and there that writing for the theatre was fun.

He also now wanted to finish college. Since his father still refused to pay for his education, my mother did so, feeling it was important Tom get his degree. He enrolled at Washington University of St. Louis, not far from where we lived, to earn credits needed to enter the senior class the following year.

At the university Tom met a young man named Clark Mills McBurney and they worked together on plays in the cellar of Mrs. McBurney's house, which they called "the literary factory." Here Tom read Rimbaud, Lorca, Rilke, Melville, Hart Crane and now, without my interference, *all* of D. H. Lawrence.

I only met Clark Mills once when Tom brought some friends home for the afternoon and I said "Hello" and "Good-bye" to him. I know he was considered the school poet.

In the "literary factory" Tom wrote his first two full-length plays. *Candles to the Sun* was a drama of violence in the coal mines of Alabama, and *The Fugitive Kind,* a story of characters in a flophouse. There he also wrote a short story about a very fat woman, mistress of a Southern plantation, who was seduced by her small, lithe overseer, the kernel of his later one-act play, *27 Wagons Full of Cotton,* and eventually the movie *Baby Doll.*

Tom did seem to have a propensity for plump women at one time. I remember a photograph in his room of a tremendously fat woman. I asked what he saw in her.

"Why, she's good-looking," he said, surprised I didn't think so.

He would also admire a woman we would pass on the street whom I'd consider downright fat.

I take some credit for launching Tom on his career as a playwright, although he has said, "My conversion to the theatre arrived as mysteriously as those impulses that enter the flesh at puberty." Perhaps his "conversion" was not quite as mysterious as he would make it, but rather, achieved in large part through hard work. At any rate, twenty-six years ago, in the spring of

72

1936, I noticed in the newspaper that the Webster Groves Theatre Guild, a theatrical group in a suburb of St. Louis, was offering a prize for the best one-act play. I suggested to Tom, "Why don't you enter this contest?"

"Look at the deadline, Mother," he said, reading the announcement. "I'll never make it. It's nearly here."

"You can do it," I urged him, remembering the speed with which he often wrote.

The next thing I knew, he was in his room and I heard the typewriter going like mad. And the second thing I knew, several weeks later a letter arrived.

APRIL 21ST, '36

THE BOOK SHELF
WEBSTER GROVES, MO.

MY DEAR MR. WILLIAMS:

It gives me great pleasure to tell you that your play "The Magic Tower" has been awarded the prize in the Webster Groves Theatre Guild Contest. The decision of the judges was unanimous.

My warmest congratulations to you, and may your pen continue to flow freely!

Very truly yours,

MARY GAYLORD COBB
Contest Chairman
Webster Groves Theatre Guild

Six months later Tom's play was presented to the public. A clipping from the St. Louis *Star-Times* of October 19, 1936, reports on backstage activities just before the curtain rose on the Webster Groves Theatre Guild presentation of three one-act plays. It told how Howard Buermann, author of the first play, *Debt Takes a Holiday*, stood talking with Louise Francis Butler, author of the second play, *The Third Act*. Then it said, "Howard Williams [they got Tom's first name wrong], whose 'Magic Tower' took first prize, cannot be found."

They didn't look very hard, for Tom was sitting in the audi-

73

ence with Rose, Dakin and myself (naturally his father was not there). He was a disappointed young man when he walked to the stage to receive the prize and was handed a sterling-silver plate with his name engraved on it, rather than money. He came back to his seat and with rather a disgusted air handed the plate to me saying, "Here, Mother, you can have it." I have treasured it, along with the original script of *The Magic Tower*. Tom's first critical review was a rave.

> Thomas Williams's "Magic Tower," the prize winning play, is a poignant little tragedy with a touch of warm fantasy. It treats of the love of a very young, not too talented artist and his ex-actress wife, a love which their youthful idealism has translated into a thing of exquisite white beauty. They call the garret in which they live their "magic tower" and are happy there until the artist's belief in his star fails. Then the magic tower becomes a drab garret once more; and tragedy, like a gray woman, glides in, to remain.
>
> Exquisitely written by its poet author and beautifully directed by David Gibson, this play evoked the emphatic response of the audience throughout, in spite of the fact that Elizabeth Rush should *not* have been cast in the role of the heroine. Her nervous acting and hurried speeches failed to convince, largely, wc believe, because hysterical parts are her métier.

I think it amusing that the heroine of Tom's first prize-winning play was *not* a hysterical woman, since he has been accused of writing only about hysterical women.

I have not kept many of my own letters but I saved one I wrote my parents shortly after the play was produced.

Sunday

DEAREST MOTHER AND FATHER:
With the family all out, I have a few quiet moments for writing. Cornelius left on a western trip of three weeks

74

Friday. Rose, Tom and Dakin have gone to Mrs. Ver Steeg's for supper. "Gypsy" and I were invited, too, but I thought that too many from one family, and made excuses for us.

Last night Tom and I went to the "Little Theatre" to see "The Cherry Orchard" by the Russian author, Tchekov. It was too much for amateurs to handle but we enjoyed it. I think Rose wrote you that Tom, Dakin and I went to the Webster Groves' Little Theatre play. At the end of the second act, the prize was awarded to Tom over the foot-lights. It is a sterling silver plate for cakes or sandwiches with the inscription "Prize, one act play, contest Webster Groves Theatre Guild—1936." It was raining so that we could not see the road both coming and going. Dakin did the driving.

Thursday I had two callers from the board of Jefferson Chap., D.A.R. who informed me I had been selected from the chapter with the whole-hearted approval of the entire chapter to be the next Regent. It seems that I have met the requirements of all the "hard-to-please" older members. They approved of my "minutes" and the "way I read them," my "tact," "charm," "graciousness," etc. They remained for two hours and a half and when they left I had promised to undertake the job. There's no telling what I've let myself in for and I am quaking in my boots!

We have been looking at houses again but I didn't like the ones Cornelius showed me. He is thinking of borrowing the money and buying one if we can find one under ten thousand in a neighborhood where I could dispose of it in the event of his death, he said. He will see Mr. Bock on this trip and on his return we will decide.

I went to "Stix" to get some gloves like mine for mother but they did not have her size. I'll try some other stores.

Tom and I went to the Cathedral today and dropped Rose off at St. Michael's. Dean Sweet has taken up cudgels for the fourteen thousand here who have been thrown off relief and have no jobs. Appalling!

Tom broke his new glasses and owes his dentist nine dollars and Dr. Alexander ten. Isn't it the limit!!!!

I enjoyed my little visit with you. Lots of love.

EDWINA

"Stix" is the department store, Stix, Baer and Fuller, which now has branches in the suburbs; "Gypsy" was the dog.

That year Tom also won first prize of $25 in the senior division of an original verse contest held by the Wednesday Club of Saint Louis. This was a competition started eleven years before by Sara Teasdale. I'm still fond of his winning poem, "Sonnets for the Spring."

SONNETS FOR THE SPRING
(A Sequence)

I. *Singer of Darkness*

I feel the onward rush of spring once more
Breaking upon the unresistant land
And foaming up the dark hibernal shore
As turbulent waves unfurled on turbid sand!
The cataclysm of the uncurled leaf,
The soundless thunder of the bursting green
Stuns every field. The sudden war is brief,
And instantly the flag of truce is seen,
The still, white blossom raised upon the bough!
(Singer of darkness, Oh, be silent now!
Raise no defense, dare to erect no wall,
But let the living fire, the bright storm fall
With lyric paeans of victory once more
Against your own blindly surrendered shore!)

II. *The Radiant Guest*

These past few months my house has entertained
Guests of an oddly uncongenial kind:
With bitter words the atmosphere was strained
Among the cluttered chambers of my mind.
But now I hear them fluttering in mad flight
Down sun-invaded corridor and stair;
I hear them uttering shrill cries of fright
As they discover April on the air!

76

Now the regenerate heart renounces gloom,
The gospel of futility forswears,
Proclaims a holiday, decks every room
With laurel such as only April wears. . . .
The house is clean, the door is opened wide
Upon the radiant guest who waits outside!

III. *A Branch for Birds*

And when the spring returning in her time
Shall find my hand no longer at the door,
Nor any echo of the lyric rhyme
Which I had offered in her praise before,
She'll wear no mourning for my vanished sake
Nor breathe for me an unaccustomed sigh,
But over me her lovely hands will shake
A few white raindrops as she passes by. . . .

Then I, with fingers curled into the earth,
And passion gone as smoke from long dead fires,
Shall not endure the rapture of rebirth
That April of the living heart requires,
But shall myself, as any rooted thing,
Put forth a branch where summer birds may sing!

Isabel, always proud of Tom, believing he had inherited his poetic ability from one of her ancestors, Sidney Lanier, wrote Tom a congratulatory letter.

SUNDAY, MAY 24TH

DEAREST TOM:—

I scarcely know how to write to you about your beautiful sonnets. I deeply appreciated your mother's sending them to me and should have written weeks and weeks ago, but they came as I was preparing to go to the meeting of our Presbyterial in Chattanooga where I was to teach Genesis and I was literally inundated with work. I did so long to have *time* and *words,* fitting words, in and with which to tell you just how I loved your verses. I loved best the first one—"Singer of Darkness" tho' all three just thrilled me. Oh, son, I do so rejoice in this gift of yours and I know you will hold it inviolate—Never cheapen it—make it count for all that is noble and fine and for that which contributes to the very best.

Then your father wrote that you had taken a prize for a play—That coming hard upon the prize for the sonnets made me feel you were advancing by leaps and bounds. Is there any way for me to get hold of a copy of your play? I will take the very best care of it if you have one and will promise to return it to you as soon as it can be read carefully.

Tom, I am so eager for you to get a place in some great Publishing House—some place where you can be with kindred spirits in the great world of literature, and I say this fully aware that there is no kindred quite as dear and close as the ones with whom you dwell today—But you must do everything to get on with your work—but not at the expense of your health.

My dear love to all of the family. Let me hear what you plan to do when you finish at Washington University. Oh, I long for you to go on and on—and son, never let anyone discourage you by attempting to measure your success by the money you make.

This poor world has sordid ways of counting things—but take the high way, Tom, and never mind the world.

With dearest love to my dear singer—

AUNT BELLE

One of Tom's best-known short stories, "The Resemblance Between a Violin Case and a Coffin," is dedicated to Isabel's memory. In it he writes, "This was the name of a sister of my father's who was a famed beauty in Knoxville. She was probably the one woman in the world by whom my mother was intimidated and our occasional summer journeys to Knoxville from the Delta of Mississippi were like priestly tributes to a seat of holiness, for though my mother would certainly never make verbal acknowledgment of my aunt's superiority in matters of taste and definitions of quality, it was nevertheless apparent that she approached Knoxville and my father's younger sister in something very close to fear and trembling."

I was never in awe of Isabel. Perhaps Tom stood a little in

affected her worse than him. I think it must be a form of influenza. We had Dr. Simon come out several days ago and he left a prescription but Mother is still not able to get up and is taking wine and raw eggs to recover her strength. There is an awful amount of sickness in St. Louis now.

I guess you have heard all about my getting the poetry prize. I bought copies of the papers for you and I believe Mother sent them before she took sick. It is almost too much publicity as everyone I see has to ask me about it which is getting tiresome. I put the money in my savings account. It will go with the twenty-odd dollars I already had. If I get a little more for my writing I may be able to attend summer school.

Dad has been talking about taking Mother and Dakin on a touring trip East this summer—to Washington and Virginia and home by way of Knoxville. I hope he decides to do it—it would be a wonderful thing for Mother—and you could come up here with us, though I'm afraid this place would not be much cooler than Memphis.

We have planted grass and flowers but I'm afraid this sudden cold spell may damage them badly. Tell the Rhodes and everybody hello for me—

With a great deal of love from us all,

Tom

5/10/36

Dear Grand:

This letter is addressed exclusively to you, since it is Mother's Day. I hope you don't think we had failed to remember you on this occasion. As a matter of fact, nobody realized it was Mother's Day until Rose came home from Church and mentioned that it was. Then I wondered if anybody had written to you and nobody had so I am now trying to make amends for this inexcusable lapse on our part. Dad is out of town now on a three weeks' trip to the West Coast and Susie is taking a week's vacation so Mother and Rose are kept pretty busy with the cooking and housework. Today we took our Sunday dinner out. We went to the Dean Sisters and had hamburgers and cold drinks

81

which were delicious—but made us appreciate the dinners Susie usually cooks for us on Sunday! Gyp didn't have anything to eat, though he was in the car with us. He begged so pitifully that the waiter finally brought him out some scraps of ham and a lump of sugar—which seemed to satisfy him.

Yesterday Dakin and I took a trip to the country. A young girl whom I met at the Wednesday Club—she writes poetry—had invited me out for the afternoon. We had lunch and Dakin went horseback riding. It is a lovely country home on the Missouri River and they have invited me to come out whenever I wish. They're awfully nice, cultured people.

It is beautiful around our place now. The ivy is out, covering the house, the grape arbor blooming, and the roses right on the verge. The grass keeps me busy. I have to mow the front and back yard several times a week. I didn't know a yard could be so much trouble. However it is worth it. We are going to put up our croquet set in a few more days.

This next week-end Mrs. Ver Steeg is driving Rose, Dakin and I out to her country place on the Mississippi. We're taking a picnic lunch and will spend the day out there. Dakin thinks the little girl, Patsy, is crazy about him —he gets more conceited every day! He has been given a part in a play at school. An English part so he is cultivating the English accent and Piccadilly air which is an awful trial on the rest of us.

We are looking forward to seeing you some time this summer.

With much love from us all,

TOM

8/6/36

DEAR GRAND AND GRANDFATHER:

Each day I've planned to write this letter but something came up to prevent. I know that sounds like a bad excuse now that summer school is out and I have so much time on my hands, but we have really been quite busy here. I still have my little "study" down in the basement and spend most of my time writing down here. It has been quite pleasant—cool—ever since Grand left and we had one all-afternoon rain which has helped the vegetation.

Nothing out of the ordinary has transpired lately. Mother is busy with D.A.R. correspondence and putting up plum jelly. She's made two big lots of it. Dakin listens to the baseball game all day. Rose went out to the Nunns' yesterday to a luncheon they are giving for Francis's guest, a girl from Nashville, and Rose is giving them a luncheon this Thursday. Jiggs eats and sleeps and plays with his new rat. He grows a couple of inches every week, I believe, and is so fat now that the floor shakes when he goes bounding around.

My story came out in "Manuscript," but Mother and Rose are not used to modern writing and were very displeased with the subject, which is an affair between a crude Arkansas couple, and so Mother forbids me to send the magazine to anybody. She thinks it is too shocking. It is supposed to be humorous but she and Rose don't take it that way.

My little country girl friend came in last week and spent nearly the whole day with us. She is nice but terribly boring. Says when she starts to school (Washington) next Fall she will drop in all the time—but not if I can help it!

We got Grand's violin yesterday. Hope you found everything okay in Memphis.

With much love,

Tom

During Tom's senior year at Washington University, Willard Holland, organizer and director of a little-theatre group called the Mummers, telephoned Tom one day. The Mummers were presenting Irwin Shaw's *Bury The Dead,* and because it ran short of the customary two hours, Mr. Holland was looking for a curtain-raiser. Tom wrote a one-act play for them called *Headlines,* although he was not even given credit as author on the program.

But then the Mummers presented his two full-length plays,

offering *Candles to the Sun* that year and *The Fugitive Kind* the following year. Of *Candles*, the St. Louis *Post-Dispatch* critic wrote that it was a drama of "poverty, degeneracy, accidents on the fifth level below ground, a strike and a brutal murder, ending with beans for everybody, hope and the singing of 'solidarity forever.'"

Tom was just happy his plays were produced. He was never one to argue with a critic even though he might feel the critic had not understood what he was saying.

With a play called *Me, Vashya!* Tom entered a contest at the university sponsored by the drama department. It was about a munitions maker in World War I and it did not win. No longer interested in anything but writing, Tom started to receive poorer grades in some of his classes. He failed Greek because he was not interested; Tom was brilliant enough to pass any subject if he wanted to.

He decided to leave St. Louis and get his degree at the University of Iowa where he wished to attend a seminar in playwriting conducted by the late Professor E. C. Mabie. My mother again agreed to pay the tuition, and Tom set out for Iowa.

Right after his departure, my husband and I were faced with a drastic decision. Rose had grown more withdrawn and helpless, and her fantasies of being poisoned and murdered, more intense. Cornelius decided to commit her to a state mental hospital.

One of the psychiatrists in charge was very understanding and genuinely fond of Rose. Each time she seemed worse, we would ask, "Isn't there anything you can do?" and he would reply, "I'll try something else."

Finally, he called in two other psychiatrists. After studying Rose, they advised a lobotomy, which, they said, was a new way of helping the mentally ill. This is a very delicate operation on the brain which destroys the chain of memory, in large part, so that one lives without being tortured by fantasies. However, as I found out, it also causes the loss of that part of the psyche that spurs one on to be independent in body and spirit.

One of the psychiatrists told Cornelius something I do not

think he should have. He said to my husband, "Rose is liable to go down and get a butcher knife one night and cut your throat."

That was all Cornelius had to hear, for he was terribly afraid of dying. He was in poor health because of his drinking, and once a month would have to go to the hospital for treatment. Each time he returned he would swear off drinking but this vow would last only a few days. He also suffered from insomnia and sometimes would stagger into my room late at night moaning, "Send for the doctor, I'm dying."

Rose was afraid of her father but I don't think she ever would have attacked him, as he feared she might. She was too gentle to engage in violence, even had she wished it. Rather, she wanted the violence in the house restrained.

When we visited her in the state hospital, it was as though she was shutting everything out of mind. The only time I ever saw my mother cry was when Rose stared at us through the bars with a blank face.

The psychiatrists convinced Cornelius the only answer was lobotomy. A noted surgeon was about to perform the operation on thirty selected patients at no cost to them, and the psychiatrists indicated Rose could be one of the chosen few, whereas if the operation were to be performed at a private hospital, it would cost thousands of dollars. They tried to make me believe this was the only hope for Rose, that otherwise she would spend the rest of her days a raving maniac in a padded cell.

I now think the lobotomy for Rose was a grave mistake. We all believed at the time that this operation might completely cure Rose, as we relied on the advice of a local psychiatrist. We had no idea of the permanent damage it is now known to do to the personality. During those days, some psychiatrists looked on the operation as a wonderful new discovery that would control madness. But now they do not perform it except on the very old and the very hopeless, realizing it destroys something essential in a person's character.

Rose is no different today than at one stage of her illness. She is less excitable, but someone always has to be with her to take care of her. Without the operation, I feel Rose might have been

85

able to come back entirely with a different kind of help. They know so much more today about how to treat this kind of sickness.

Cornelius never visited Rose after the lobotomy. To him, it was as though she disappeared from the earth. I think Tom always felt as though he had failed Rose, that had he been on hand when the big decision was made, he might have been able to stop the lobotomy.

He had lost Rose, in a measure, when she grew into womanhood, but now he lost her in a more final way. Tom's sense of loss and loneliness, first, when Rose started to have delusions of being murdered, and then after the lobotomy was performed, must have been devastating, although he never talked much about it. I think his was a grief beyond words, as he saw his beautiful, imaginative sister whom he had always idolized, partially destroyed.

Fragile, lovely Rose, to Tom must seem a broken creature, to use one of his similes, like a soft moth that flew too near the flame and suffered severe crippling.

As the curtain line of his only comedy, *Period of Adjustment*, Tom puts these words into the mouth of Isabel, the bride of a few days, a nurse who was fired because she fainted at the sight of blood:

"The whole world's a big hospital, a big neurological ward."

To Rose, this certainly has been true, for she has had to live in a psychiatric hospital all these years.

Just before the operation I fell ill, seized by a deep depression, and Mother came to stay with me. I didn't think I could ever get out of bed again; I really had about given up after all the wretched years. Then I looked at my poor mother sitting by my side so patiently, not saying a word, and I thought, What a coward I am. I decided not to bring any more sadness into her life and somehow managed to climb out of bed and go the rest of the way. I don't know how I did it. It hasn't been easy.

My two children, Rose and Tom, met the tragedy in their lives in different ways. One became a brilliant writer, the other succumbed to mental illness. Both had original minds, always expressing themselves in unusual imagery. To Rose, the word "tragic" became her favorite expression. She would write us letters saying, "It is tragic," about almost everything. After the lobotomy, when she visited the new home of a friend of mine and I asked what she thought of the house, she shook her head and said, "It's just tragic."

It is sad to see a loved one die physically. But I think it even sadder to see a loved one die spiritually and mentally. I had to watch this in Rose. They say a flowering tree is most beautiful the year before it dies and it seemed the last year Rose spent at home, dying spiritually, when I was fighting to keep her out of a sanitarium, she never looked more beautiful. Her face held a faraway expression as she sat on the ground for hours, her lovely eyes reflecting the blue of the sky, that cloud of auburn hair falling softly around her shoulders. My heart was heavy.

I think I gave up hope when she would no longer visit Mother and Father. Now there seemed nothing in life to interest her. Her aunts in Knoxville tried to help; Ella asked Rose to go to New York with her on a shopping trip but Rose refused her invitation.

After the lobotomy, Isabel wrote a letter to Cornelius.

AUGUST 7TH, 1937

DEAREST BROTHER:—

My heart and my prayers have certainly been burdened with dear Rose as she is sent for this treatment which we trust will mean restored health to her. I think you did the only thing you could wisely do to take the course which alone held out hope for her recovery. I do pray that God will empower it in her behalf. I know how your hearts have ached and oh, I do so wish I could be of some help and comfort to you.

I know your new home is lovely and I do wish I could come out to see you, but as that seems impossible please remember that we are counting on your visit home in September—I do wish all four of you could come—I have not seen Tom since he was a child and I so long to see him.

I have so much confidence in his success as a writer. I know he will one day really distinguish himself—

Honey, please let me know when the Friedman Shelby shoes are on display in Knoxville—I should so like to see the Fall line, and perhaps order a pair or two.

With dearest love for the dearest Brother I ever had—and for all who are his—

Will and I leave for *Fairfield Inn, Sapphire, N. C.* this coming Wednesday. Please write me there right away and keep me in touch with Rose's condition and with the family in every way.

ISABEL

How little we really know our loved ones, I thought, as I read Isabel's letter. "The dearest Brother I ever had," indeed.

We had moved into a new house hoping the change would bring Rose back to this world but our attempt had failed. Rose was now lost to all of us, forever.

Life is as unpredictable as a dream. Once I was young and gay and danced night after night with beau after beau, the belle of the ball. Then a handsome young man from a fine family came along, fell in love the first time he saw me and asked my hand in marriage. How was I to know this charming youth would turn into a man of wrath and that I and my children would live by his side consumed by terror? How prepared was I to meet an anguish I never dreamed existed, not in my wildest nightmare?

6.

"Well, We All Have to Paint Our Nudes"

T OM enjoyed the University of Iowa and particularly Professor Mabie's seminar. He earned extra money by waiting on tables in the cafeteria of the university hospital. He wrote me his greatest ambition in life, next to having a play on Broadway, was to balance a tray on one hand. I don't think he ever achieved that ambition.

His letters reflected his happiness.

225 N. LINN   IOWA CITY
SUNDAY EVENING

DEAR MOTHER:

Apparently people in the Dramatics Dpt. are not supposed to be Godly as they even have us working on Sunday morning. I am taking part in a "living newspaper," a series of skits dramatizing current events. I play a Negro chairman of a church convention condemning Hugo Black and the Ku Klux Klan. First rehearsal this morning.

My registration was held up five days because my credits had not come from the University of Missouri, only from Washington. I had to wire Columbia to have the credits forwarded. I wrote Holland about this delay and he apparently became very alarmed because he sent Prof. Mabie, head of Dramatics Dept., a long telegram urging him to admit me and also got Colvin McPherson, dramatic crit. of the Post-Dispatch, to send a Special Delivery letter. All of which was quite unnecessary as the delay was purely routine and I was attending classes just the same. Holland even sent my new play up special delivery for me to show Mabie. I had to send it back to him immediately as he had not finished having it typed. The Missouri credits have now arrived and I am fully registered. I only have to meet two requirements, two hours of science, probably astronomy which I will take next term. All the rest are electives, that is, whatever I choose to take. So my courses are all in the English and Dramatics Dept. The lectures here are far better than any I've heard previously. I'm studying Shakespeare and the Modern Drama, Stagecraft, Experimental Playwrighting and a comprehensive survey of English literature. In stagecraft I get practical experience in backstage work, building sets, etc. Dakin would love this school as everyone is obliged to do some acting whether he wants to or not. The theatre is the most completely equipped in the world and the rehearsals I have seen have been as good as professional.

The A.T.O. chapter entertained me twice this week, for lunch and dinner and want me to move in the house. They offer me room and two meals for $22 a month by which I would save slightly but the house is too far from the campus. It is considered one of the best chapters on campus. But I find the more interesting people are outside of frats and sororities here. At our table here, for instance, we have mostly graduate students and English majors, a very cosmopolitan bunch, representing the Bronx, Manhattan, Canada, Pennsylvania, California, Mississippi, and Alabama. There is even a Russian, very communistic, who comes up to my room after every meal to talk art and politics.

I have learned of a private laundress who does shirts for 8¢ each which sounds fairly reasonable.

Much love to you,

Tom

Dear Mother:

I only have time for a few lines before supper. I got your letter this morning and was pleased to hear the encouraging news about Rose. Does the Doctor also feel that she has improved? I wish that I could see the new Buick: I think they are about the handsomest cars on the market now.

I have had quite a dramatic time about my rooming-places. It happens that the Faculty Adviser, who supervises rooming-houses, is an A.T.O. I met him shortly after my arrival here and, hoping that I would move into the A.T.O. house, he got me out of my contract in the place where I was staying. It turned out to be rather disagreeable. They did not provide a study-lamp or clean the place properly. However I made no promise to move into the A.T.O. house and so when I was released from my contract I moved directly into the present place which is very satisfactory. Two nights ago a large delegation of A.T.O.'s called at the house and said they thought I was obligated to move in their house—they lowered their former price two dollars so that the room rent would now be ten dollars a month and breakfast and lunch for twenty-five cents which is extremely cheap—evidently they are in bad financial shape—but I still do not want to move in much as I am well-satisfied here and fraternity life no longer has the appeal it once had for me. However I may decide to move in with them if they can assure me of rides to and from the campus. The house is located rather far out.

I had a short play presented very successfully last week and another one will be put on next week, a satire on Hollywood producers. They are giving it the best director and a cast consisting of the university's best players and so I think it will turn out fine. It is about an ignorant Jewish movie-producer revising a great classic for the movies. "American Prefaces" are still holding my short-story. The editor says it is "going the rounds" which means I suppose that every one in the English faculty is passing judgment on it. They have also asked to see some of my short plays. There are several very well-known literary figures on the campus, all of which I have met. Prof. Mabie, head of the dramatics department, is a brilliant man but slightly unbalanced at times. He has been confined occasionally in the university hospital's psychopathic ward—he has terrible tantrums. On one occasion, when he attended the final dress rehearsal of a play, it displeased him and he threw his glasses at one of the actors: kept them all rehearsing from eight o'clock that night till noon the next day and made the author re-write the last act of the play.

I am glad Dakin got a part in the one-act plays: they will probably be pretty awful, but the experience will help him. Tell him I recently saw a book by Prof. Carson, "The Theater of the Frontier," in the University library—the girl who was reading it said it was extremely dry, but Carson would probably be flattered to know it is on the required reading list in one of Mabie's courses.

Holland wrote me a very encouraging letter about the new play. Said he read it to the Mummers and received "God! What a reaction!" It seems they are very enthusiastic about it and are going to give it all they've got—he is planning to run a feature article about me and the play pretty soon in one of the papers and wants me to have a picture taken.

When you send my next board and room checks, about the twenty-third, please make them out to me as I am planning to take my meals somewhere else. The diet at Scott's is too starchy: potatoes three times a day seven days a week. I find I can eat more reasonably and better food at the campus restaurants. I will buy a meal ticket to last me a month.

I have to buy some materials for stagecraft amounting to about three dollars—those are my only book expenses. I ought to buy them right away as we are supposed to be using them now.

Hope you are all well,

With much love,

Tom

P.S. Will you please send me the stagecraft money by return mail as we are supposed to be using the materials now—for designing.

P.S. Yes, I got the suit and it fits fine.

DEAR GRAND AND GRANDFATHER:

I don't know when I've received a more welcome gift than that delicious box of candy. Grand, it was absolutely the best home-made candy I've ever eaten. I've been quite selfish about it—concealed the box in a corner of my closet so that it will be entirely for my own consumption. I get frightfully hungry in the evenings and of course in a fraternity house you can't raid the ice-box like you can at home—so a box of candy is a really heaven-sent gift.

Well, I got through the first term quite well with an A, two B's and two C's. The A was in Experimental playwriting, for which I have Mr. Mabie, who is nationally famous, head of the dramatics department. He is a splendid teacher but unfortunately has a brain tumor which cannot be removed and which causes him to have occasional periods of mental trouble.

Right now I am having a series of short plays broadcast over the radio every Tuesday night. I'm sending you the announcement of the first one. I will send others to you or Mother later so you can save them for my legendary scrapbook. I am going to have a short story and some poems published in "American Prefaces" in one of the spring issues—I will send it when it comes out.

The Memphis Episcopal clergy has certainly been getting some publicity lately. There have been front-page stories about Dean Noe's hunger-strike or whatever he calls it in all the Iowa papers. I was shocked to hear of Rev. Bratton's

93

suicide. He and Canon Douglas and Dean Noe have certainly had unfortunate careers.

We have had remarkably mild weather since the holidays. It has been almost spring-like the last two weeks. But it rains continually and freezes which makes the walks bad. Grand, I wish you could drive up here with Mother and Dakin some time in the spring. I believe they are planning to come.

With much love,

TOM

Monday 4/25

DEAR MOTHER:

The Easter boxes were overwhelming, almost like a personal resurrection. I'm sorry I haven't had time to write more letters this month but when you glance at the reading-list for my departmental English final you will readily see what has deterred me. It covers all of literature from the Bible to Babbitt and unfortunately they are mostly things which I knew only by reputation or read way back in my remote childhood. However it has been very helpful as they are things which I ought to have been acquainted with and now I *am!* I'm happy to say the Exam is already finished—I had it Saturday—it is given early so it won't interfere with the other finals which commence about the twenty-third of May, and so you can take it over in case of failure. You can take it as many times as you want but you *have* to finally pass it to get a degree in English. My new English teacher is Dr. Rufus Putney, son of the local clergyman—nice but a dull teacher.

My new play is completed and turned over to the playwriting class. They are reading it individually in Mr. Conkle's office and there will be a round-table discussion this week which should be extremely helpful. I am very hopeful about this play, as it is well-constructed, no social propaganda, and is suitable material for commercial stage.

Dr. Conkle is a changed man since "Prologue to Glory" achieved such an unexpected success in New York. He has been ground under Mabie's thumb for years, and had lost all his personality—but since this success he has shown a miraculous transformation in character. His voice, appearance, everything is completely altered, and he has turned into a first-rate teacher as well as dramatist. He was always an excellent writer but paid no attention to commercial requirements which had held him back and caused him to be under-estimated by everyone around the campus. He has gotten marvelous publicity, even broadcast on Rudy Vallee's program and illustrated in "Life." It was produced by the WPA which are now holding "Candles to the Sun." I will send them "Fugitive Kind" soon as I finish re-writing it. Conkle and I have always gotten along well so I am hoping that if he likes my new play he will get his agent—the best in New York—to handle it for me.

I'm glad to hear Dakin is stepping out socially. They have no T.K.E. chapter on this campus but one of my best friends here is a member from Drake and he says they are very scholarly and well-balanced.

The little dog next door had an accident recently—struck by an automobile and spent several days at the veterinary but I see this afternoon he has returned to his yard, apparently none the worse—except that his ears go flat every time he peeks around the corner of the house! I picked him up after the accident and his howls were so dreadful and he was so cowed that we all thought he had a broken back. It is comforting to know that Jiggs is in good health and staying in the backyard.

Our Easter weather was abominable but it has now turned very nice.

I never pay any attention to those anthology rackets. They print some good poems but of course the bulk is made up of very mediocre stuff, so it is no distinction to appear in them, certainly not three dollars worth. If I ever become known as a playwright I may be able to cash in on my poems and might as well save them for that possibility instead of giving them away now. I have collected a group of new lyrics which I will send to "Poetry" this spring. Enclosing one I think you might like since it is on a floral subject—was suggested by a beautiful painting of Hovsep

95

Pushman's now being exhibited in the Memorial Union, called "Enchanted Roses."

With love to all,

Tom

P.S. The cake arrived in perfect condition—is still fresh—served at a little supper party we had Sunday night.

That spring Isabel died and although we all felt bereaved, it was Cornelius, of course, who suffered the greatest loss, for he and Isabel had always been close. He went to Knoxville for the funeral; I did not go but wrote Ella of my sorrow. The extent of Tom's grieving may be measured by the fact that he later dedicated one of his finest short stories, which I have already described, to Isabel, the only time, I believe, he dedicated a story to any member of the family.

Ella wrote, thanking me for my letter.

MAY 22, 1938

Dear Edwina,

Your sweet letter came a day or two ago and I do feel that Isabel is radiantly happy in a fairer land, and sorely as I miss her I wouldn't have her back if she had to live paralyzed and a hopeless invalid. Through the last 4 days of her illness she was literally surrounded by a wall of prayer. You have no idea of the different groups and churches that were praying for her not only here but in Chattanooga, Atlanta, Columbia, S.C., and other places where she was known. But God always knows best, and her work on earth was done.

The weather has been very changeable. Three days this past week it was over 90 and we have had heavy storms.

Love to you and all the family. I would like to hear something about Rose.

Affectionately,

Ella

During his year at Iowa, Tom wrote two more full-length plays. One, called *Spring Storm,* he read aloud in class. It was a play about love and Tom recalls that when he finished reading it, Professor Mabie's eyes "had a glassy look as though he had drifted into a state of trance," and there was complete silence in the classroom, a silence of embarrassment.

Finally Professor Mabie remarked in a kindly voice, "Well, we all have to paint our nudes."

Tom's second play, *Not About Nightingales,* dealt with a prison riot that actually occurred at that time after a group of convicts were literally burned alive while being "disciplined" in an oven-hot room. Tom said he has never written anything to compare with this in violence and horror.

Tom was still going under the name I gave him, not yet having adopted "Tennessee," which he first used when "The Field of Blue Children" appeared in *Story* Magazine in 1939.

People ask me all the time why I named my son Tennessee. I didn't. To me, he is Tom. He has tossed out a number of reasons over the years as to why he took the name Tennessee.

One time he told Mark Barron, Associated Press drama critic, "I got the name of Tennessee when I was going to the University of Iowa because the fellows in my class could only remember that I was from a Southern state with a long name. And when they couldn't think of Mississippi, they settled on Tennessee. That was all right with me, so when it stuck, I changed to it permanently."

Another time he said Thomas Lanier Williams sounded too much like William Lyon Phelps. Still another, that as a youth he had published some poetry which he later decided was "bad" and, feeling his original name more suited "to an author of sonnets to spring," changed it. He also gave as reason that "the Williamses had fought the Indians for Tennessee and I had already discovered that the life of a young writer was going to be something similar to the defense of a stockade against a band of savages."

In 1938 when he was still "Tom," at the age of twenty-seven, he received his Bachelor of Arts degree from the University of Iowa. He came home and finished work on *Not About Night-*

ingales, for the Mummers intended to produce it. But the depression took its toll of this semiprofessional theatre group and they disbanded before production started.

Tom then decided to go to Chicago to try to find work with the WPA Writers' Project. He made a desperate effort to get on the Project but did not succeed because, he said, his writing did not contain enough social protest and he could not prove his family was destitute. Before long, he returned to St. Louis.

It was still the depths of the depression and difficult to get any kind of a job. Tom did not want to remain in St. Louis. Even though he had not a cent, he decided to try it on his own some other place, not willing to take his father's contempt or miserliness any longer.

He set out for New Orleans and when he left, I had the feeling this time, in one sense, he was never coming back to us.

7.

"Indians Would Be a Great Relief"

TOM found New Orleans a complete contrast to St. Louis, a city he hated. To him, it was the most colorful, fascinating place he had ever seen, including all the cities in Europe he had visited with his grandfather.

He was, I recall his words, "crazy about the city" and walked miles exploring it completely from the squatters' shacks along the river to the elegant mansions of the residential districts and the campuses of Loyola and Tulane.

He reveled in Audubon Park, lush with graceful palm trees and live oaks delicately draped with Spanish Moss, and was entranced by the flower-filled courtyards of the old houses in the French Quarter, with their fountains and wells, balconies and small stairs winding to the second floor.

He moved into the French Quarter, paying only $3 a week for a room. He also found the food amazingly inexpensive, breakfast costing a dime and lunch and dinner fifty cents each. He told me the cooking was the best he had encountered away from home and he was luxuriating in raw oysters, shrimp, crabs and lobster, fulfilling his passion for seafood.

He met both struggling writers like himself and writers who had arrived, such as Roark Bradford and Lyle Saxon, author of *Fabulous New Orleans* and at that time head of the Writers' Project there. Tom hoped to find work either with the WPA Theatre or its Writers' Project.

Before he left for New Orleans, while visiting his grandparents in Memphis, he entered a play contest sponsored by the Group Theatre in New York, about which he had learned through a newspaper announcement. He sent them his four long plays, *Candles to the Sun*, *The Fugitive Kind*, *Spring Storm* and *Not About Nightingales*. He also submitted several one-act plays grouped together under the title *American Blues*. They included *Moony's Kid Don't Cry*, *The Dark Room* and *The Case of the Crushed Petunias*.

In *Moony's Kid Don't Cry*, a man who formerly worked in the forests and now holds a monotonous job rebels against the added burdens of a new baby and a nagging wife, wanting to return to where "there's space to swing an axe in!" He accuses his wife of forcing him into marriage and is about to walk out on her when the wife shoves the sick baby into his arms and he suddenly becomes concerned with his son, his rebellion forgotten. *The Dark Room* tells of a social worker interviewing an Italian woman about her delinquent children; the mother has hidden one of her daughters, who is pregnant, in a dark room for six months. Although the daughter's lover has been forced by his parents to marry another girl, he continues to visit the daughter in her darkened room.

The third play, *The Case of the Crushed Petunias*, focuses on a repressed Boston woman and a gay young man who, after destroying some petunias in her garden, proposes they ride in a convertible to Cypress Hill, the cemetery, to make love.

Knowing Tom had little money, I sent a few dollars and he wrote to thank me and say the money was not yet needed but "will be stashed away." He told me of a couple he had met and liked; the husband was an artist who painted modernistically and was brilliant and goodhearted. "He has a red beard and often forgets where he is going when he leaves the house," wrote Tom.

He informed his grandparents he had moved to a rooming house "owned by a lovely Mississippi lady" for $10 a month at 722 Rue Toulouse in the heart of the French Quarter. He also told them he was busy revising a play for the WPA Theatre in New Orleans. A card to me added the information that the new landlady provided 25-cent meals and the play being revised was *The Fugitive Kind*.

My father was intending to visit Tom, as he was to visit him often in later years. A card from Tom told Father where he might stay. Then another followed, expressing Tom's regrets that Father could not come because of a bad cold. Tom wrote, "The weather here, when good, is *very* good—but when bad, is horrid," adding, "hope my description of the Quarter didn't frighten you—it really isn't so bad."

722 Rue Toulouse was actually owned by three ladies who had seen better days and now lived on the second floor of this old house amidst their antiques. They were marvelous cooks and Tom so enjoyed his 25-cent meals that he persuaded them to open a restaurant on the first floor. He thought up the slogan, "Meals for a Quarter in the Quarter," and offered to be cashier and help serve.

The restaurant proved a success until one of the old ladies lost her temper. It happened one night when she was trying to sleep above the first floor which she had rented out; it became the scene of a party that turned into bedlam.

DEAR MOTHER:
It is just as well Grand and Grandfather decided to delay their visit, as we've had a very hectic time at 722 Rue Toulouse. As I've probably mentioned, the land-lady has had a hard time adjusting herself to the Bohemian spirit of the Vieux Carré. Things came to a climax this past week

when a Jewish society photographer in the first floor studio gave a party and Mrs. Anderson expressed her indignation at their revelry by pouring a bucket of water through her kitchen floor which is directly over the studio and caused a near-riot among her guests. They called the patrol-wagon and Mrs. Anderson was driven to the Third Precinct on charges of Malicious Mischief and disturbing the peace. The following night we went to court—I was compelled to testify as one of the witnesses. Mrs. Anderson said she did not pour the water but I, being under oath, could not perjure myself—the best I could do was say I thought it was highly improbable that any lady would do such a thing! The judge fined her fifteen dollars. One of the other witnesses was the wife of Roark Bradford, who wrote Green Pastures, the famous Negro play. Her dress was ruined at the party. I went to see her afterwards to assure her my part in the affair was altogether unwilling—she was very nice and cordial and assured me there were no hard feelings at least toward me. I also met Mr. Bradford and Sam Byrd, a New York producer. As all my plays are in New York I had nothing to show him. I'm using my colorful experiences here as the background for a new play which is well under way.

The process of certification for the Writers' Project will be complete the fifteenth of this month and I expect Mr. Saxon will put me on at once, as he seems very much concerned and sympathetic about my precarious situation. He gave me a list of trade journals yesterday, that I might get temporary writing jobs from. I'm making a round of their offices. One of the radio stations is doing a weekly ghost story and they're going to produce my spook radio drama which I luckily got back from KXOK. They don't mention payment but of course it may lead to something—the radio stations here are in a pretty bad shape, in fact everything is except the business which caters directly to the tourists.

I hope I will get at least some encouraging news from the New York contest. It should be announced the fifteenth. I already know twice as many people here as I ever knew in St. Louis—some of them highly influential such as the Bradfords and Saxons—so I ought to get a break.

Mrs. Anderson's unpopularity has wrecked the Eat Shop —I don't think she can ever re-open it. But Mrs. Nesbit plans to start a new one when she returns from Florida. Mrs. Anderson plans to sell the place for $350-lease on the house and out-right sale of the complete furnishings, many of which are valuable antiques. If you come down here, you might be interested.

I'm completely out of funds now—so could use a few dollars if you're not in the same predicament.

Hope you're all well and Dakin successful in his scholastic and social enterprises.

With much love,

TOM

The effect of New Orleans on Tom was a profound one, even though he did not stay long, returning however during the following years. He became acquainted with a new kind of life in the French Quarter, one of wild drinking, sexual promiscuity and abnormality. Here he was surrounded by the lost and lonely people about whom he later wrote. He has said of New Orleans, "My happiest years were there . . . I was desperately poor . . . hocked everything but my typewriter to get by . . . New Orleans is my favorite city of America . . . of all the world, actually."

I was surprised one day to receive a letter from Tom postmarked San Antonio, Texas. He wrote he was on his way West, driving out with a young man whose relatives owned a squab ranch near Los Angeles. Tom gave addresses along the way where I could write and I sent a letter telling him I was glad he was enjoying the trip and enclosed a small check.

From San Antonio he wrote his grandparents a card explaining, "I've got a free ride to Los Angeles & Hollywood with a musician going to work there. Swell trip. With love—Tom."

Swell or otherwise, it must have been quite a trip! Neither of the two young men had much money and it finally reached the point where they could not pay for gas or shelter. In later years, Tom was reported as having siphoned gas out of a car on this journey but I believe he could never be guilty of such an act and anyhow I don't think he could operate a siphon if his life depended on it. He has no mechanical skill.

But he did tell me they stopped one night at the house of a huge Indian woman who, with fine redskin intuition, announced she kept a shotgun for handling deadbeats. Forewarned is forearmed and about four in the morning, the two destitute young men crept out of the house and into the Ford. They stepped on the gas only to hear the car treacherously backfire. They managed to roll a few hundred feet before a double-barreled charge of buckshot whirred through the air a few inches above their heads. The Indian lady was true to her word but luckily not her aim.

Whenever my mother could, she sent $10 in a letter to Tom, stitching the bill to the paper. She knew this meant he would eat for a few days. My father's pension as a clergyman did not stretch very far so Mother was sacrificing to help Tom.

En route, he stopped at Phoenix and wrote his grandparents, "We have nearly completed our leisurely trip to the west coast, been on the road over 2 weeks. Spent several days in Phoenix, Ariz. and here at Palm Springs, resort of movie millionaires—both delightful spots. This morning we are driving on into Los Angeles where I hope some type of employment will be obtainable."

Then followed a card announcing, "We arrived here a little later than we expected. Just got in Los Angeles last night. I'm going to see Sam Webb, one of Dad's salesmen, who will probably help me get located . . . Staying at the 'Y' for a day or two —I found your letter here at Gen'l Del.—hope you don't disapprove too much of my wanderings!"

Another postcard arrived soon after, saying, "I have an address now—811 E. New Jersey in Hawthorne, a suburb of Los Angeles. It is practically out in the country, a pigeon 'ranch.' We killed & picked 100 squabs yesterday—today delivered them at markets. I enjoy this rustic life for a change. Sam Webb called and thinks he can get me a job selling shoes—my plays are still in New York so I haven't contacted the film studios yet. Will write a letter soon."

A third card told more about the "pigeon ranch" in Los Angeles County, "owned by the uncle of the fellow who drove me out here." Tom wrote, "They took me in like their own nephew and I'm only paying a few dollars a week for room and board there. Sam Webb hopes to get me work in a retail shoe store until I've tried my luck at the movie studios." He wanted to work at Metro-Goldwyn-Mayer.

In the meantime, it was back to shoes as Mr. Webb got Tom a job at Clark's Bootery in Culver City, a half block from the MGM studios. Tom bought a secondhand bicycle for $5 and each day bicycled back and forth the twelve miles between Culver City and Hawthorne, since there were no trolleys connecting the two places. He wanted to stay with the Parrotts because the board was so reasonable.

I was relieved when Tom stopped riding bicycles for I lived in terror he would be run over. Years later a newspaper interview carried the story he had once run into a cow on his bicycle. I imagine he was as terrified as the cow, perhaps more so.

Important things continued to happen to Tom just around his birthday, as though the gods were sending him a gift. On the evening of March 20, 1939, six days before he turned twenty-eight, he bicycled from the shoe store to Hawthorne to find a telegram from New York.

THE JUDGES OF THE GROUP THEATRE PLAY CONTEST ARE HAPPY TO MAKE A SPECIAL AWARD OF ONE HUNDRED DOLLARS TO YOU FOR YOUR FIRST THREE SKETCHES IN AMERICAN BLUES.

It was signed: Harold Clurman, Irwin Shaw and Molly Day Thacher.

A letter from Miss Thacher, of the play department, followed, explaining that, under the terms of the contest, the judges had planned to award only a first prize of $500 and this had gone to Roman Naya for his full-length play, *Mexican Mural*. The judges felt, however, that *American Blues* was "so outstanding that it deserved recognition, and at our request the Group Theatre has made possible this extra award."

Miss Thacher ended the letter, "I hope the winning of this award will be the beginning of a fruitful association with the Group Theatre, that you will keep us in touch with your work and that it will not be too long before you come to New York to get acquainted at first hand with our theatre. Sincere congratulations from Harold Clurman, Irwin Shaw and from me."

Tom wrote his grandparents, "I had a pleasant surprise this week—got a congratulatory telegram from the Group Theatre in New York and a $100 checque as a special award for my group of short plays, 'American Blues' which I sent from Memphis. I am now working in a retail shoe store and like the work pretty well—small salary—$12 a week. Much love—Tom."

When Cornelius heard of the award, he sent a letter, one of the few he ever wrote Tom. Written on International Shoe Company stationery, it was signed not "Father," or "Dad," but "C. C. Williams."

St. Louis, Mo.
March 31, 1939

Dear Tom,

I got a pair of our woven shoes for myself today, that were samples, and they had an extra pair, which I am sending to you today by parcel post. They are made in two widths, narrow and broad, and we only had the broad in samples, which is about like a D width, which is a little broader than you wear in a shoe, though I imagine they will fit you all right.

I knew you just had white shoes I lately sent you, plus the shoes you carried out there with you, so these no doubt will come in very handy.

I hope you are getting along nicely in your work, and we were all very proud you won the $100 prize.

Hoping this finds you well, and with love from us all,

Affectionately,

C. C. Williams

Mr. Webb had written Cornelius about Tom's award, the letter arriving when Cornelius was away on a short business trip. His secretary called me, knowing I'd be interested, and read me the letter in which **Mr.** Webb said, "Any boy who would ride a bicycle twenty-four miles a day to work is bound to succeed."

I wrote my parents, telling them of this letter, saying nothing could have pleased me more than Mr. Webb's writing to Cornelius in praise of Tom. "You know how horrid Cornelius has talked to Tom, and about him," I wrote. "I just hope it won't prove to be too much for him. I don't forget what he has been through." After the insults Tom took from his father, I figure he can sail through any words critics might hurl.

Then came a letter from Tom, thanking me for a birthday gift and telling me he had received the check from the Group Theatre "so you may now inform my St. Louis public." He was working hard all week in the shoe store, nine to six daily and nine to nine on Saturdays, and expressed the hope he could arrange to get "at least an afternoon off—the work is pleasant compared to office work but consumes all my time."

This award turned into a thread that led to exciting developments. A number of literary agents now sought Tom out, having seen the notice in the newspapers. He wrote his grandparents, "I have a great deal of correspondence on my hands with N. Y. agents who want to handle my plays."

Not long after, he resigned from the shoe store and left the "pigeon ranch." He and the musician set off on their bicycles for Laguna Beach where they lived most of the summer on Tom's $100. Tom truly had a vacation, swimming and bicycling, writing only a little. He looked so young he had difficulty convincing bartenders he was over twenty-one, he said.

He had been at Laguna only a short while when a very important woman entered his life long distance—Audrey Wood. Audrey, who has since become a good friend of the family's, along with her husband William Liebling, wrote Tom from New York at the suggestion of Miss Thacher, asking if she could represent him as literary agent.

Audrey had faith in Tom from the start; after reading his plays, she sensed his talent. She helped him immeasurably, for it is not easy to find a foothold in the theatre; half the time you cannot even get plays read. Audrey has earned every penny of her commissions, for she is diligent and capable. I think the relationship turned out to be mutually very satisfactory.

Audrey went right to work for Tom. She sold his short story, "The Field of Blue Children," to *Story* Magazine for $25, and suggested he apply for a Rockefeller grant. This meant Tom could spend all his time writing, without having to sell shoes or pluck feathers from squabs at two cents a squab. Audrey sent him a Rockefeller Fellowship application blank.

But the grant was still a dream and Tom's money had run out. Mother sent him enough to pay his bus fare home and he arrived after a short stop in Taos, New Mexico, where he visited Frieda Lawrence whom he had always wanted to meet.

While at Laguna, Tom had started work on a play which he finished that autumn in the attic of our house (he moved from basement to attic as we changed houses). He called the new play *Battle of Angels;* he has described it as "the emotional record" of his youth, a play that released and purified the psychological storms of his adolescence.

He sent it to Audrey and followed up the mailing of the script with a visit to New York. He wanted to find a job there, not necessarily writing, but any kind of work, and to meet Audrey with whom he had only corresponded up to that point. When she walked in one morning he was sitting on the bench in her office and shyly introduced himself. Both Audrey and he tried to find him a job, Audrey even calling Macy's to see if they needed someone in any department. But this was the depression and there just was nothing available. After a few discouraging weeks, Tom returned to St. Louis to continue writing short stories and poems, a few of which were published in magazines.

I don't know the exact date but in one scrapbook reposes a yellow card from *Poetry.*

This contribution is one that particularly interested us. The editors would like to send a personal answer expressing their appreciation of its exceptional quality. But the staff is limited, and time is lacking for correspondence. We thank you for the privilege of reading it and hope that you will submit other manuscripts for consideration.

The editor signed his name, Peter De Vries, and added the note: *Not quite. Come again.*

That December, Tom received a long-distance telephone call. It was from Audrey. When he hung up he told me excitedly his Rockefeller grant had come through for $1,000 over a period of ten months. He said, "Mother, they want me to come to New York." I felt very happy for him, feeling this an important step in his career.

This time Tom took off for New York with more assurance. He enrolled at the New School for Social Research where Theresa Helburn and John Gassner were conducting a seminar in advanced playwriting.

DEAR MOTHER AND DAD:

Ashamed I haven't written earlier to acknowledge the shoes and rubbers. The rubbers are very ingenious and I wear them quite a bit lately as the streets are sloppy with half rain and snow.

What with attending the playwrighting seminar on my new scholarship, finishing a new play and revising the last act of the old one, I'm kept extremely busy.

The plays this season have fallen like sparrows. Even Odets' new play got terrible notices—the one I watched through rehearsals—and is just staggering along. They may not have money enough to produce anything more this season. There are about six plays that are terrific box-office successes and sold out solid for weeks in advance. The others can't even get an edge in. If Lillian Gish in "Life With Father" comes to St. Louis—it's on the road now—be sure to go. It is one of the hits here and is screamingly funny.

What kind of a car is the new one?

With love,

TOM

DEAR MOTHER:

It is nearly two A.M. so I'm sure you'll excuse me from writing a very long letter, but I want to write it now as I never know when I'll find another occasion. So many interesting things to do that the days slip by unnoticed. I spend every afternoon watching the Group Theatre rehearse. Evenings I usually visit some of the many fascinating people I've met or else take in a new play. This afternoon I received two passes to the new Elmer Rice play "Two On An Island"— given me by the Dramatists' Guild. Tonight I went to a poetry reading by W. H. Auden, the most famous English poet, and spent a couple of hours talking to a group of the best New York poets who were also in the audience. I'm afraid this city would not do for me to write in—there are too many diverting things going on. I have worked a good deal, however, on the last act of my new play and I have a feeling the Group will be pleased with it. Clurman, their head director, introduced himself to me at the rehearsal yesterday and said he had my new play on his desk and would read it as soon as he gets the present Odets play on the stage. After seeing some of this season's productions I don't see why my work should be neglected much longer by the commercial theatre. There is a pitiful lot of plays going on right now. Except "Juno and the Paycock" which was magnificent. I was standing out in front opening night of that play when Audrey and Liebling came along— Liebling gave me a box-seat. I sat directly over Robert Benchley, John Beal, Elissa Landi and several other notables and Audrey said I had the most conspicuous position in the house. It was the only really good play I've seen so far and is a revival of an old Abbey Theatre success.

I meant to start this letter with thanks for the package. I got it at the desk as I came in tonight—the two shirts and the gloves were especially welcome. My checque was sent me on the twenty-second so I came out okay financially for the month. It is horrible the circumstances in which some people are living in New York. I met a group of young writers who had had nothing but black coffee for several days and were sleeping in an unfurnished room. Mr. Vinal, editor of

Voices, is trying to keep them from starving. We chip in the money we would spend on an evening meal and buy food enough for the whole bunch—they have a double burner in the room—came up here from Georgia to *sell* poetry.

I distinctly remember mailing Rose's coat. Surely it must have reached her.

I hope you will take your trip South pretty soon. I'm sure it would do you a lot of good. I suppose Grand and Grandfather are leaving for Florida.

Much love,

TOM

Audrey later told me about the opening night of *Juno and the Paycock,* presented by the Abbey Players, when she and Liebling saw Tom standing in the lobby all alone. Liebling asked if he were going inside and Tom replied he did not have a ticket but just came to see the celebrities. Liebling managed to get him a seat in a box and Tom evidently had the time of his life. He single-handedly carried the audience with him, he so obviously enjoyed the play. His hearty laugh rang out often and so spontaneously that the sophisticated audience found itself easily joining in.

About this time Tom wrote his grandfather of his new life in New York.

DEAR GRANDFATHER:

I am dreadfully sorry to hear of your suffering from eczema and having to postpone the trip to Florida. I was hoping you were already there and reveling in the sunshine. Perhaps you should have come to New York with me as the winter has been delightful. Today so warm I have my window wide open for fresh air while I am writing and the castles along Fifth Avenue are radiant with sunlight. I have just finished a new short story which I am pleased with and am making minor revisions on my new play while waiting for the Group Theatre to take some action on it. I feel that this play will be produced sooner or later, whether the Group Theatre takes it or not, as it contains some very strong drama—a little too strong, perhaps, for most producers.

An enormously wealthy young Jewish girl I met in St. Louis has just returned to New York and called me from her apartment. She had two telephones and was talking over both of them at once—a bit of Hebrew ostentation which made me smile. I like the Jews but they do have some funny traits. It is just like Bernice, for instance, to drop one letter out of her name to make it sound Aryan without changing it sufficiently to prevent people from recognizing herself as the author.

Life here is very pleasant. I get up and take a shower and a quick swim, write several hours, then take another short work-out in the gym, go out for dinner and then attend a play or exchange visits with various interesting people that I have met here. Certainly no stagnation as there is in the middle-west. However I don't think I would stay here while working on another play—there are too many pleasant, enticing distractions. The attic in St. Louis or a cabin on the beach or the desert is best for that purpose.

I am going out now to deliver some short scripts to Audrey and visit an editor of Harcourt-Brace whom I know.

I do hope your condition will be relieved when you've kept to your diet a while and that the Florida trip is only a little deferred.

With much love to you and Grand,

Tom

The students at the New School planned to stage one of Tom's plays and a note about it appeared in the drama column of *The New York Times,* possibly the first mention of Tom on that august page. I wrote on top of the column, as I pasted it in the scrapbook, "From G. B. Shaw to T. Williams!" The column's first item announced that *Geneva,* Shaw's fiftieth play, would close Saturday night at the Henry Miller Theatre after fifteen performances, and its next-to-last item, ten paragraphs below, reported that *The Long Good-bye,* by Tennessee Williams, would have its first showing at the New Theatre School on Feb. 9 and 10.

Another newspaper carried the announcement in a small story all by itself with the headline SHOW PRIZE PLAY and identified Tom as having won a $1,000 Rockefeller Foundation playwriting scholarship.

Fleet Munson, the critic, saw the student production and sent Audrey a letter which she, in turn, gave Tom and he mailed to me with the note: "Letter shortly. Very busy with writing. Tom."

FEB. 14, 1940

DEAR AUDREY WOOD:

Last Saturday night I had the good fortune to watch a group of not too fumbling student actors perform a piece called THE LONG GOODBYE. I cannot know how it was to be a member of a Provincetown audience in the early days of O'Neill but I do know that I have been profoundly moved by the playwriting talent of one whose ability is as clearly recognizable.

I am told that THE LONG GOODBYE is but one of Tennessee Williams' lesser works, not considered worthy of much attention by such prize awarding bodies as the Group Theatre. Well—I am glad you are handling him because I think you've got something there . . .

I'm sure you know how good Mr. Williams is but even so, I am impelled to add my small word. Gentle him, for pete's sake. He's a honey. Don't let the drones get him.

Best greetings,

FLEET MUNSON

This one-act play of Tom's was written in flashback form as a son, a sensitive young writer, recalls his mother suffering from cancer, then committing suicide, and his sister, who liked the gaiety of night life, becoming a prostitute.

Audrey had written across the top of Mr. Munson's note: *Dear Tennessee: I thought you would enjoy this as much as I did.* As I reread Mr. Munson's kind words, I thought to myself, the drones never did get Tom. Anything but.

While attending the spring session of the advanced playwriting course, Tom gave Mr. Gassner, who was a director of the

113

Theatre Guild as well as his instructor, a new draft of *Battle of Angels*. Mr. Gassner liked it well enough to show to Miss Helburn and Lawrence Langner, powers in the Guild, with the hope they might produce it. This was Broadway's prestige organization for the production of plays. Any playwright accepted by the Guild was assured at least an audience among producers from then on.

Tom must have gone through what, to a writer, is a time of exquisite torture as he waited for the Guild to decide. He had been planning, when the seminar ended, to take a trip to Mexico and write there, living on his grant. He also wanted to visit New Mexico again to consult Mrs. Lawrence about a play he wished to write about her late husband. But his plans changed.

DEAR MOTHER:
My Mexican trip has been postponed, at least till the Fifth of April. The Theatre Guild has taken a sudden, unexpected interest in my new play. Audrey called up yesterday morning and said their play-reader, John Gassner, who is also my instructor at the New School, was "tremendously excited over it" and wanted Elmer Rice, the playwright, to look at it soon as he got back in New York, April 2nd. I saw Gassner this afternoon and he confirmed Audrey's report and said it was the best play he had read in a year and if the other two readers, who took it to Nassau with them, liked it as well as he, there would be a production next Fall!! It seems that fortune is certainly with me, as this happens just when the Group Theatre has gone broke on Odets' new play which has closed, a complete failure. The Theatre Guild has long been the outstanding theatre in New York, though lately the Group had challenged them. However they have had five straight hits this season, Katharine Hepburn in "The Philadelphia Story" which has been running a year and is now going on tour, Hemingway's "The Fifth Column" with Franchot Tone, just opened and a big success and Saroyan's "Time of Your Life" which is still running, Lunt and Fontanne in a new Sherwood play and a new play by Saroyan. If they should produce the play

114

it would be the best possible production. So I am in a state of great suspense and regardless of the outcome, will certainly need a Mexican trip to relax me when things are settled. Audrey also went with me over to Harper's this afternoon—they are reading my short works and want me to write a novel. Said if I wrote fifty pages on one which they liked, they would give me a contract with advance payment. But I don't feel in a state to start a novel right now. I told them I would be very glad to sell them some short stories to pay my boat-fare to Mexico. The writing and theatre world is a flock of sheep. They never get interested until someone else is. You have to distribute things around several places to work up any enthusiasm.

Spring is here today, I went out without a topcoat as the streets were quite warm and sunny. I suppose New York will be more pleasant now. I hope so as I have grown pretty tired of it in the last few weeks. The people here are all living such artificial lives—Indians would be a great relief!

Forward this letter to Grand as I have not written them lately.

Much love,

TOM

TUESDAY PM

DEAR MOTHER:

I am exhausted but very relieved as the preliminaries seem to be more or less settled. The Guild had a meeting at the class this afternoon, the play was thoroughly dissected and many changes were suggested, but Miss Helburn (one of the heads) took me home in a cab and said they would pay me one hundred dollar option on the play tomorrow which is the first step toward a complete sale. I haven't got the details straight but they may pay me this amount each month till the play is produced. In the meantime, however, I have to do a lot of revision to meet their requirements, many of which seem foolish to me at the present moment, but I am not telling them so. It appears that they are genuinely excited over the play and their intentions are quite serious. So I think we should come to some satisfactory compromise about changes. Of course I hate to go back to work on an old play when I want to write new ones. But you can't have cake and eat it. I told Miss Helburn I was planning to leave for Mexico and she thought that when the re-writing is done and work toward a production really gets under way, I could go.

I'm going to pack a box of winter things and mail them to you. I plan to leave by the Cuba Mail Line, landing at Vera Cruz and going to Mexico City for a while and then on over to Acapulco which has marvelous swimming, fishing and resting. They say it never gets hotter than 86 although summer is not the tourist season down there. And then one American dollar buys $3.60 in Mexican money so I can live very cheaply while down there.

If I leave Thursday afternoon, I will send you a wire giving next address, probably care of Wells-Fargo in Mexico City or Vera Cruz.

Much love to you all,

Tom

On May 8, I received a telegram from Tom.

> THEATRE GUILD SIGNS REGULAR CONTRACT TODAY. MUST
> STAY NEAR NEW YORK. FALL PRODUCTION LIKELY. THANKS
> FOR BOXES. INFORM GRAND AND GRANDFATHER. THANKS
> FOR BOXES. LOVE
>
> Tom

The boxes contained some of his summer clothes I thought he might need either in New York or Mexico.

A card arrived a few weeks later with a picture of the RCA building in Rockefeller Center rising high above the statue of Prometheus in the Sunken Plaza. He wrote, "Spent week in Lake George—now back old address. Plans looming for Fall production if war doesn't kill the theatre. Love, Tom."

Soon afterwards, however, he left for Mexico by boat to work on revisions for *Angels*. He wrote, "If I didn't need a complete change so badly, after these weeks of tension and scurrying-about making 'contacts,' I would come home for a short while before leaving. But a week on the ocean seems too marvelous to delay." He fell ill in Mexico and sent a wire from Acapulco on September 17.

UNEXPECTED EXPENSE. PLEASE WIRE TWENTY DOLLARS. REPAY PROMPTLY.

TOM WILLIAMS

This was one of the few distress calls he ever made. It was a Sunday and I wondered how on earth I could find the money, for there was not a cent in the house. But a friend to whom I appealed came to my rescue, lending it to me, and I wired it via Western Union.

Then I received a letter from Tom back in New York, telling me he planned to go to Provincetown, probably until the end of the month. The Guild was showing his play to a number of leading actresses, among them Miriam Hopkins, who, he said, he hoped would be interested. "She is Southern and has great feeling—will probably see her tonight at one of the summer theatres," he wrote. "She has my script and has promised to read it this week. They are all afraid of the other woman in the play who has a dangerously good part."

He continued, "I don't think the Guild will announce any production plans till after the actress problem is settled. I am not told anything at all. They had so much trouble with Saroyan interfering in his productions that I suppose they think it is best to keep the playwright as ignorant as possible till everything is settled.

"It is very warm and muggy in N. Y. so I'm anxious to get back on the Cape. Hope you are comfortable in the new home."

The "new" home had quite a story behind it. Cornelius and I had been driving to the house in which we lived, which was rented, as all our homes had been, one day just after he had taken his regular monthly "cure" at the hospital. I had said not a word about his drinking and he was evidently feeling very grateful for my not scolding him. Suddenly he said, "I'm going to buy you that home you've wanted all these years."

"You mean it?" I asked in disbelief.

117

"I do," he said emphatically.

I realized I had caught him at the right moment, so I said, "Well, here's the house."

We happened to be passing a three-story home at 53 Arundel Place, of Georgian Colonial architecture, with a FOR SALE sign on a lawn abloom with jonquils. I felt we could live in such a house with a minimum of friction. My mother had become very ill and I wanted to ask her and my father to live with us, but our present home was too small.

We stopped the car, got out, looked at the house, bought it. Cornelius scarcely would have done this had he not been in a chastened mood. "When the devil was sick, devil a monk he would be, But when the devil was well, the devil a devil was he," applied to my husband. Afterwards, Cornelius regretted his generosity and every time he got drunk he'd sneer, "Well, you really put something over on me, didn't you?" It rather spoiled the gift.

I fixed up the third floor for Tom, making a bedroom-studio out of its large room. I suspect a great many landlords in New York would think it palatial, for it had dormer windows and space for a desk, a work table and a chair in addition to the bedroom furniture. Tom used it whenever he came home.

Dakin was then in his second year of law school at Washington University. He had been an honor student all through high school and college. When he told his father he wanted to study law, Cornelius said he would not pay for three years of law school. Dakin said, "Dad, if you'll let me take just two, I'll study hard, go to summer school and make the three years in two," which he did. He attended the University of Colorado summer school in 1939 and 1941, where he sat next to the man who became President Kennedy's first Supreme Court appointee, Justice Byron (Whizzer) White. After Dakin received his law degree he went to Harvard Business School for a few months before being called into service in World War II.

As Tom had hoped, Miss Hopkins was interested in starring in *Angels*. Miss Helburn wrote him in October that Miss Hopkins, in a talk over the telephone from Hollywood, said she

118

would like to play the lead but was not sure she could get free of film commitments. "If she cannot we will have to wait for our other star possibilities," Miss Helburn stated.

But Miss Hopkins managed her freedom and Margaret Webster was signed to direct the play. A trial run was announced for Boston and an opening on Broadway early in 1941. Mark Barron, referring to Miss Hopkins and Miss Webster, wrote in the columns of the Associated Press that Tom's play was "swinging into rehearsals with as high powered a lineup of talent as even Bernard Shaw or Eugene O'Neill could command." This was part of an interview with Tom that started out, "Tennessee Williams is a young playwright with the soft, warm drawl of Mississippi in his voice and the footloose urge of forty-eight states in his feet."

Tom wrote he was getting his own way with the production, but only after much fighting. "The lady has a strong will. I have had to develop a strong one also to manage her." He may have been referring either to Miss Hopkins or Miss Helburn, for he told me his original script was covered with red ink, all changes suggested by Miss Helburn.

Then a reassuring card arrived.

Dear Folks—Everything going nicely—We open in Boston Dec. 29 or 30 for 2 weeks—then Washington and New York. Will be on road with play probably about 3 weeks. Much work and excitement and of course suspense! Will try to get off a letter and a few Xmas things this week. Suggest you come up *after* N.Y. opening as opening night will be terribly hectic in N.Y.—Much love—Tom.

But Tom was wrong. It was opening night in Boston that was to prove the hectic one.

8.

"Death or Madness Are Nearer
Than a Myth"

TOM'S first play destined for Broadway opened the night of December 30, 1940, in Boston. A city less likely to receive it with open arms could scarcely have been chosen.

Battle of Angels, a play Tom dedicated to D. H. Lawrence, was, as Tom told a newspaper reporter, "a sex play with cosmic overtones," with "a good deal of what Philip Barry calls 'good violence.'" Its hero was a young writer gathering material for a book about "Life," named Valentine Xavier (the very name of one of Tom's ancestors on his father's side, a sixteenth-century Basque who was a younger brother of St. Francis Xavier).

The hero is described in the play as about twenty-five years old with "a fresh and primitive quality, a virile grace and freedom of body, and a strong physical appeal." He wears a snakeskin jacket as he wanders into a town in the Mississippi Delta and before long becomes sexually intimate with a married woman, Myra Torrance. She gives him a job in a confectionery store owned by her villainous husband, Jabe, dying of cancer in his room above the store.

Val also attracts two other women, Vee Talbot, the sheriff's wife, a religious fanatic and an artist, and Cassandra Whiteside, a society girl who seeks surcease from the pain of her empty life through sexual promiscuity. There is also a woman from Waco, Texas, who descends on the town, gun in hand, claiming Val raped her, although he tells Myra she seduced him, becoming enraged when he refused to remain in Waco.

Myra becomes pregnant, confesses it to Jabe who then shoots and kills her, telling the townspeople Val murdered his wife. Val tries to flee but is caught by the angry mob who burn the store to the ground, tear off all his clothes, throw him into a car and ride him to the "lynching tree." There they tie him, then turn a blowtorch on him, burning him alive in the death he most feared (he had told the woman from Waco that he hated fire because as a boy he suffered a severe burn which left a scar on his leg).

This was quite a play for Boston, including as it did scenes of seduction, adultery, nymphomania, shooting, lynching, flood and fire. The premiere started peacefully, as the elegantly dressed subscribers to the Theatre Guild filed into the theatre and settled with an air of dignity into their seats. They watched the action unfold, not appearing too shaken until the scene when Vee Talbot unveiled her portrait of Jesus, which bore a remarkable resemblance to Val. Shocked whispers sounded throughout the audience, followed by a few hisses, and some even stood up and indignantly marched out of the theatre.

Then a physical catastrophe occurred. At the dress rehearsal, there had not been enough smoke to make the fire convincing as the confectionery store burned down, and those in charge of the smoke pots decided to make sure opening night would suffer no anemia of flames. When it was time for the mob to set fire to the store, billows of smoke poured forth, cascading over cast and audience alike. An already angered audience took this as the last flaming straw and spluttered its way up the aisles, talking loudly of the indignities thrust upon it. When Miss Hopkins came out to take a bow, waving her hands before her face to clear away the fumes and coughing apologetically as she smiled, she saw mainly the backs of the first-nighters as they pushed their way out of the theatre. Only the balcony applauded.

Before the play opened, Miss Helburn had sent Tom a telegram saying, SAINT MICHAEL AND ALL GOOD ANGELS BE WITH YOU!, signing it CONNECTICUT UPDYKE (her married name coupled with the state she adopted à la Tennessee). But it was as though the very devil plagued Tom's *Angels*.

Most of the critics did not understand what Tom was trying to say. One called it a play "about a half-wit living a defensive life against predatory women," another referred to it as "dirty." There was, however, some faint praise. One reviewer remarked the play held occasional lines of beauty, another that the atmosphere was realistic, and a third that there were good character touches in some of the minor roles.

Personally, I think what most disturbed Boston, a highly Roman Catholic city, was the idea of Vee Talbot painting the young wanderer in the resemblance of Jesus. This must have struck the Catholics as sacrilegious. After a week of deliberation, irate city officials demanded this scene be deleted and other "offending" lines be cut.

Miss Hopkins, who played the role of Myra, was quick to rally to Tom's defense. She was quoted as suggesting it would be a good idea to pitch the Boston Council, which had censored the play, into the harbor as patriots had once done to British tea. As to the play being "dirty," Miss Hopkins declared, "That's an insult to the young man who wrote it. It's not a dirty play. I wouldn't be in it if it were a dirty play. The dirt is something in the minds of some of the people who have seen it. They read meanings into it according to their own suppressed feelings."

Tom, still hopeful the play would open on Broadway, returned to New York to work on revisions. He wrote me, "I am O. K. I was fully prepared for our difficulties in Boston—disappointed, of course, but feel that in the long run things will work out better. The play is not ready for New York, due mostly to my ill-advised efforts to make it a starring vehicle satisfactory to Miss Hopkins rather than to my own best judgment. . . .

"The Theatre Guild had promised to continue my advance royalties until the script is repaired which is very decent of them I think. I will probably leave town in a few days to work in peace."

There was much interest in New York in the play, scheduled to open on Broadway in a few weeks. Dorothy Kilgallen in *The Voice of Broadway* wrote:

> The play upon which they will pass judgment after Gertie's show is launched tonight [*Lady in the Dark*] is one starring the sultry, ash-blonde Miriam Hopkins—a play which is reported to be, if not good, at least good and hot. . . . From all sides poured the information that it was a sizzler calculated to send Puritan audiences out of the theatre muttering, "Well, I never did!" and to spur the notoriously alert Boston censors to a frenzy of scene-banning.

But after two weeks in Boston, the Theatre Guild announced it would close the play there and postpone the New York opening. The Guild sent a letter of apology to Boston subscribers, refunding money to those who had not as yet seen *Angels,* and explained, "The play was more of a disappointment to us than to you. *Battle of Angels* turned out badly. But who knows whether the next play by the same author may not prove a success?"

> In view of the unfortunate publicity caused by the Boston censor's protest about *Battle of Angels,* we feel it is only fair to give you the Guild's reasons for producing the play. We chose it because we felt the young author had genuine poetic gifts and an interesting insight into a particular American scene. The treatment of the religious obsession of one of the characters, which sprang from frustration, did not justify in our opinion, the censor's action. It was, we felt, a sincere and honest attempt to present a true psychological picture.

Tom wrote me the play closed because "non-poetic audiences did not quite understand the production, an allegorical play." So many of his plays have been allegories.

One of Tom's boyhood hometown newspapers (he had one in Columbus, one in Nashville, one in Canton, one in Clarksdale), the Clarksdale *Register,* wrote an editorial attacking the play, calling it a "dirty" story. This must have hurt Tom almost as much as the Boston verbal assault. Margaret Webster wrote him a very understanding letter shortly after the closing. She said she was sorry to hear "the tale of our Boston immorality penetrated to Clarksdale," adding, "I must admit that for a week or two I scanned the papers, fearful of seeing a headline YOUNG AUTHOR LYNCHED IN HOMETOWN!"

She commented, "I'm glad your grandfather remained sympathetic. He must be a very swell person." Father always championed everything Tom wrote and he particularly liked *Angels.* I think secretly Father got great delight out of Tom's putting to poetic purpose the fire and brimstone ministers use in their sermons to pulverize parishioners from the pulpit.

To further cheer Tom up, Miss Webster described some of her current activities at the Guild and the plays in production there, reporting the author of one "is making them all realize with more vivid appreciation the fine qualities of Tennessee!" She added, "My author, Mr. Euripedes, is fortunately dead. As the old rhyme goes,

> The great thing about Clive
> Is that he is no longer alive.
> There is a good deal to be said
> For being dead."

She concluded with, "My love, dear Ten. I do hope that the operation will finally turn out to have been perfectly successful. I have had two eye operations myself, and know how unfunny they can be. Let us know when you will be around again. Meanwhile write good, and all lovers of the English language will have cause to love you."

124

And as P.S. "Are you using carbons? Are you wearing your red flannel underwear? Do you need some more pencils?"

The operation to which she referred was on his left eye. For years Tom suffered from a cataract over the eye and this was to be the first of four operations, none of which resulted in saving his sight. Today he is able to see out of his right eye only, which is quite a coincidence considering Cornelius had vision only in one eye.

Thus *Angels* closed before I had a chance to attend it. Insult was added to injury when someone at the Theatre Guild handed Tom a small check with the warning, "Now, don't think we're going to take care of you the rest of your life."

I asked Tom what he had answered. He said, "I was so stunned I couldn't say anything. I just turned on my heels, Mother, and left."

As it happened, however, the Guild did continue to "take care of" Tom, not for the rest of his life, but for two months, as he wrote me from Key West where he landed after the eye operation. He was given a check for $200 and told to go somewhere and rewrite the play.

2/12/41

DEAR FOLKS:

I should have given you some warning of this radical change of address but decided to go the day that I left. My doctor said no further treatments were necessary and I was free to leave town so I packed up immediately and took the first train to Florida. I met the Parrotts in Miami and Jim drove me on down here to Key West which will be my headquarters for the next month or two.

I am stopping in the 125-year-old house you see on the envelope. It belongs to an Episcopal clergyman's widow, Mrs. Black—he had Grace Church in Memphis. She is renting me the servants' cabin for eight dollars a week. The Theatre Guild is advancing me living expenses for the next two months in which time I am to complete my re-write of "Angels" and send it back to them. Then, if they are satisfied, they will renew the contract, and plan a second production. They are having a run of hard luck as their two new productions "Cream in the Well" by Lynn Riggs and "Liberty Jones" by Phillip Barry both got an unanimously bad press and are doomed to failure. I am going to rest for a week or so before I start any more writing as I am pretty tired out.

Unfortunately the weather in Florida is extremely bad right now. I don't advise Grand and Grandfather to leave till it changes. In Key West it has been so cold I have slept under blankets the past three nights since I got here—no sun at all. A cold rain and wind—but this is expected to break by tomorrow.

The doctor seemed satisfied with the result of the operation. I can distinguish light and dark much more clearly and there is some visibility of objects but it will take several more weeks to know whether or not the vision will return enough to be useful. The cataract absorbs gradually after the operation. Sometimes it stops at a certain point and a second "needling" operation is necessary to complete it. This can be done any time afterwards. Doctor said there was nothing in McGrath's report that would preclude the good possibility of sight being restored eventually —I am glad that I had it done though it was quite a bad ordeal. I suffered very severely for the first few days after the operation and they had to give me typhoid fever injections to combat the inflammation in the eye—it seems an artificial fever will accelerate absorption. The injections gave me high fever and chills that nearly shook me to pieces! I got wonderful attention at the hospital, though, they were in and out of my room every five or ten minutes, so there was absolutely no reason for anyone to come up. After I was released from the hospital I went to stay with some friends who gave me excellent care till I was able to look out for myself. Several columnists carried reports of my operation so I received a great many sympathetic calls. Everybody in New York has been marvelous to me— considering what a hard-boiled town it is supposed to be.

I left all my summer clothes in St. Louis. As it will be very warm here when the wind changes, I wish you would send me my white linen suit and the dungarees which I wore in Mexico. Also any sport shirt which I may have around the house.

I think Grand and Grandfather would like it here.

Much love,

Том

The place where Tom was staying was called the Trade Winds, a tourist home owned by a lifelong friend of mine, Marian Black. Her daughter, Marian Black Vaccaro, has since become a very good friend of Tom's.

Mrs. Black informed me, knowing I was worried about Tom, that, although depressed, he was trying to write. The maid would sweep up stacks of crumpled paper thrown to the floor and bring them to Mrs. Black saying, "There ain't nothin' on these pages. Can't I throw them away?"

"No," Mrs. Black would order. "They might be valuable. Tom might have written something he wants to save."

She told me one page held the seven words written over and over, "My head is a block of stone."

Tom must have felt all his hopes had crashed with that Boston debacle and that he had failed our faith, too, for we had been looking forward eagerly to his play on Broadway.

But he managed, as he always has, to pull himself together. He set about rewriting the play, hoping the Guild would produce it. He never gave up on *Angels,* working on it spasmodically for years. It finally appeared on Broadway sixteen years later as *Orpheus Descending,* about seventy-five percent rewritten, Tom estimated, and in 1960 as the movie, *The Fugitive Kind,* starring Anna Magnani and Marlon Brando, which had no connection except the title with Tom's earlier play of the same name.

About three weeks after he arrived in Key West, Tom seemed in a far better frame of mind. (The Mrs. Lippmann to whom he refers is Alice Lippmann, an old and dear friend of the family's.)

DEAR MOTHER:

I was vastly pleased with everything in the box especially the sweater which feels very comfortable these windy nights. I also received a box from Mrs. Lippmann, a box of candy.

It is now really warm here, the sun and the swimming delightful, and the island has become a haven for the intellectual society from New York. I've met a record number of celebrities lately at suppers and cocktail parties, such people as Max Eastman, John Dewey, James Farrell, Benedict Thielen, Mrs. Ernest Hemingway (divorced), the famous artists Arnold Branch and Doris Lee, playwright Arthur Arent and the poet Elizabeth Bishop. They are all busy entertaining each other and having political quarrels. I prefer my writing-desk or the beach to this type of social activity which I got enough of in New York.

Are Grand and Grandfather still planning to come South? I believe the cold spell is broken now even in the northern part of the peninsula. I may run up to Miami for a few days, it is only three hours drive over the famous Over-seas highway, a long bridge extending between the keys. Miami is only pleasant for a brief visit, it is terribly over-run with tourists.

I work some every day on "Angels" and several new dramatic scenes I've inserted will probably enhance its value. Also working on new material. The Theatre Guild's two recent plays barely got through the subscription season and were mercilessly assaulted by the critics—both serious, poetic plays which have not had a fighting chance this season. Drum-beating, flag-waving, and pure musical comedy entertainment are the chosen fare. The dice will be loaded against us till after the war—but of course popular stuff dies quickly and the future accepts more readily what the present rejects. I am thankful that the Guild continues my allowance till I have finished re-writing.

I will let you know immediately if I leave on a trip.

Much love,

TOM

We then received a picture postcard of the Trade Winds, a two-story house topped by a widow's walk and surrounded by

My mother as a bride

Tom's grandmother,
Mrs. Thomas Lanier Williams

Me as a child . . .

. . . and later as a debutante

Just before my marriage

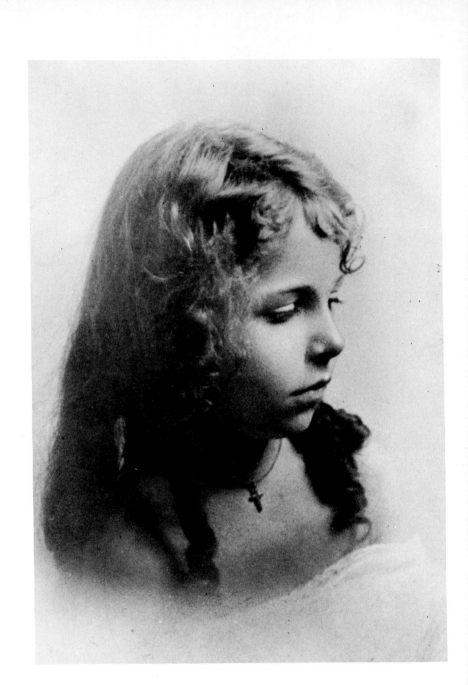

Rose as a child

Family portrait with Rose and Tom

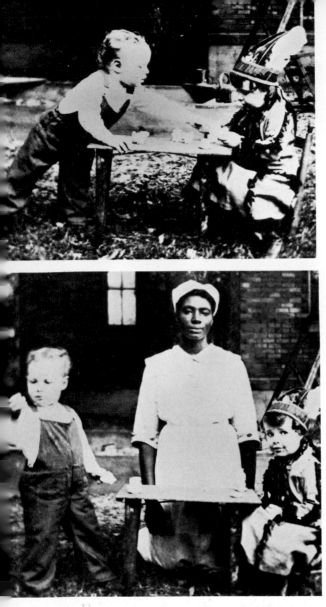

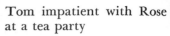
Tom impatient with Rose at a tea party

Tom observing something as usual, with Ozzie and Rose

Tom as a child

Ozzie the storyteller, and Tom

My husband, Cornelius Coffin Williams

When I became Regent of the D.A.R. in St. Louis, in 1936

Tom as a boy

Dakin as a boy

Rose as a young lady

The cover of the first magazine in which a short story by Tom appeared

A "gag" picture after Tom won the National Academy of Arts and Letters award

George Platt Lynes

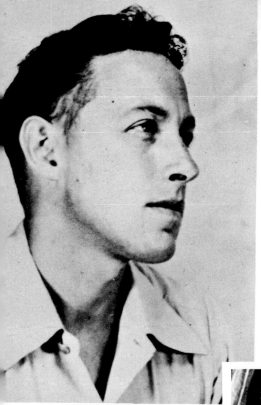

Tom in his early twenties

My father in his later years

The house on Arundel Place. *Below:* Tom's present home in Key West; the lady standing outside is my cousin's wife, Mrs. Horace Dakin of Hannibal, Missouri.

Left: Mother and Father on a stroll in St. Petersburg, Florida. *Right:* Tom and Father about 1947.

Dakin and a proud mother,
1957

Mother and sons in Holly-
wood, 1961

Dakin, Tom, Dakin's wife
Joyce, Christopher Isher-
wood and myself in Holly-
wood, 1961

Tom on his way to Europe, 1960

palm trees. Tom wrote, "This is where I am living. Cabin just behind house. Very simple life—write in morning, beach in afternoon. Where are G. and G. F. going: I may visit them. Love, Tom."

A week later he received a telegram informing him the Rockefeller committee had granted him an additional $500 to write a new play, the money to be given at $100 a month. Audrey obtained this for Tom.

He left Key West for New York where he submitted his revision of *Angels* to the Guild. They told him they had decided to abandon production. Whereupon he rented a room at the YMCA and started a play with Donald Windham, a young writer he met the year before. Donald had the idea a short story by D. H. Lawrence called "You Touched Me" would make a good play, and Tom agreed to work on it with him.

Tom also got busy on a play of his own, *Stairs to the Roof*, subtitled *A Prayer for the Wild Hearts That Are Kept in Cages*. It was a fantasy based on his experiences in the International Shoe Company. Its hero was a meek young man who revolted against the domination of his wife and employer. He fell in love with a young woman who worked at the company and, as the play ended, they climbed the "stairs to the roof" which he discovered in the company building, on their way to colonize another world, one of happiness and laughter.

That summer, Tom again went to Provincetown to swim and to start another play, *I Rise in Flame, Cried the Phoenix*, based on the last hours of D. H. Lawrence, about whom, for years, he had wanted to write. This play describes Lawrence's relationship to his wife, telling how he wanted to die alone, yet even in his fear and hatred of women, called out for his wife with his last breath.

At the summer's end, Tom decided to go to New Orleans to work. There he received two encouraging letters. Mr. Gassner wrote, "I hope everything turns out well for you, and that you can reward those who have had faith in you. Meanwhile, you can tell them—if my name and opinion mean anything to them— that, regardless of the outcome I think you have written one of

the most promising scripts I have read in years." He was referring to the ill-fated *Angels.*

Then Audrey sent him a letter from John Tebbel, managing
editor of the *American Mercury,* who had written, "Williams
is sort of D. H. Lawrence and Hemingway and Thomas Wolfe
rolled into one and leavened by a style which is not at all eclec-
tic. I have a feeling that he'd be a better novelist than a short
story writer. He has something to say and knows how to say it,
which is more than can be said for nine-tenths of the American
writers currently practicing."

Tom left New Orleans to spend a few weeks in St. Louis after
I wrote him that his grandmother, now living with us, was
dying of cancer, having wasted away to eighty-three pounds. He
had always adored her, and she, him; the first large sum of
money he earned writing was sent to me with the instruction to
give it to "Grand," which I did not do—I kept it in the bank for
him. He wanted desperately to be a success while she was alive.

He returned to New Orleans where he completed his play on
Lawrence and continued work on *Stairs to the Roof.* The latter
he took to New York in January and gave to Audrey, then he
and Donald worked further on their play.

Tom underwent his second eye operation, this one performed
in St. Louis. It was not his eye, however, that kept him out of
military service. When he reported for his preinduction physical
examination, it turned out to be a very brief one. The doctor
listened to his heart and promptly classified him 4-F. Tom has
always been fearful of a heart condition ever since his collapse
in St. Louis, although doctors have assured him the palpitations
are more the result of anxiety than of a defective heart. Actually,
he would have been classified 4-F because of his poor eyesight.

Tom did not get far with *Stairs to the Roof.* David Merrick's
reaction was fairly typical.

JUNE 14, 1942

DEAR MR. WILLIAMS:
    Audrey Wood sent over your play STAIRWAY TO THE
ROOF. I found it interesting and beautifully written. How-

130

ever, I think it is unlikely that you can get a Broadway production. I don't think a producer would be likely to risk a more than average amount of production money on a fantasy or semi-fantasy at this time. Not unless it had a chorus of pretty girls and a part for Gertrude Lawrence. Certainly not for one with some meaning to it. You told me that you were aware of the fact that your work was uncommercial, so I don't suppose this opinion will come as a disappointment.

I don't think I should advise you to write about more commercial subjects because I feel that you write so well and with so much genuine feeling in your present form. Let's just hope that soon they'll get around to wanting something better.

I'm looking forward to reading your latest play and I hope Miss Wood will be free to send it over soon.

Have a pleasant summer and good luck on whatever you're writing.

Very truly yours,

DAVID MERRICK

Weeks passed and still no producer seemed interested in *Stairs*. Tom never did get a Broadway production for it and it eventually appeared at the Pasadena Playhouse March 25 to April 7, 1945, staged under the direction of Margo Jones, who also directed it two years later, February 26 to March 9, 1947.

To support himself, Tom now took a variety of menial jobs, including dishwashing, operating an elevator on the night shift of an apartment building, selling books at Frances Steloff's famous Gotham Book Mart, a job which lasted only one day, and reciting poetry in Greenwich Village, where he attracted attention by his startling eye patch. A friend painted a white, staring eye on the black patch he wore for a while after his operation, and it looked quite Daliesque.

Tom decided to spend the summer in Macon, Georgia, with two friends, Paul Bigelow and Jordan Massee. I came across some notes he kept while there, in which he describes the depths of despair to which he plummeted after his first elation

131

at getting out of New York. Now that Tom has achieved a success I believe beyond his most daring dream, I trust he will not object to my including evidence of his feelings at this trying time. His words can only serve to inspire others not to give up. They show the true artist is never vanquished, no matter how high the odds against him.

The notes are headed "The Macon Period" and are not necessarily in order.

SUNDAY

Been here a week and one day. I guess it's what I wanted. Quiet. Easy.

As for work—I've done some good scenes (comedy) in "You Touched Me!"

WED. EVE

Read play to Paul and he liked it and made helpful suggestions. We hit a solution for the last scene. Swam and worked with bars. Came home in tolerably good humor.

I am a problem to anybody who cares anything about me— most of all to myself who am, of course, my only ardent lover (though a spiteful and a cruel one!).

A period that is rich in neuroses is also rich in invention. I will probably get a good deal of work done this summer before the culminating disaster or the regeneration takes place—which will it be, I wonder?

Mother writes that Grand is frail and thin and that she hopes I'll come home before I go back North.

Oh, God—there is too much to hurt, you can't think of it all— You have to evade and evade. You have to skip rope lightly!

FRIDAY

I thought it was Sunday—because I had been writing a Sunday scene. Went well—

Paul and I battled a couple of hours over my criticism of his 3rd Act—I found it too rhetorical and stuffy. I hope he will pull it in shape. It could be beautiful.

The nerves much better—feel tired but well.

I have the material for a short novel in my mind.

Maybe I'll write it this summer—psychologically *impotent lover—a song recital*—heat—sleeplessness—*neuroses*—racial trouble in South—a feeling of impasse—*helplessness*—closing in—*lostness*—the effort at *"keeping face" with a set of uncomprehending people*—one who seems to know—the *struggle for contact*—the water out of reach—the cold frigidity and the ennui—final surrender—*the armoire closed.*

Good material. Macon swell background.

Well—I must go swim.

WED. MIDNIGHT

Just closed the book on "Pale Horse, Pale Rider," a fine story. Pretty close to the way it might be. The reality of loss was caught perfectly. The mockery of going on afterwards.

Today wrote not long but well. The invariable day. I will need to dip myself in something cool after this period in Macon. I will be nearly reduced to powder. Yes, it's like being a piece of toast forgotten in the toaster.

But after all I am my own incinerator mostly. And the work goes well. If I grow old and dry and all my hair falls out, it is no exceptional thing.

Tomorrow—a picnic in the country. I will eat and go off by myself. I don't want to be nice to a bunch of more or less nasty people. Endurance is what I ask for, that's about all.

SUNDAY NOON

Some nice times lately. The picnic—swell food & beautiful scenery.

TUESDAY

Yesterday was nice. Three of us drove out to the lake and had a nice evening of it and at the end Bill and I talked for a long time about our mental difficulties and drank beer. He has the same problem I have though it is different, too. We called it the "mental double exposure"—the intrusion of self-consciousness into experience. Apparently he has suffered a good deal, though perhaps he is still an amateur beside me.

Today the writing slowed a bit.

I began to feel qualms about "Dragon Country." It is too heavy and lacks grace and charm. Too macabre.

133

A sombre play has to be very spare and angular. When you fill it out it seems blotchy, pestilential. You must keep the lines sharp and clean—tragedy is austere. You get the effect, with fewer lines than you are inclined to use.

A sad letter from Mother—The old man is being devilish. I read "Desire Under the Elms." Incredibly bad writing, it seems to me. I go to bed early—desire to work in morning. Play "You Touched Me" remains untyped. No word from Audrey. Horrid cold—head full of mucous. Foul. Well—I am a dull boy tonight. Bon nuit.

WED.—JULY 8—MIDNIGHT

I have just read "Maria Concepcion" by Katherine Anne Porter—a truly great story. Elemental and rich.

I did much writing today—my heart is not good—I should rest more.

Reminiscent. I looked back through my life—starting with the summer of 1938 that I graduated from Iowa. Chicago— New Orleans—California—and all the shuttling times since— the travels, the people—the anxieties, hardships, events, disappointments, fevers, kaleidoscopic shifts and changes—What a four years it has been! A lifetime in itself—not one moment of rest, hardly a bit of real peace in it all; But good! And terrible— a liberation. A fight. Well, here I am, still living—and going on. Not young anymore.

If one dared to face it, what a thing he would see!—this life.

I am writing a dramatization of "The Malediction"—goes well. Will finish tomorrow—though I ought to rest.

I would like to spend August in another place—Will I be able to? How? Not back in N. Y. or St. Louis. Yet.

MONDAY

Returned from a week-end trip to Atlanta. Paul not back from Sea Island. Play untyped. I return feeling weak, very weak, and ill. The cold has gone on my chest and this morning I observe traces of blood in the sputum. My knees shake on stairs. I go without coffee which adds to my depression.

Later—I go out for a bite to eat at the Pig'n Whistle as a divided being—one who lives at #1 Brimstone Drive in Perdition. I am being silly.

Let us not complain of the bed we prepared for ourselves. They say if you smile it improves your disposition.

Later—I lie on a couch in the hall and the great trees throw the wind through the windows like rushes of cool water. I read about Jack London, a hot and violent man, beautiful in his youth and his power, who wrote the brawling objective life of a young America. Not my kind but I like him.

WED.

I wake at 9:30—bright. the peculiar blue devils occupy my waking fancy—Paul is up—suggests we go have coffee—against my prudent judgement, I will.

Later—I wrote a little today. It was good enough but no true liberation. All of my actions these past few days—since coming to Macon—have been cramped and conscious—Why?—I see a terrifying vista of time like this—no real escape anywhere; effort and endurance—thirst of the body and of the heart that I cannot slake any longer. Am I beginning to walk across a long desert under a merciless sun?—If I am become my enemy at last—my own relentless antagonist—what is the use? No. I know that finally death will seem the only complete, undivided thing left. And I will take it. It will be forced on me.

THURS.

My last day of work for a while. I feel too shaky to add more. How will I fill the days?

Later—Read "Time"—News appalling—

What a world, what times confront us! Russia, Egypt crumbling—I cannot see ahead nor can anyone. But I suspect it will be especially hard for us who are not made to be warriors. Our little works may be lost.

Here in Macon the crickets make the only noise at this time of night.

A new phase for me—tomorrow no coffee, no work. I will try to sleep late and read. Of course I will be weak and depressed. More depressed. I do not think there will be anything but endurance this season. Survival is enough—at least may have to be enough. I do not think of love—only a few primary needs—and work—and the various little tricks of evasion. Goodnight.

135

SATURDAY MIDNIGHT

I only laid off work 1 day—Today wrote "Dragon Country."
I wistfully hope that tomorrow unless I feel better I'll lay
off again. Tonight I am aching all over—half my bones crack-
ing—felt about to collapse after supper.

But days without work here are utterly void.

It is curious how I have so little urge for the bed—of roses—
flying creatures—bugs—in the room—hate them—Just made a
savage and successful attack on one—The sum of living organ-
isms in the universe was reduced by one—I will go to bed now,
drinking a glass of milk and maintaining some equanimity for
the morrow. So long—10.

SUNDAY NIGHT

Well, I never did like Sunday so I shouldn't complain now.
I'd like to live a simple life—with epic fornications.

I think I will stop writing poetry.

Looking through the collection, it appears to be mostly crap
with just enough quality to make it more distasteful.

Sometimes I delude myself horribly.

I glance at that big black book of verse and think that I
must be an important poet. Well, I'm not—so there.

Maybe my plays are a little bit better. I hope.

Well, I ache and my joints crack and my head aches, too.

I try to make a long play out of "Dragon Country"—Maybe
I can.

MONDAY

Lunches are discontinued at the house next door. I have
iced coffee and I feel somewhat better. The sky is overcast, it
will likely rain. I return to the gable to read and smoke and
let time drift away. I do not feel that I shall ever give battle
to anything hereafter but such feelings are evanescent, have
always been so before.

I read "Rasputin," life at the tragic court of Russia. Material
for drama. A non-realistic play. Stylized. Something like Eisen-
stein's film, "Alexander Nevsky." Gypsies, dancing, an atmosphere of the Gothic and of the weird quality of Russia. Short
scenes. Prince Yusupov, a murderer with a guitar—Rasputin's
death speech. The mystic and the voluptuary.

The afternoon passes—and I am growing stronger. Soon I will go out to the library and then swim.

TUESDAY

I get up and drink 3 cups of coffee with Paul. What suicidal folly!

I come home to write. And the story is wooden, the writing is awkward, only the idea is good.

I seem to have no ear or else too much. It smoothes out to a drone or it doesn't have any even rhythm at all. I think of Saroyan and how beautifully and effortlessly he puts words together—I feel hopeless.

Yes, of course, I *am* hopeless, hopeless, HOPELESS!!

And youth is gone.

And I am sick and weary and only sleep is simple.

TUESDAY—2 A.M.

(or rather, Wed.)

Well, there is nothing to do but go on working.

I have to consider my family and their love—and be brave and enduring as long as it is humanly possible.

We mustn't think about disaster. I'm afraid it could only be messy and prolonged—what happened to my sister.

That way—no—I don't want it.

And so tonight I turn back to the little boy who said, "Now I lay me down to sleep."

I appeal to the darkness above me to stir and give help.

I am sleepy—I will probably sleep.

Tomorrow—coffee—*write*.

Oh, no, I can't make peace. I can't accept a little or nothing. I will struggle and lunge which may only tighten the bonds. I won't ever make a good captive. No, I won't make a good end of it, either. I guess what I will do is drive beyond safety—till I smash—Cleanly and completely the only hope.

THURSDAY EVE.

Wrote a new poem of no special importance—"Speech"—went swimming—Bought & read "Time." The narrow vista remains, I must be cautious. Exercise my gift for evasion.

Called everybody I knew—out. Walked a good ways with Paul—feel fairly quiet—a storm is coming up to cool things off.

137

Tomorrow I swim at the lake. To bed—I will try sleeping in hall.

Later—Just now woke up with nightmares—the vampire dream, a frightful thing, the scene was the exact hall in which I was sleeping.

SUNDAY

hot—furiously—

I try to work on the play.

One little 2-page fragment of pretty obvious humor about the only result.

Ennui and no vitality.

I quit—

Had better lay off for several days.

What shall I do? The swim Saturday did nothing to help.

Pity of self? No. A savage contempt for self. Yet I shall go on. Necessarily helpless. That's how it goes. I will fill my belly and put on a shabby little performance for people.

En Avant!

And now I must make a sensible plan of action unless I *am* determined on messy destruction.

I must quit the effort to create for a while and retrench on something like mere endurance. Make a solemn compact with myself and on no account break it—to relax for a while and vegetate and let my nerves feed up. I don't dare do otherwise for death or madness are nearer than a myth.

MONDAY

Whew!—Quite devastating the condition of my nerves. Wrote in morning. Noon found me literally staggering.

A swim at the Y helped some—had a hair cut and I *am* now back and determined to let everything go at all costs—

Knots in my head loosening up a bit and I will not allow them to tighten—not if I have to lock my door on the world and live alone for the rest of my life.

Later—I spent the evening rooting among my papers—journals. What a struggle these past few periods have been!

What a long-drawn fever!

I will go out now to get cigarettes and return to bed.

I'd better make some money so I can move again.

Tom returned to New York in August and Audrey told him she was having little luck with *Stairs*. So again he headed South and the next I heard he was working as teletype operator with the United States Engineer Corps, typing from 11 P. M. to 7 A. M. for $120 a month.

He thought he would keep this job only until something broke for him in New York. He wrote me that he had bought a bus ticket to St. Louis but at the zero hour his courage failed. He just could not come home yet. His dread of his father still made a psychological horror of homecomings for him.

Once again, he felt emotionally exhausted. He had submitted to endless examinations as a prerequisite for his job, filled in stacks of papers, been fingerprinted and sworn in twice. It all made the job demeaning to him. He loathed the idea of man being reduced to an object.

Thus, it did not surprise me that by November Tom had quit and was back in New York. I sent him a package for Christmas which was returned, since he had moved elsewhere. He wrote me the new address, and I tried again. Tom has always been difficult to keep up with. I warned him the penalty for not giving his draft board a change of address was four years in jail.

Dakin had sent Tom a Christmas card which was also returned. The war was well under way and Dakin had been inducted into the Army. He had come home briefly for Christmas, looking well but complaining about the food. He said Jiggs, our dog, got better food than he did. He was working very hard to get an appointment to Officers' Training School and it looked as though he would have it before long, for he was one of eight selected to appear before the board out of a class of two hundred, recommended by his Commander.

Tom was trying to get a job of any sort to earn money. I have never felt a false pride about the kind of work he accepted in times of need. I admired him for being willing to work long hours at little pay. I do not admire a man who sits back and lets someone else take care of him, as some of Tom's friends have done.

Again he began recording his day-to-day feelings.

SAT. JAN. 24

I guess this sorry little notebook will serve to record what's left of the apparently dwindling 8th period in New York.

My money is running out and I am unable to settle on a course of action. I drift on.

My heart just now acted oddly.

Now I must not look for happiness but endurance. It is strange and interesting to think that what is now so unknown, so dark, the solution of the situation I am in, will resolve itself in only a few days time.

The night seems hostile.

SUN. NIGHT

Nothing has happened to change the situation except that I certainly won't get up in time tomorrow to try that job at the book store.

Blank space is the future but if you don't dive you get pushed in anyway.

So here we go.

No cigs. Mood reasonably black.

Hate this hotel. A sort of middle class Ritz.

Spent eve. with —— and ——, a tall blonde fille de joie and a former burlesk dancer. Very fresh and clean looking and genuinely child like. Has no money and just drifts through time as I do. I like her very much.

One lives a vast number of days but life seems short because the days repeat themselves so. Take that period from my 21 to 24 yr. when I was in the shoe business, a clerk typist in St. Louis at $65 a month. It all seems like one day in my life. It was all one day over and over. Ben in "Stairs to the Roof." The best way to have new days is to travel or work with intensity on a long creation. The progress of the work gives time a perspective. Yes, we must not go over and over our same day unless that day is deeply satisfying which it rarely is. One cannot hope for a life of continual movement and change and so must devise a good and deeply satisfying day to repeat. A day involving love

140

and creation and security and a beautiful open country. New Mexico.

Help me, dear God, to find what I need.

Good night.

MONDAY

Well, at least a glimmer of light appears and the die is cast that I shall at least remain in N.Y. till the money gives altogether out.

Horton Foote, the playwright, told me about an elevator operator's union which he thinks will get me a job. I will see in the A.M. Also will move back to the Y.

Eventful day. Met William Saroyan and went to Cornell production of "Three Sisters." Both disappointing. Saroyan is likeable enough with his somewhat calculated but fresh candor and probably has for many a charm. I felt too much space between us. As for 3 sisters it just didn't have any effect whatsoever. Nobody connected with it seemed to feel the play as an entity.

So stupid tonight and the pen's no good. Better quit. So we light the last cigarette before sleep.

The air is pregnant with change.

As, indeed, it was. No sooner had Tom managed to land a job as usher at the Strand Theatre at $17 a week, than Audrey called. She had somehow obtained for him a contract as script writer for MGM in Hollywood. He was to be paid $250 a week for six months. He sent me a telegram on May 5, 1943.

SIGNED CONTRACT MGM. SALARY THOUSAND DOLLARS A
MONTH. LEAVE THIS WEEKEND. LOVE

TOM

He had not pulled down the plum for which he hoped, a play on Broadway. But he was on his way to a moment of glory. He could now walk past Clark's Bootery, just down the street from the studio, with the feeling he was done forever with the plucking of poultry feathers and the selling of shoes.

9.

"I Am More Faithful Than
I Intended to Be"

Tom's first assignment for MGM was to write a script for Lana Turner titled *Marriage Is a Private Affair*. He worked on it for several weeks, then handed in what he believed a good script.

The powers-that-be read it, informed him that while his dialogue was fine in its way, it was not for Lana. I think they meant it was too highbrow.

He was then asked to write a scenario for a film featuring the child star, Margaret O'Brien. Tom's reply was frank if hardly the height of diplomacy. "Child stars make me sick," he announced.

He worked instead on an original script about an aging Southern belle and submitted it to the studio with a note advising that it eventually would run twice as long as *Gone With the Wind*. The studio turned it down with the comment that since *Gone With the Wind* had just been produced by Mr. Selznick, they were not interested in a second version.

Tom called Audrey and asked her to request the studio's permission for him to go East to see one of his plays produced experimentally. The studio's answer was, "Yes, he may go— on one condition." When Audrey asked the condition, the studio replied, "That he never come back!"

Although Tom was then dropped by MGM, who no doubt thought he was hopeless as a screen writer, his contract called for a minimum of six months' employment, so he continued to receive his $250 a week, most of which he sent to Audrey to bank so he would have it in reserve.

He rented a cottage at Malibu and, taking his original script with him, began to convert it into a play entitled *The Gentleman Caller*. If I were to choose the one most important writing act of Tom's life, this would be it, although they all were important, each in its own way.

While Tom was out West, Mother became perilously ill. I wrote she was fading fast and if he wanted to see her alive, he had better fly home at once, which he did. He just about walked into the house when she died, literally in his arms. It was as though she had hung on until he arrived. That very day she had insisted on practicing three hours on the piano, refusing to give up her beloved music. I never saw my mother idle. If she didn't have anything better to do, she would take up a piece of sewing.

After the funeral, Tom returned to Malibu to finish his play. When his Hollywood contract expired, he journeyed East to give Audrey the completed play. He had renamed it *The Glass Menagerie*.

At this time Tom learned he was to be presented with a $1,000 award from the National Academy of Arts and Letters. *Battle of Angels* had not been in vain, nor his one-act plays which were receiving wide recognition, presented by various little theatre groups. The citation read:

> To Tennessee Williams, born in Mississippi, in recognition of his dramatic works, which reveal a poetic imagination and a gift for characterization that are rare in the contemporary theatre.

It was a time of tributes. His play *Moony's Kid Don't Cry* was included in *The Best One-Act Plays of 1940,* edited by Margaret Mayorga. He was also represented in the third volume of a series, *Five American Poets, 1944,* published by New Directions, which has since become his publisher.

After reading *The Glass Menagerie,* Audrey deliberated as to which producer should see it first. She decided on Eddie Dowling. No other producer ever had a glimpse of the script. Mr. Dowling carried it home, read it, decided he wanted to produce it and act in it as leading man. He took an option and set about raising money.

Stung by his Boston experience, Tom was not counting any chickens until they were hatched on Broadway. He wrote me, "Money is coming in slowly on the play. The chance of a spring production is quite off now." He was staying in New York, he said, only until the presentation of the National Academy of Arts and Letters award on May 19th.

"Then I will either come home for a while, or go first to one of the nearby beaches," he wrote. "I have been thinking of taking a summer course in a university, maybe Washington and in the Italian Renaissance which is the period setting of the play I am working on now. I'm going to write for the Washington summer catalogue and see if they offer such a course. Sewanee might also be suitable."

He said he wished I could be present at the Academy ceremony. "It will apparently be very impressive," he wrote. "Eudora Welty, who got one of the awards, is from Jackson, Mississippi."

He also informed me, "I have gotten several very respectable-looking portraits from Mr. Lynes which you will like much better than the one I sent. In fact, I look quite elegant in them and might pass for a member of café society."

The photograph he originally sent us, taken by George Platt Lynes, was striking but a gag. Tom was posed like Rodin's "The Thinker," wearing an old sweater with its sleeves completely out at the elbows. His father took one look at the photograph and sent him a telegram ordering him not to dare use it. Its substitute showed Tom clad in a conservative business suit sitting with bored, sophisticated expression in a round, stream-lined chair. It was, indeed, elegant, as he said.

Despite advice from theatrical friends that *The Glass Menagerie* would never be a success because of its fragile plot and unhappy ending, Mr. Dowling went ahead trying to raise money. Some of the backers wanted Tom to change the ending and allow the sister and gentleman caller to fall in love but he firmly refused. Finally Mr. Dowling persuaded Louis J. Singer, a banker who had put money into a few Broadway productions, to invest $75,000 and the four parts of *Menagerie* were then cast. Mr. Dowling was to be the son, Laurette Taylor the mother, Julie Haydon the sister, and Anthony Ross, the gentleman caller.

Chicago was chosen for the out-of-town opening. Tom asked me to come up and I was delighted, both at attending my first premiere and at the feeling my son needed me. His father did not want to go and since he always threw a pall over everything where Tom was concerned, I am sure Tom was just as pleased. He said he didn't think his father would like the play anyhow.

There's a little train that goes directly to Chicago called the Wabash and I boarded it alone, arriving about six hours later in Chicago during one of their frozen spells. It takes courage to brave Chicago in the middle of winter, especially for a Southerner. The streets were solid sheets of ice, the temperature zero and the wind cold and violent.

I arrived in time to see a rehearsal and witness the friction that seems part of the birth pangs of every play. Mr. Dowling wanted to sing the bawdiest verse of "St. Louis Blues" in the scene where the son staggers home drunk. Tom objected, saying to me, "He's trying to make it funny, Mother. I've got to stop him." Mr. Dowling gave in to Tom.

Then Mr. Dowling and Laurette engaged in a quarrel or two, usually under their breaths, and Laurette, who was trying to make a comeback in this part, would retire for a while to the nearest bar to recover. When Jo Mielziner arrived to light the show, he found that the color of Julie's second-act dress faded

145

under the lighting and Julie, Mr. Dowling and Tom dug into their pockets to collect $20 to buy Julie a light-proof dress.

Laurette was a genius in the rapidity with which she acquired a Southern accent. Describing herself as "a Southerner out of Ireland," she said she had never been below Washington, D.C., except to Florida, but she had visited Southern Italy, if that helped. At first she kept charging up and down the stage, her head wrapped in a bandanna, looking like a Southern mammy and talking like one. I whispered to Tom, "A Southern lady doesn't sound like a Southern mammy imitating a Southern lady." Laurette toned it down for the opening and thereafter.

She tried at first, according to a newspaper interview, to learn a Southern accent by imitating Tom. At one point he interrupted her to say, "Youah ayaccent's too thick, Miz' Tayluh."

"But I'm trying to imitate yours, Tennessee," she said.

"*Mah* accent?" Tom said in surprise. "Ah don't hayev any ayaccent."

The evening of the premiere was the night after Christmas, Tuesday, December 26, 1944. Everything seemed against the play, even the weather. The streets were so ice-laden we could not find a taxi to take us to the Civic Theatre and had to walk. The gale blowing off Lake Michigan literally hurled us through the theater door.

Tom went backstage, unable to sit still, to find everyone gripped by a slight case of opening night d.t.'s. It had taken twenty-four hours to erect the single set because the man slated to supervise had gone off on a binge and could not be located. Laurette was discovered a few minutes before curtain time dyeing an old bathrobe she was supposed to wear in the second act, because she suddenly did not like its shade.

I am sure both Tom and I said our prayers those crucial moments. Tom prays each night before an opening. He believes in God even though he doesn't go to church. I think within himself he is quite religious, for sin never triumphs in Tom's plays. The transgressor is always punished, usually by death.

I had not read *Menagerie,* knew nothing of its story except the snatches I glimpsed at rehearsals. After the curtain went up,

146

I became lost in the magic of the words and the superb performance of its four players. You couldn't call Laurette or Julie pretty but they imbued their parts with a strong spiritual quality.

This was the first of Tom's plays I had seen, unless you count *The Magic Tower,* and I was thrilled to think he had created a play without a wasted word and one in which every moment added drama. I don't think there's been a play like it, before or since.

The audience, too, seemed spellbound throughout and particularly when Mr. Dowling stood to one side of the stage and uttered the words, "I didn't go to the moon, I went much further—for time is the longest distance between two places. . . . Oh, Laura, Laura, I tried to leave you behind me, but I am more faithful than I intended to be! I reach for a cigarette, I cross the street, I run into the movies or a bar, I buy a drink, I speak to the nearest stranger—anything that can blow your candles out!"

At this moment, in the center of the stage behind a thin veil of a curtain, Julie bent low over the candles in her tenement home as Mr. Dowling said sadly, "—for nowadays the world is lit by lightning! Blow out your candles, Laura—and so goodbye. . . ."

And the curtain dropped slowly on the world premiere of *The Glass Menagerie.*

At first it was so quiet I thought the audience didn't like the play. A young woman behind me clapped wildly, as though to make up for the lack of applause, and I heard her remark indignantly, "These Chicago audiences make me mad! This is a beautiful play."

Then, all of a sudden, a tumultuous clapping of hands broke out. The audience had been recovering from the mood into which the play had plunged it. Gratefully I turned to the young woman, who I later found out was a student of English at the University of Chicago, and asked, "Would you like to meet the author? I'm his mother." When Tom arrived to take me backstage, I introduced the young woman, breathless with excitement, and we invited her to go behind the scenes with us.

147

I wanted to congratulate Laurette, who had brought down the house with her amazing performance as Amanda Wingfield, the faded, fretful, dominating mother lost in the dream world of her past, bullying her son into finding a gentleman caller for his abnormally shy sister.

I entered Laurette's dressing room, not knowing what to expect, for she was sometimes quite eccentric. She was sitting with her feet propped up on the radiator, trying to keep warm. Before I had a chance to get out a word, she greeted me.

"Well, how did you like you'seff, Miz' Williams?" she asked.

I was so shocked I didn't know what to say. It had not occurred to me as I watched Tom's play that *I* was Amanda. But I recovered quickly.

"You were magnificent," I said quietly to Laurette.

Someone mentioned to Tom the opposite receptions given *Angels* and *Menagerie* and he explained this by saying, "You can't mix sex and religion . . . but you can always write safely about mothers."

To which I say, "Ah, can you, Tom?"

Over the years both subtly and not so subtly, I have often been reminded that the character of Amanda was rooted in me, and this is not generally meant as a compliment. The critics have described Amanda in such inelegant words as "an old witch riding a broomstick," "a raddled belle of the old South, sunk deep in frustration," "the scuffed, rundown slipper that outlived the ball," "a simple, sanely insane, horrible Mother, pathetic and terribly human and terribly real" and "a bit of a scold, a bit of a snob."

Tom's own description of Amanda as stated in the play held that she was "a little woman of great but confused vitality clinging frantically to another time and place. Her characterization must be carefully created, not copied from type. She is not paranoiac, but her life is paranoia. There is much to admire in Amanda, and as much to love and pity as there is to laugh at. Certainly she has endurance and a kind of heroism, and though her foolishness makes her unwittingly cruel at times, there is tenderness in her slight person."

148

Tom has contradicted himself when asked if the play were based on his life. Once he told a reporter it was a "memory play," adding, "My mother and sister will never forgive me for that." Another time he said, "It was derived from years of living." Then again, he denied it was autobiographical, calling it "a dream or fantasy play. The gentleman caller is meant to be the symbol of the world and its attitude toward the unrealistic dreamers who are three characters of the play."

I think it is high time the ghost of Amanda was laid. I am *not* Amanda. I'm sure if Tom stops to think, he realizes I am not. The only resemblance I have to Amanda is that we both like jonquils.

Laurette objected because in one scene the word "jonquils" appeared a dozen or so times within the space of a few minutes. "It sounds like too many jonquils to me," she said. "Can't you cut out a few jonquils, Tennessee?"

"Laurette," Tom said, "it's got rhythm. I need all those jonquils."

She practiced the lines at home, "sort of sang them to myself," she reported. She returned to admit, "Tennessee, you were right."

One evening Audrey and I took Laurette to dinner. We were discussing why she wore those pathetic, fringy bangs as a hair style for the part of Amanda.

"I have an awfully high forehead," Laurette explained. "I wanted to cover it up so I could look like a silly little thing."

I took off my hat and said indignantly, "My forehead is just as high as yours."

Audrey said right then and there I confessed to being Amanda. As a joke, sometimes I call myself Amanda in front of friends. One of them, taking me seriously, rebuked me. "I wish you'd stop doing that, Edwina. People will believe you."

"Not those who know me," I replied.

I never woke Tom up with that sugary chant, "Rise and shine, rise and shine." Nor did I matchmake for Rose, who was quite able to find her own young men and, incidentally, I don't think marriage necessarily the culmination of a woman's life, for some

149

of the happiest women I know have never married. Nor did my husband walk out on me.

At the Chicago premiere, after congratulating Laurette, we returned to the hotel for a late dinner and to wait for reviews. Tom wanted to take me to a midnight service at the Episcopal Church but the weather was so ferocious we still could not find a taxi. Julie joined us for dinner; Laurette refused, saying she was all in. Margo Jones, who was helping Mr. Dowling stage the production, was supposed to meet us but never showed up. Margo, who became a good friend of Tom's, was one of the most enthusiastic, talkative persons I have ever met. The death of this dynamic woman was a tragedy.

As we waited for the notices, the excitement was subdued but intense. Tom must have been reliving the agony of *Angels,* yet also gripped by new hope that the critics would like this play.

His hope was fulfilled. One by one the reviews came in, each more superlative than the last.

Claudia Cassidy of the Chicago *Tribune* started off: "Too many theatrical bubbles burst in the blowing, but 'The Glass Menagerie' holds in its shadowed fragility the stamina of success." She said further, "If it is your play, as it is mine, it reaches out tentacles, first tentative, then gripping, and you are caught in its spell."

In a later column she wrote of Tom's play, "Things like this remind you sharply how much of your life you spend on the dreary treadmill of inertia that is the theatre's and music's second best. It's harder to accept the shoddy substitute after your eyes and ears have had such rich reminder of the real thing."

The late Ashton Stevens, in the Chicago *Herald-American,* said Tom's play "removed this first-nighter so far from this earth that the return to mundane desk and typewriter finds him unaccustomedly dizzy in the head, to say nothing of the heart. Fifty years of first-nighting have provided him with very few jolts so miraculously electrical as the jolt Laurette Taylor gave him last night." He had not been so moved, he declared, "since Eleanora Duse gave her last performance on this planet."

He described the play as "a lovely thing, and an original thing. It has the courage of true poetry couched in colloquial prose. It is eerie and earthy in the same breath. . . . Its unforced wit is as pure as its understated pathos."

I realized Tom did not need me much longer in Chicago. He had, at long last, won his fight with his father; he was a success in the field he had chosen. I stayed a day or so, then took the Wabash back to St. Louis. The train arrived at one in the morning and to Cornelius' credit, he met me at Union Station. I think he was anxious to hear about the play, having read the reviews.

He went to Chicago by himself a few weeks later to see *Menagerie* and found it sold out. The play broke the jinx hanging over Chicago's Civic Repertory Theatre, which now had a full house every night. They put a chair in the aisle for Cornelius because he was the playwright's father. He did not believe I was Amanda; he was a very literal man and he had not left home, nor did the lives portrayed on the stage resemble ours in any way, he thought.

It had been impossible to get a commitment for a Broadway theatre before the Chicago opening but after the reviews, a number of theatres asked to be the locale of the debut of *Menagerie* in New York. Mr. Dowling chose the Playhouse. Tom went to New York before *Menagerie* opened to discuss the presentation of a second play, *You Touched Me!* with Audrey and potential backers. He was receiving royalties from Chicago of $1,000 a week, his first real money after living from dollar to dollar all his life.

He wrote asking if I would attend the New York opening saying, "If you can go, Mother, I would like to give you the trip as a much-delayed present." He added, "Writing and so many social invitations that I have to turn half of them down have kept me constantly busy."

But I did not get to the New York premiere the night of March 31, 1945 (again, near Tom's birthday, five days after he turned thirty-four) because Cornelius said since we had both seen the play, it would be a waste of money. Tom sent a telegram the day after *Menagerie* opened. It was April Fool's Day, but far from a fool's day for him.

PLAY RECEIVED BIG OVATION.
REVIEWS NOT OUT TILL MONDAY.
LOVE

TOM

I thought it most unkindly the newspapers mentioned a missing button. They described how "the audience shouted 'Author, Author!' and rose as one man as the lights dimmed on the last scene." They said that "for fully five minutes, evening gowned dowagers joined the gallery—clapping, shouting, whistling, shrieking approval." One critic lost count at the twentieth curtain call. Finally Mr. Dowling walked up to the footlights "and assisted modest Author Williams to the stage."

Photographers were "shooting" Tom from all angles. He was dressed, according to a reporter, "in a gray flannel suit with a missing coat button, a conservative pale tie on a water-green shirt." The reporter summed up, "with his hair cut short, Mr. Williams appeared more like a farmboy in his Sunday best than the author of a Broadway success."

I read ruefully of that missing button. I was sorry I hadn't been there to sew it on. Poor Tom—no one to look after his wardrobe. He was accustomed to having his grandmother or me watch over his clothes, about which he was quite careless. He would be a trial to anyone who tried to take care of him. Frank Merlo, his man Friday, who cooks for him, runs the house, drives the car, packs when they go on trips, has my sympathy.

I imagine Tom has been an occasional tribulation to Audrey. Once she went to his apartment to take him to see an important producer and found him searching through piles of paper, trying to find a sock. He fished all over, even underneath the radiator, but no matching sock.

"Put on another pair," Audrey finally suggested.

"I haven't got another pair," he confessed.

It was hopeless to try to find a small sock amidst the mountains of manuscripts, so Audrey's husband, Liebling, went out and bought Tom another pair.

After the New York opening of *Menagerie,* Tom sent a second telegram.

REVIEWS ALL RAVE. INDICATE SMASH HIT.
LINE BLOCK LONG AT BOX OFFICE. LOVE
TOM

It was a double triumph, one for Tom, one for Laurette. She had been engulfed by what she told *Time* Magazine was, she supposed, "the longest wake in history" after her husband, the playwright J. Hartley Manners, died in 1928. She appeared on Broadway only once in the thirteen years before *Menagerie,* in a revival of *Outward Bound.* She was linked in the popular mind with a play in which she had starred thirty-three years before, *Peg o' My Heart,* and another, *Alias Jimmy Valentine,* in 1910. Now there would be a third for which the public would always remember her.

Just after the premiere, a friend called to ask if I had seen Walter Winchell's column that morning. I had not and, curious, took a look. Near the end I read, "The first gesture of Tennessee Williams following unanimous raves of his 'Glass Menagerie' was to sign over half rights to his mother." Contracts arrived in the mail the next day, notifying me I was half owner of all the rights to *Menagerie.* From that day to this Tom has never mentioned his gift, nor the part of *Sweet Bird of Youth* he also gave me.

For both Tom and me, *Menagerie* was a turning point, one that arrived after years of enduring an intolerable situation at home. When Tom gave me half of *Menagerie,* Cornelius was not at all pleased. It meant I would be out from under his domination. He kept gloomily prophesying I would land in jail. "You're going to slip up one of these days and Uncle Sam will get you for taxes," he would threaten.

"Uncle Sam isn't going to get me," I'd reassure him. "I've already given him his share."

153

Tom's success was a bitter pill for Cornelius. The son he always berated as a failure, whom he taunted as "Miss Nancy" when he was growing up, because he wasn't an athlete, whom he had pulled out of college when he failed R.O.T.C., was now achieving a financial income far beyond his father's. Life can be beautifully ironic.

The New York reviewers called Tom's play "enchanting," "hypnotic," "sheer magic," "theatre at its best," "completely perfect." *Newsweek* Magazine described it as "a simple, sentimental story that offers Saroyan's fresh approach to people without Saroyan's facile dismissal of the people's problems." Burton Rascoe wrote, "Here is make-believe so real it tears your heart out. . . . The play hurts you . . . hurts you all through. It arouses in you pity and terror."

A few weeks after it opened, *Menagerie* won the New York Drama Critics' Circle Award as the best play of the season, the critics voting for it in a record fifteen minutes. It was the first time in the group's ten years that a play was chosen on the first ballot. Louis Kronenberger was the only critic who did not vote for any play, and in a column in *PM* he explained why. He thought Tom's play "interesting, sometimes absorbing theater, with a pretty honest core" but "it was fancied up with otiose and irritating stage tricks, and its good writing is offset by its bad (which is often extremely bad)." What distinguished *Menagerie* was Laurette's superb acting, "to which I would gladly offer a prize; but that is not the same as offering one to Mr. Williams," said Mr. Kronenberger. He liked best George Kelly's *The Deep Mrs. Sykes,* adding, "but not enough of it is good."

Tom admired that play too, for when he heard he received the award, he said he thought *The Deep Mrs. Sykes* should have won it. Tom sometimes is very humble, perhaps too humble.

Laurette won the Drama Critics' unanimous award for the best dramatic performance of the year. When a stagehand told her about both awards just before the performance was to start that evening, she shouted in glee, "We've won it, we've won it!" and announced, "From here on I'm just kicking the clouds around." Of Tom she said, "It couldn't have happened to a nicer guy."

There was no holding *Menagerie* back. It won the Donaldson Award, sponsored by *Billboard,* the tribute of the profession itself, the result of a poll of 2,000 theatre people from stagehands to stars. It won the "Sign" Award, presented by the National Catholic Magazine. It was chosen as "the command performance" for the Roosevelt Birthday Celebration at the National Theatre in Washington in January, 1946. Tom received the $1500 Sidney Howard Memorial Award given "to a new American playwright who, having had no previous substantial success in the theatre, has had one or more plays produced in New York during the current season." The citation stated Tom had "brought a vigorous new talent into the theatre. He has the sense of poetry and of character of which great drama is made."

Tom gave a big party in New York, sending out formal invita tions which requested "the pleasure of your company for tea and cocktails on Friday, April 27th, 1945, from five to seven at Sherry's to meet

Mrs. Edwina Williams
Miss Laurette Taylor."

He reserved rooms at the Royalton for his grandfather and me and I invited all my friends to the party. Laurette and I, however, found ourselves deserted in the receiving line. Father stole the show as he entertained everyone, which he loved to do and at which he was a master. I was seized by a fleeting pang of grief at the thought Mother was not there, for her part in this marvelous moment of Tom's life was a great one.

By the end of the year *Menagerie* was still news. Jack O'Brian, of the *Journal-American,* noted that more than 3,350 delicate little glass figures had been smashed "to some glass-carver's heaven," 125 gallons of coffee had been consumed, 156 pint jars of Boston baked beans and 250 loaves of bread eaten, while five cartons of cigarettes went up in smoke, mostly inhaled by Mr. Dowling (this was during the war when it was difficult to get cigarettes and envious looks were often cast at the characters

155

onstage as they puffed away). The gentleman caller had chewed 1,300 pieces of gum and Laurette had stuffed 832 powder puffs down Julie's bosom.

The fall of 1945 saw Tom with *two* plays on Broadway. *You Touched Me!* had its first production at the Play House in Cleveland, Ohio, on October 13, 1943, under the direction of Margo Jones. It then moved to The Playbox at the Pasadena Playhouse from November 29 to December 5, 1943, still under Margo's direction.

Now it was scheduled for Broadway where Guthrie McClintic and Lee Shubert were to produce it. It had gone through five drafts since Donald Windham and Tom started to dramatize it in 1941, adding an exclamation point to the title of the story as originally created by D. H. Lawrence. The final draft had been written after a visit to Taos where Mrs. Lawrence made suggestions.

This play, an allegory, told of the love of a young RAF flier for the the daughter of an old alcoholic sea captain who adopted him. The captain represented a progressive social attitude as pitted against his sister, a bitter, conservative spinster who opposed the boy's courtship. Edmund Gwenn played the captain and Montgomery Clift, the aviator who eventually won the girl by accidentally touching her and awakening her desire for him. But even they could not save the play from the verbal ax of the critics who compared it to *Menagerie* and decmed it inferior.

It seemed to me several of the critics had made up their minds in advance. At the opening I sat behind a group of them. After the first act they turned around and, not knowing I was Tom's mother, asked, "Do you like this play?" perhaps wanting a woman's reaction.

"Why, yes, I do," I said. "Don't you?"

"No," they said.

A friend with me whispered, "Tell them who you are," but I did not.

"It won't last a week," announced one of the critics.

After the play I stood in the rear of the theatre next to Tom as this group of critics walked past. Their faces fell when they realized who I was.

I told Tom what had happened, saying, "Wasn't that amusing?"

"I see nothing amusing about it," he said darkly.

Menagerie had closed only five months when Laurette died at the age of sixty-two, on December 7, 1946, of a heart attack in her suite at the Hotel Fourteen. She had been stricken with a slight attack the previous February but missed only five days of performance. In an article Tom wrote the spring of 1946 for the Sunday magazine section of *The New York Times,* he spoke of his love for Laurette.

"For me to love her was remarkable because I have always been so awkward and diffident around actors that it has made a barrier between us almost all but insuperable," he said. "In the case of Laurette Taylor, I cannot say that I ever got over the awkwardness and the awe which originally were present, but she would not allow it to stand between us. The great warmth of her heart burned through and we became close friends. . . . I am afraid it is the only close friendship I have ever had with a player."

Laurette often had not been well when she played Amanda, Tom said, but was determined "to beat her ill health, often continuing with her performance when a person of ordinary spirit would not have dared to."

But she died knowing she had made a comeback that would go down in theatre history. *Menagerie* proved a miracle play for many of us. The film rights were sold for a goodly sum. Tom's original script went for $6,000 at an auction sale. *Menagerie* also brought me my first and only trip abroad.

Tom suggested I go to England for the British premiere of *Menagerie* in 1948 and Dakin and I decided to travel by boat. Although I was fearful of being seasick, the ocean turned out smooth as glass. Dakin danced the nights away and we both made many friends. We went first to Brighton where the play was given its British tryout. There we met Helen Hayes, who was starring in it as her first appearance in England.

After the Brighton premiere, we retired to our hotel room when suddenly there came a rap on the door. I opened it and there stood Helen, shyly holding out a sliver of soap. Soap was a treasure in England at this time; the hotel did not offer any and I had been wondering how I would get clean. I accepted the sliver gratefully, thinking what a gracious gesture this was, for Helen was dead tired after the performance yet still had the energy to think of someone else.

Tom, the wretch, left three ladies in the lurch opening night in London. Audrey, who had come over with Liebling, Helen and I awaited all day his return from Paris where he was visiting. Every hour on the hour we received a telegram saying, "Missed the last plane. Will take the next." It was only a short hop across the Channel and we thought he would surely arrive in time for the opening, but when the final curtain fell, still no sign of Tom. A telegram was waiting for me at the Hotel Savoy.

DEAR MOTHER. JAKE A BOUT FOR ME TONIGHT
IF I AM NOT THERE.   LOVE

TOM

The operator had inelegantly twisted the words "take a bow."

When Tom finally appeared the next day he gave no excuse, merely said he had been delayed.

At the opening, two women sitting directly behind me were discussing the play between the acts.

"How do you like it?" asked the first.

"I don't," retorted the second. "It's just too beastly real."

After the play we all went to a party at the home of Lady Sybil Colefax, a noted London hostess, who died two years later at the age of seventy-six. *The Manchester Guardian* called her "the last of the gay and skilled London hostesses." Famed for the celebrities she knew in politics, literature and the theatre, she was holding this after-theatre party in honor of Helen and the absent Tom. I had received an invitation from Hugh Beaumont, managing director of Tennent Productions, Ltd., saying, "I am sure you will find many old friends at the party to celebrate the opening of this thrilling theatrical event."

It was an elaborate affair with the finest of food, much of which, I suspect, must have been black market because there were still drastic shortages in England. Noel Coward was there and John Gielgud, now Sir John Gielgud, who directed *Menagerie* in London. Upon being introduced to me, he said he was happy to meet Tennessee's mother, and in the course of conversing, he commented, "When Tennessee throws his head back and stares at me through those lowered lids, I know he's seeing right through me."

He, too, had been struck by this gesture of Tom's as he observes people intently, the same gaze with which he once studied the blue morning glory. Sometimes when he throws his head back, he just stares at the ceiling, and then again he throws it back when something amuses him and he laughs. I love to hear him laugh because it is always so genuine and comes as a surprise. Most of the time he is quiet in a crowd.

Helen came to the party with her husband, Charles Mac-Arthur and their daughter, whom Charles was taking to the Riviera. I thought him a very handsome man and the daughter very beautiful, and was shocked by her death not long after.

The party over, I found myself being driven through London in a horse-drawn coach belonging to Lady Sybil. It was not the elaborate carriage of Natchez days but it was a coach nevertheless.

And as the horses clopped along the silent street, I thought how swiftly time took away the years. One grows older so fast, you're hardly a descendant before you're an ancestor.

10.

"Thee Had Seventy-Four Gentleman Callers"

I WAS named Edwina for my father's father, Edward. I was born in Marysville, Ohio, at the home of my mother's parents, but I remember nothing of the North in my early life.

According to reports, I was a squalling baby with a terrible temper. Mother claimed I drove her to teaching piano and voice, I was so obstreperous, and to work to pay a nurse was easier than taking care of me. Thus she became one of the first women to do what the majority do today, embark on a career. My father was proud of her teaching. I think, also, he appreciated the money it brought in, for as a teacher himself, then a clergyman, he was not very well paid during his lifetime.

I was late in talking, it seemed I was late in everything, even growing hair. When they posed me for a baby picture, they draped my grandmother's cape over my head so my bald pate would not show. But I was a very merry baby, at least for the purpose of being photographed. I usually had my mouth open, laughing, when the camera clicked.

My earliest memories begin at the age of five or six when I was in first grade at the Shelbyville Female Institute, a high-sounding name for a boarding school for a few little girls from Mississippi. Shelbyville is located not far from Nashville.

Father was superintendent of the Institute, in the residential part of town, and we lived on the campus. Every place in this sleepy old Southern community was within walking distance, though the ladies did not bestir themselves walking anywhere. Each had her own horse and buggy with a colored man to drive.

Shelbyville would not allow a railroad to go through it and still won't, because it did not want to be touched by the commercial hand of railroad or factory. It was a lovely town with wide streets, on both sides of which spacious residences were set back in the midst of large lawns filled with old forest trees. The huge columns of the Colonial-style courthouse supported porches on its four sides. There were seats on the lawn for the men of both town and country who gathered at the courthouse for business and to while away summer days after tethering horses, mules and oxen to the hitching posts.

The small red brick Episcopal Church with its square tower peeped out from among the trees, and on Sundays the street in front was lined with carriages and landaus as Negro drivers with silk hats sat on the high seats awaiting the end of church service.

Duck River flowed past Shelbyville and on it cruised a little steamboat, the *Alpha Omega*. In the spring, the members of Mother's bridge-whist club would board the boat and it would chug up Duck River as they all ate picnic lunches and told stories. Once they threatened to put Mother and Father off on the riverbank if I didn't come up with a good story, so I produced an exciting one, not wanting to abandon my parents.

I read a lot as a child and also made up fairy tales. My father put some of them in a folder (which has been lost) and labeled it *Written by Edwina,* giving my age and the year. He evidently

161

expected some talent from me, poor man. But he lived to see his grandson become a writer.

Father took pride in me for other reasons. He spoiled me, that I know. I was an only child and rarely was required to do anything I did not want to do, as far as he was concerned. Maybe that's why I'm not of more account. When Mother wanted me to practice the piano, he would say, "Now, Rose, she doesn't have to, if she doesn't want to." Or when she wanted me to learn to cook, he insisted, "If she has the intelligence of a Southern mammy, she'll be able to cook if she ever needs to."

My mother was never very demonstrative, the least demonstrative person I've known, but she felt things deeply; some of the most demonstrative people seem, to me, to feel the least. My father was more expressive of his feelings, never hiding the fact that he enjoyed living.

We left Ohio when I was a child. My grandmother, with whom my parents were living, wanted to go to a warmer climate, because she had trouble with her bronchial tubes. Mother's father, a merchant who had made and lost several fortunes, was now retired, so he pulled up stakes in Ohio and moved South, buying one of the mountain ridges of Chattanooga, now the site of many splendid homes.

Father was born in Harveysburg, Ohio, a little village just outside of Cincinnati, coming from a large family of five sons and four daughters. When he was a boy, his parents moved to nearby Waynesville, a small Quaker community of rare beauty. It was built to resemble a vast park, with no fences around the houses and each home set off by a large lawn. Like Shelbyville, it, too, scorned a railroad.

Father was partly of Quaker descent. One day I happened to be reading aloud an item in Walter Winchell's column that referred to "the odd monicker of the New Yorker buried at 2nd Street's Marble cemetery. His name is Mr. Preserved Fish."

"Isn't that a strange name?" I said to my father.

"I see nothing strange about it, Daughter," said Father. "He was your great-great-grandfather." The Quakers often bestowed these quaint names on their members.

162

Father's father was a doctor much admired in town and I remember him as a kind and gentle person. All the Dakins were either doctors or lawyers; my great-grandfather was Judge James Dakin of Cincinnati. None of Grandfather Dakin's five sons took to medicine, having an example in front of their eyes, I guess, of the difficult life of a country doctor. My grandfather never sent out a bill; his account books were filled with such transactions as:

1 delivery — 1 turkey

I seemed to be a favorite of Grandfather Dakin's since I was named for him, but because we lived, for the most part, in the South, we didn't see much of him. His wife died when I was small, so I scarcely knew her.

Mother was of pure German stock on both sides. Her mother was a beautiful old woman (old when I knew her and not for long, at that) named Elizabeth. She carried herself very proudly and considered herself superior to the rest of the Germans in Waynesville where she lived.

Father fell in love with Mother the first time he saw her. She was riding her own horse through the streets of Waynesville. At the time, she was fourteen and he seventeen, but he made up his mind to wait for her.

Her name was Maria Rosina Francesca Otte, but everyone called her Rose. After a high school education in a convent, she went to the Conservatory of Music in Cincinnati. When my father asked for her hand in marriage, Mother's father did not approve. He pointed out Mother would never make a poor man's wife, since she had been brought up in luxury and Father didn't seem to have much prospect of earning a lot of money.

Father had attended Eastman's Business School in Poughkeepsie, New York, where he bowled over the Vassar girls, he was so handsome. Then he attended several teachers' colleges, intending to teach. But he decided to take a temporary job as accountant in a furniture store because it paid well and he wanted to marry and support Mother. He was afraid she would not wait for him if he prepared for the Episcopal ministry, what he now really wanted to do but which would have been even more poorly paid than teaching.

When he moved with his in-laws to Chattanooga, Father started to teach, then was offered what seemed to him quite a step upward in the educational hierarchy—the position of superintendent of the Shelbyville Female Institute. Mother was given charge of the music department at the Institute. I remember her at concerts, looking regal as she swept across the stage to seat herself at the piano, then removing her jewelry, for it would have been difficult to play with dangling gold bracelets and heavy rings. Her pupils played well too, for she was a disciplinarian and made them practice.

Every now and then, Mother would hire a landau, which had two coachmen, and repay the calls of the ladies living in the nearby mansions, each one of whom had a weekly "at home" day, stated on their calling cards, when they would serve tea. Mother, too, had her "at home" day at the Institute, although I don't believe it was as often as once a week. What with all the "at home" days, the ladies were kept busy without needing to do much else.

Mother would walk out of the house to the landau in her stately manner, beautifully dressed. I recall especially a gown of black lace over crushed strawberry silk, with bonnet to match, and a black parasol lined with the crushed strawberry silk. To look at Mother you'd think she was the Queen of Sheba, although she might often be wearing old dresses she had made over.

I'd swing on the front gate and think how lovely she looked, and once I told her, "Mother, when I grow up I'm going to marry a rich man so you can have your own landau."

I am quite sure Mother and Father stayed in love over the years. They had disagreements but never any violent arguments. Mother always held the upper hand but Father never seemed to mind. He depended on her and felt confident she would somehow manage things.

At the Institute, Father also taught Latin and Greek, English and mathematics. When not instructing, he presided as head of the school. He would sit at his desk and keep an eagle eye on the girls. He was young-looking and small in stature and when he first arrived, the girls thought he would be a pushover. But it didn't work out that way with Father, who had high personal as well as scholastic standards, and before long the girls stood in awe of him. Teachers would threaten, "I shall send you to Professor Dakin," and this brought better behavior at once.

Father had all the girls stepping swiftly and learning their lessons. In spite of his jovial disposition he could be determined when he wanted order. He was quite severe about one thing with me. I had to know my Latin grammar. He would sit down holding the Latin book and make me decline all the verbs. But he gave up on mathematics, for I could never master that mystifying subject.

In one way I was spoiled but in another, I was not. I gave my parents complete obedience. I wouldn't cross them to my dying day. That is, after the one time I did.

They had to be pretty strict with me since they were both so busy all day; Mother would start teaching music before breakfast and go through until evening. Some of my friends who lived in Shelbyville would often ask me to go home with them afternoons. But I had been instructed, "Edwina, don't leave the school grounds!" I certainly would have been a lonely child had I not enjoyed reading or playing games with my dolls or writing fairy stories.

I was also forbidden to go to the rear of any of the school buildings. Built before Civil War days, the school had luxurious grounds surrounded by a high rock fence covered with vines. In the fall the giant oaks would shed their leaves, which were raked and heaped in piles. One of our greatest joys was to run, then jump into those big feather beds. The leaves would fly to the corners of the yard and would have to be raked up again, but the gardener didn't seem to mind. The colored people never hurried. I must have imbibed that feeling of leisure from those around me as I grew up, for I have never hurried. I have always taken everything that happened in life with calm, feeling that

165

what I might gain at one end by hurrying, I would lose at the other and not reach my destination any faster.

The once I disobeyed my parents occurred on a day I must have felt in a rebellious mood. Janiel Bell, a friend, asked me to her home for about the twentieth time and I decided this afternoon I would defy the commands of Mother and Father. I sat down and took off shoes and stockings, compounding the crime, for walking barefoot was another forbidden act. It was also a direct way of punishing myself, because the town had just scattered sharp rocks on the road to keep down the mud, and by the time I reached Janiel's house my feet were raw and bleeding.

Mrs. Bell stared at my bloody feet and asked, horrified, "What on earth are you doing barefoot, Edwina? Do your parents know where you are?"

I was not very communicative, one way or another, and it wasn't long before Mrs. Bell had her horse and buggy hitched up and I was driven back over the rock-strewn road.

My father was frantic, certain I had been kidnapped, which families always seem to fear when a child disappears, although most of the time nobody in his right mind would want the child. Once I had this feeling of fear with Tom. He was three months old at the time and couldn't even turn over by himself. We were vacationing at a resort and I thought it would be safe to leave him on the bed while we went for lunch.

When I returned, there was no Tom in the room. The first thought in my terrified mind was that he had been kidnapped.

Suddenly I heard a small muffled cry. Following the sound, I looked underneath the bed and there was Tom. He had fallen between wall and bed. The chambermaid had not swept under there for months, and Tom's little face peered up at me covered with cobwebs and dust. I was so relieved he had not been kidnapped—yet who would have wanted to kidnap him? We had no money. But it was my greatest fear, as it had been my father's when I disappeared years before.

Just about the time Father had searched the school grounds in vain and convinced everyone kidnappers had made off with me, I appeared in Mrs. Bell's horse and buggy. I fully expected a whipping, the first of my life. Instead, Father took me on his knee and simply told me in a quiet voice how much he had suffered. That was punishment enough, that and my sore feet. I never disobeyed again.

The school found itself deep in debt after being purchased by a lady who came down from the North and ran it in slipshod manner. Neither Mother nor Father received any salary for a year, after which the Institute collapsed. Father was offered a job as superintendent of schools in Shelbyville which he accepted, and we forsook the Institute as home to board at one of the rambling old mansions.

Clare Singleton, the daughter of the family at whose house we boarded, became my best friend, and her brother John my first sweetheart. From him, I received my first proposal, when he was nine and I, eight. Mother was taking violin lessons in Nashville and Father and John drove there one day to pick her up. On the way John confided to Father, "In all seriousness, Mr. Dakin, I'd like to ask Edwina's hand in marriage." He was an avid reader and no doubt was quoting precisely from the printed page a recently read courtship scene.

Father laughingly told me he had been asked for my "hand in marriage," and from then on embarrassment set in between John and me. He even stopped carrying my books to school. I met him years later when I visited his sister and he decided he was in love all over again and became one of my more serious beaus for a while.

The year of my first proposal, Father was offered a position at Woolwine, a young men's college in Tallahoma, Tennessee. We moved there for a brief stay but one which was to prove very important to his life. This was to be his final teaching job.

Father had a rich speaking voice and greatly enjoyed reading aloud. I never knew anyone to read as much as my father, from classics to the latest novels. I'm sure Tom got some of his love of books from Father. He could also recite poetry by the yard; people today don't memorize poems the way they used to do.

Because of Father's mellifluous voice, he was often asked to be a lay reader in church. One Sunday, Bishop Charles Todd Quintard, Tennessee's second Episcopal Bishop, came up to Father after the service. He said, "Dakin, I've got to have you in the ministry. I'm in need of clergy like you."

Father confessed he had always wanted to be a minister, had even written to the Bishop of Ohio in earlier days telling of his desire to go to theological school.

When he informed Mother of Bishop Quintard's interest, and mentioned his old, frustrated wish, she asked, "Why didn't you tell me that's what you wanted to do?"

"I was afraid you wouldn't wait for me," he said.

He was hesitant to change professions, for he knew his earnings would be less. Furthermore, Mother would have to give up her own income and devote herself entirely to the many chores of a minister's wife. It was a great sacrifice for her but she wanted Father to work at whatever made him the happiest.

Thus Father became a minister. He attended the Sewanee Theological Seminary at the University of the South in Sewanee, Tennessee, and was ordained by Bishop Quintard on March 23, 1895, in the library of Fulford Hall, on the Mountain, as they called it. In the following years he served many parishes throughout Tennessee and Mississippi, for he felt a clergyman should not remain too long in one parish. He became so popular he had trouble breaking away, because the parishioners would beg him to stay. I think, too, Father had a good deal of the wanderlust in him.

The same dear bishop who persuaded Father to become a minister was also a very impractical man. He was pleased when Father was called to one small town that needed him, not realizing the town was bankrupt and could not pay its minister. Some of Father's kin living near Cincinnati heard of our financial predicament and wrote that a parish near Springfield, Ohio, needed a rector. Father accepted this offer at a time the bishop was in England trying to get grants for his Church, even though Father knew the bishop would be dismayed at his leaving the state of Tennessee.

The Ohio parish was out in the suburbs and there, too, my parents had to leave me alone a great deal because the church catered to business people and held many meetings at night. When Father found out I might be sitting next to a colored child in school—Ohio was more liberal than Tennessee about segregation—he said, "You shall go to Wittenberg College." This was a junior college which accepted younger girls.

I had to pass an entrance examination which consisted of translating long passages from Julius Caesar, but with my early training in Latin, this was easy. What became hard was studying German, which I took at the school because Mother thought I should learn the language of her parents' native land.

I went to Wittenberg a year, then transferred to Harcourt Place, a boarding school for wealthy girls who wanted to prepare for Wellesley and other large Eastern colleges. The headmaster at Harcourt was in search of a few outstanding scholars and since I had earned the reputation at Wittenberg of being studious, I was offered a scholarship—the only way I could have attended Harcourt, because Father could not afford to send me there.

Harcourt was the scene of my first three years of high school. This was my first experience living away from home and I enjoyed it once I recovered from a few spells of homesickness. We were permitted to leave the school only for holidays.

Although I always managed to earn high grades, I cannot say I liked to study. I studied because I had to. What kept me from really digging into schoolbooks was knowing I would not go to college. Not only could we not afford it, but most girls in those days, unless they were planning a profession, did not bother with higher education but aimed frankly at getting married.

There were three schools for young men in town—Kenyon College, Kenyon Military Academy and Kenyon Theological School. Up until the time I was a full-fledged junior, I had dates only with the boys from the military academy. But by then, I felt myself a bit old for military students. My appearance in a school play helped me out of this dilemma.

Harcourt was whipping into dramatic shape a simple little comedy called *Six Cups of Chocolate*. I don't know whether a professional or one of the girls wrote it, for I never heard of it before or since. It had a leading part for a Southern girl and I seemed the proper choice. The night of its official presentation a number of young men from Kenyon College were in the audience and somehow I turned out to be the hit of the evening. I think they liked my Southern accent.

I remember one line, even to this day. The high spot of a particular scene was reached when I delivered the parting shot, "If he had been down South, my pa would have fixed him!" It was a telling line, for after that, when I would meet a young college man walking around Harcourt campus, he would call out teasingly, "What would your pa do to me if I were down South, Miss Dakin?"

It wasn't long before my first college man invited me to the Harcourt prom, the occasion of the year. Because of the three men's educational institutions nearby, there was never danger of being a wallflower at a dance, what with twelve men to every girl.

But the school authorities objected to my going to this dance with a college man. They did not want to forbid me outright and decided to give me special examinations, hoping I would not pass and thus be proved frivolous, so that they could deprive me of the dance. They devised what they thought a stiff test in history, which didn't faze me at all for I liked history, and an even stiffer one in Latin, my strongest subject; by then I had translated Caesar several times. If they had examined me in mathematics, I never would have made it to the prom.

When the examination scheme failed, they wrote to Father asking if he thought it proper for his daughter, only a junior, to go out with a college man. He replied he saw no reason why not. Luckily, Episcopalians do not think it a sin to dance and have a good time.

Mother gave her approval by sending a new dress with a low neck, which I wore with a green sash, and long, white kid gloves. The other girls, from wealthy families, may have had more expensive gowns but they could not have been any happier. I whirled around the floor in cotillions and figure dances and waltzes, my green sash streaming out behind me, having the time of my life. It was a program dance and you did not know with whom you were going to dance next but you knew every dance would be taken.

From that night on, college men sent me tickets to football games, which we attended chaperoned by teachers, and invited me to other dances. The principal of Harcourt stopped me one day in the corridor and warned, "Now, Miss Dakin, don't allow your little head to be turned." She thought I was thinking too much about the young men, which, perhaps, I was.

But we girls, although flirtatious, were never forward nor allowed the men to be. We were highly circumspect. One time I accidentally dropped my calling card on the street and a young man I knew returned it, saying in horror, "Miss Dakin, look what I found lying in the street—your calling card!" Men were extremely courteous and attentive. In one sense, it was a wonderful step forward when women fought for and won suffrage, for the woman of today would not be where she is without it, but I think although women gained something, they also threw away a great deal in demanding supposed equality.

Mother could not bear the Northern weather for too long, and when I was about to enter my last year of high school we moved to Cleveland, Tennessee, near Knoxville. The bishop was delighted to welcome Father back to his state and found him a beautiful old church. I regretted leaving Harcourt, for I had formed deep friendships there which endured many years. Most of the women have since died; I have begun to think of myself as the last rose of summer.

I attended Tennessee Female College in Cleveland. This was the end of the Gibson girl era and the students all wore their hair pompadour style. Father, however, insisted I wear mine straight back to make me look more intellectual, so I plaited my hair, turned it up and tied a bow on it. I also wore knee-length dresses when most of the girls appeared in longer ones, but I did not feel self-conscious. I was younger than the others and did not resent Father wanting me to dress in a way he considered appropriate for my age.

My amateur theatrical career blazoned at Cleveland as I appeared in several school plays, including one called *A Bachelor's Dream* in which I played the bachelor's first sweetheart. But I was not unhappy to move farther south when Father got a new parish at Port Gibson, Mississippi. There ended my formal education. I must admit I was not in the least sorry, for I had as much as most girls.

From then on, I was launched on a social whirl. I spent the happiest years of my life at Port Gibson, a plantation center located between Vicksburg and Natchez. It was called "Port" although it wasn't a port at all, for the Mississippi River flowed five miles away. The colored people told the story that when the Lord made the earth he had a lot of water left over and he said it could go where it pleased, and it went where it pleased and that's the Mississippi. Once it had flowed through Port Gibson, then it "went where it pleased" and wandered over to Lyons.

The state of Mississippi reminded me of a great big county. It had no large city and all the towns seemed joined by a feeling of intimacy and informality. The residents of Port Gibson were very kind to us; I have only pleasant memories associated with that little town.

The prominent families living on the large plantations would hold endless garden parties where we would dance on the huge verandas or stroll around the wide lawns lit in rainbow colors by Japanese lanterns.

When we moved to Port Gibson I decided it was time to become a young lady, to wear long dresses, not just to my shoe-tops but with sweeping trains. The girl who lived in the house across from us on Church Street rather enjoyed taking me down, for I heard she said some unkind things about the "newcomer," but even she could not spoil my love for Port Gibson.

One afternoon when I went calling on her, she said, bestowing one of those backhanded compliments which are tantamount to insult, "Your mother looks young enough to be your sister— you don't look at all like her daughter." She added reproachfully, "You look like your father, don't you?"

I thanked her, inwardly pleased, because I thought my father

172

extremely good-looking and believed I did resemble him more than Mother, although some people said I looked like her.

I told Father of my neighborly call and said, "She thinks I look like you."

"The old cat!" he said indignantly. "You don't at all. You look just like your mother." He thought Mother very beautiful. I thought her beautiful, too, in every way. Rarely do you find someone who doesn't think his or her mother the most beautiful in the world, but I wasn't biased—everyone admired Mother's beauty. I never hoped to measure up to her.

It was amusing to hear Father refer to the girl across the street as a "cat" for, as befitted his profession, he did not believe it proper to hold malice against anyone. He once said thoughtfully, "To be a Christian is a very difficult thing, Daughter. I try to be a Christian but I'm afraid I may have to spend a little time in Purgatory."

Father very definitely believed in "Hell," and also "Purgatory," which is primarily a Roman Catholic belief. But then he considered himself an "English Catholic" and very "high church." One of his favorite expressions was, "High and hazy, low and lazy."

I was pretty much of a butterfly in my late teens. I had good times with a number of beaus, not caring to pin myself down to any particular one, although there were some who wished to be serious if I'd allowed them to be. Many of the girls were belles in those days, with Southern men spending half their time making sure we enjoyed ourselves.

Most of the families were wealthy and could pass on estates and money to their children without inheritance taxes slicing it away. Sons knew they would be planters like their fathers before them. Cotton was everything. The young men had little to do but get up on a horse and ride around the plantation, watching overseers parcel out work, or else spend their time hunting quail and deer. My beaus had so much leisure, they would even take me for buggy rides in the morning.

What was the use of being too serious about anything in this kind of world except enjoying yourself, going to as many dances

173

as you had the strength for? The style of dancing was different then. We did not dance cheek to cheek on a postage stamp. We needed room for our trailing skirts, which we held up as we whirled around in a waltz.

After you danced until two and three in the morning, you were not too ambitious the next day. Gathering yourself together in the afternoon, you might sit on the veranda and wait for callers. Sunday was a great day for the young men to go from house to house calling on the girls. There were wonderful cooks in the kitchens who baked delicious cakes and concocted tasty chicken salad, and there was always plenty of good coffee.

If the young men wanted a special orchestra for a dance, there was Bud Scott's band which went all over Mississippi. He was a big, genial Negro who weighed about 250 pounds and led twenty colored youths who played music that defied you to keep your feet still. Old Bud Scott knew me well and he would grin from ear to ear as I walked onto a dance floor and say, "Hello, Miss Edwina."

Father was pleased I had a lot of beaus and liked them all until they became serious. Whenever one wanted to marry me, that was a different story. Father seemed to want me to become an old maid, but it never bothered me because I was not in love with anyone. We didn't fly from one lurid romance to another as young women do today. Our relationships were rather on the basis of friendship. I wouldn't have dreamed of "going steady," would have found it boring.

Tom has heard me describe these gay times. But he never heard me use the phrase "gentleman caller," for I referred to the young men as "friends" or "beaus."

Sometimes people tease me, thinking of Amanda, and ask, "Did you *really* have seventeen gentlemen callers?"

"Why, I remember a Sunday I had seventy-four!" I reply.

One time a young admirer, now happily married and a grandfather, who expected to marry me at that moment in his life, invited me to his home to meet his mother who was hoping I would become her daughter-in-law. The minister's daughter was

174

highly approved of as a match by mothers, and in addition, I was partly Quaker and so was she.

That afternoon several of us girls were holding court at her house, so a large number of Sunday callers streamed into the mansion. She was not present but finally, at supper hour, made her appearance. She walked over to me and nodded her head in satisfaction.

"Thee had seventy-four gentleman callers this afternoon," she said. "I counted them."

She had generously attributed to me the total number of men calling on all the girls.

I made "two" debuts. I always tell of this with a laugh, since a minister's daughter was supposed to be too poor to make even one. My double debut occurred when each of two sisters asked me to "come out" with her. I met Vicksburg society first with Clara Moore and again, the following year, when her sister Elise wrote, "I'd like you to make a debut with me now."

In spite of my gay life, I would return home each night at a reasonable hour and always before dark if out buggy riding, which meant alone with a man. I was never allowed to go buggy riding at night. Then I had to go with other couples in carry-alls, which had seats on both sides and a coachman up front.

Once I accepted an apparently innocent invitation from a young man to go to a party, only to find another beau of mine—who was taking someone else—calling at the house before the dance. He asked in a shocked voice, "Miss Edwina, do you know how Jenkins expects to take you to the dance tonight?"

"I imagine we'll go as we always go," I said, puzzled.

"He's bragging around town he's going to take you out in a buggy tonight!" he announced, as though this were the fate worse than death.

At that moment the young villain in question arrived at the front door—and with a buggy indeed! "He'll just have to go on by himself," I announced. "Father wouldn't let me ride with him in that."

It wound up with the two young men traveling to the dance

in the buggy and the rest of us transported in the carry-all. I suppose these things must seem pretty silly today.

But life was not only dancing and social calls. I also kept busy with church duties and chores around the house. There was no electricity then and I had to get up every morning in the world and wash every globe in the house, and there seemed endless lamps in endless rooms. I would trim the wicks and scour the blackened chimneys until they were sparkling clean.

There were no electric fans or air-conditioning, either. People who could afford a pickaninny used the little boys for air-conditioning. You would think their tiny hands would drop off as they'd stand behind you and energetically swing the fans to create a breeze and keep away the flies. They would feel proud they were chosen for the honor of serving in the big house.

I also took time out from being a butterfly to write an essay that won a prize from the Port Gibson Shakespeare Club when I was seventeen or so. The club members gave me the prize, a book, but shook their heads in disbelief that I had written the scholarly essay called "Julius Caesar, the Tragedy of an Idealist." They insisted Father must have done it. When I told Father, he snapped, "I have enough to do writing my sermons."

Soon after this intellectual victory, we left Port Gibson for a year in Natchez as Father's love of moving again took precedence over permanence. A new girl in town always creates quite a sensation and I felt like Cinderella in Natchez, where I met many new young men who called for me in the splendor of glass-enclosed carriages driven by coachmen.

The first dance to which I was asked was held at Stanton Hall, one of the famous old Civil War mansions. Dakin and Joyce, after a recent visit to Natchez, brought me a copy of the Pilgrimage Edition of the Natchez (Miss.) *Democrat*. In it were photographs and articles about some of the fine old homes, including Stanton Hall, whose description began:

> Occupying an entire block almost in the center of Natchez stands beautiful Stanton Hall, a magnificent memento of

ante-bellum taste and grandeur. It is without a doubt a most palatial home, and with the exception of Clifton, the old Postlethwaite home, is considered the finest mansion ever erected in Natchez.

The young man who took me to that first dance was a nephew of the lady who owned Stanton Hall. It had been in her family before the Civil War, but she lost it during the battles; when later she married a banker, he bought it back for her. My escort's name was Rowan Gaither. Not too long ago I read headlines in a newspaper:

MAN WHO HANDS OUT MILLIONS
BORN IN STANTON HALL, NATCHEZ

The story went on to say that Rowan Gaither, II, had been appointed president of the Ford Foundation. It was probably his father who invited me to that dance at Stanton Hall. I trust it was not his grandfather!

In Natchez, I "took" my first ride in an automobile. I can hardly use the word "enjoyed" about that experience, offered unexpectedly.

I was walking along the street one afternoon, out to pay several calls, and wearing my best and only calling costume, a champagne-colored voile dress over apple-green silk, with a green velvet belt. From my arm hung a parasol and my calling-card case. I also wore a hat edged with tiny pink rosebuds that sat on the back of my pompadour (by then I was wearing a pompadour). I tripped along demurely in high-heeled slippers, holding up my skirt.

I looked up to see a young man I knew driving alongside me in his automobile.

"Miss Dakin, do you want to ride in my new machine?" he asked.

He was the first young man in Natchez to own an automobile and at that time his was the only car in town. I was thrilled at the invitation and stepped eagerly into the automobile, which was built low to the ground. He steered it by a stick which he turned from one side to the other.

Naturally he wanted to show off so he went dashing madly through town. Ten miles an hour was a mad dash in those days. They had just watered down the dust of the streets, a daily occurrence that turned dark Mississippi dirt into black Mississippi mud. Not only had the big sprinkling cart left deep puddles dotting the road but the yardmen were out watering the sidewalks, adding to the muddy mess.

That automobile did not miss a mudhole. From the top of my rosebud hat to the last thread of my green satin slippers, I was plastered with mud. Spots even soaked through my new dress to the green petticoat.

When I reached home and stepped out of the car, Father met me at the door. He did not utter a word but his face was a thundercloud. He gave me only a look but I knew what he was thinking.

When the young man left, Father's only words were, "I hope at least he will pay the cleaning bill."

He never offered. But the champagne-colored dress was past redemption. That Mississippi mud would not come out. Father lost his investment in the dress. I had to get along for a while without a calling costume. And the young man ran into trouble with that automobile because people objected to it careening through the streets and frightening the horses to death.

For a while I never wanted to step into another automobile. I was through with the "new machine," at least until they built asphalt roads or higher running boards.

Other than that, life was quiet, its placidity broken only by such other momentous events as the installation of the first telephone. This was one long period of peace in our history, the Civil War just a memory and the First World War not even a thought.

In spite of the sorrow of later years I feel very fortunate, for I probably could not have endured what was to come if I had not enjoyed the early respite to which I think each child entitled. If there is one time in life a person ought to be free from fear, it is when he is growing up.

Unfortunately, this was not to be so for my children.

11.

"Mr. Dakin, I Am Not
Looking for a Cook"

W HEN I reached twenty-one and was still unmarried, I
considered myself an old maid. After all, it had been several
years since I'd made my two debuts.

We now lived in Columbus, Mississippi, an old town on the
Tombigbee River, across the state from Natchez and Vicksburg.
Father was minister at St. Paul's, a large, beautiful stone church
with a rectory alongside it in which we lived.

He assumed his duties on July 1, 1905, and was to serve the
church for nearly eight years before he would again move. Six
months after his arrival, his hometown newspaper, the *Miami
Gazette* in Waynesville, Ohio, asked him to write an article for
a special Home-Coming Edition.

WAYNESVILLE OLD AND NEW

ST. PAUL'S RECTORY
COLUMBUS, MISSISSIPPI

You have asked me to write you somewhat of my life and
work, of me and of mine.

When such a proposition is put to one, it is borne in upon him how very little he has done and how much he has left undone of all the plans and schemes and dreams with which he started out when he left the dear, old plain brick building upon the hill, where AT THE TIME, he supposed he had stored away all the wisdom of the ages, and that there was nothing more worth while.

They tell me the dear old school house is re-placed with one more up to date; that lamps are now a thing of the past with the tallow candles of our grand-mothers, and that nothing else but electricity will do for modern Waynesville; that out of its ashes, has sprung—Phoenix-like—a new town; that the trolley is near and some are dreaming of its being still nearer—yes, at the very door; that new residences with all the luxuries of the day have taken the place of the former simple Quaker homes and that "The apostle of the simple life" would stand aghast, could he see the interiors of some of them.

It has not been twenty years since last I viewed Waynesville, still I fear I shall have a Rip Van Winkle feeling, if I be fortunate enough to be among those at the Home-Coming of 1906.

If this be Waynesville, who be I?

Shall I like the NEW Waynesville, or shall I be homesick for the simple life of the town as I remember it? Will George Bailey say "thee" or "thou" to me, or has he changed with the changing years?

How George and Anna Lile and Anna Furnas (may Light Perpetual shine upon her!) and Maggie McComas and I labored over those wonderful orations in the third story of the OLD school house—those fearfully and wonderfully made productions which WE supposed would startle the natives—but that was 1875.

Shall I like NEW Waynesville? I almost doubt it. (Is that treason?)

There is so much that is NEW, and newness is becoming to some things—but Waynesville—well, it was just Waynesville; what it is now, I do not know.

I believe in progress for MOST things, but then, you know Waynesville is different; it is like the grand old Faith—it cannot be added to, or subtracted from for it was perfect as it was—but, as Kipling would say, "that is another story."

Be Waynesville as it may, old or new, still there are, across the river, sleeping in God's Acre, so many of my dear ones, that it will often carry us back.

I cannot write more of THEM for with Tennyson:

> "I sometimes hold it half a sin
>   To put in words the grief I feel;
>   For words, like nature, half reveal
>   And half conceal the Soul within."

I am not accountable for this feeling; I only know that it is one of the many Dakin peculiarities.

You want to know something of my present life? Well, my lines have fallen in pleasant places—it has always been so with me—and I am grateful.

Columbus is a beautiful little city, with still many of the "before the war" homes both in and near it, having suffered less from the devastation of war than the towns around.

You may recall that it was at this place that the women first placed flowers upon both Federal and Confederate graves alike, calling forth that beautiful poem, beginning:

> "By the flow of the inland river
>   Whence the fleets of iron have fled,
>   Where the blades of the grave-grass quiver
>   Asleep are the ranks of the dead;
>   Under the sod and the dew,
>   Waiting the Judgment day;
>   Under the one, the Blue;
>   Under the other, the Gray."

I feel very much at home among these delightful people; they seem to have adopted me and mine; it was easy for me to accept their adoption, for my grand-mother Bellard's people were Virginians—whether F.F.V.'s or S.F.V.'s. I cannot say, but sufficient it is that some Virginia blood flows in my veins.

But I love these dear, cultured Southern people because they are so lovable.

My surroundings are beautiful. St. Paul's church is a

stately old brick building, with a pipe organ and all that goes to properly render our Service as St. Paul says, "decently and in order."

Back of the Church is a nice brick Parish House with rooms for the Sunday school and the various guilds. The rectory nicely furnished by the Church, is a very pretty home, and I, with my wife and daughter, am very happy in it.

Of my work I will only say it is that of most clergymen, doing what, I trust, the Master may one day pronounce "good."

Wishing the "Home-Coming" all success, and hoping I may be there in person, as I am sure to be in spirit, I am,

Faithfully yours,

WALTER EDWIN DAKIN

The Daughters of the American Revolution invited me to join shortly after we moved to Columbus. I asked Father, "Can we trace our ancestry back to the Revolution?"

"Well, Daughter, I don't know," he said. "My family came over here one hundred years before the Revolution but they had grants of land from England. They were Tories. Some of them discreetly retired to Canada until the fuss was over. But if I can find one for you that fought on the side of the Revolutionists, I certainly will."

He went to the library and, by strange coincidence, discovered the young lady in charge was also named Dakin. He asked if she knew any Dakin who had fought for the colonies. She mentioned a relative, Elijah Sabin, of Quaker origin.

"That seems rather hopeless," said Father. "Quakers don't like to fight."

But they managed to dig up a Dakin who was a farmer and a very patriotic one. He had thrown down the plow to take up the musket. So I was able to join the D.A.R., an organization of which I am very proud. They do much welfare work of which people seldom hear.

The Dakins could trace themselves back to the Normans. One of our ancestors was captain of a ship that sailed to England

182

at the time of the invasion under William the Conqueror. When the wind wreaked havoc with his sails, he climbed up to untangle sail from rope. Our coat-of-arms bears the motto: *Stryke Dakyns, Ye Devils in Ye Hempe* (referring to the wind tangling the rope that was strangling the sails). The coat-of-arms also holds the words, *Sir Baldwyn Dakeny, Knt.* and the picture of a knight's breastplate with four lions, one in each corner, and his helmet. Above the latter a crown contains a hand stretching out of it with a spear, poised as though ready to strike.

In addition to joining the D.A.R., I also took part in amateur theatrical productions as I had done in school and in Port Gibson. I must confess my secret ambition was to become an actress, a musical comedy star. But ladies in those days were not allowed such careers except in amateur form.

I had always loved to sing and was part of our church choir. I would be called on to substitute for whoever happened to be ill or missing on Sunday. I told Father once, "I don't mind being the soprano or the tenor or even the baritone but I draw the line at the bass." I lost my voice when I nearly died of influenza after Dakin was born, and the illness did something to my bronchial tubes from which I have never fully recovered.

One evening in Columbus, I was rehearsing in a charity production of selections from *The Mikado* when a local lawyer, one of my most serious beaus of the moment, came backstage. He explained he had brought, as guest to the rehearsal, a young man who had come down from Memphis to plead a case in court for the telephone company, for which he worked. The young man had attended the University of Tennessee law school for a year, then enlisted in the Spanish-American War and never returned to the study of law but understood enough about it to handle the case. The young man did not know a soul in Columbus and my beau felt sorry for him. The young man had seen me onstage rehearsing the "Three Little Girls Are We" number and wanted to meet me.

"But I don't know anything about his family background," said my beau. "When I find out, if it's a proper one I'll bring him over to your house."

He called me up a few days later. "I found out all about him," he said excitedly. "He's from the very first family in Tennessee!"

He brought the young man to the rectory to meet me. His name was Cornelius Coffin Williams. He came from pioneer Tennessee stock on his father's side and early settlers of Nantucket Island on his mother's, the poet Tristam Coffin being his great-uncle.

The young man's family were makers of Tennessee history through the Williamses, the Seviers and the Laniers. The Williamses, who came from Wales, had their coat-of-arms, too. It depicted a fighting lion, above it a peacock, with the motto, *Cognoscy-Occasionem* (Know Your Opportunity—Seize It). The Williamses, Coffins, Seviers and Laniers each possessed a coat-of-arms; a cousin of my husband's painted one on each corner of his four-poster bed—much to my husband's disgust, for he never bragged about his ancestry. One time I was telling a group of men about his background while he was out of the room, and when he returned they said with new deference, "Take a chair, Mr. Williams—take two chairs!"

The young man's (after all, he was not my husband yet, nor at the time did I dream he would be) father, Thomas Lanier Williams (after whom Tom was named), was a Tennessee politician who served as railroad commissioner for the state, spending many of his days in Washington. He was appointed in 1893 as World's Fair Commissioner to represent Tennessee in Chicago. He wanted very much to be Governor of Tennessee and ran three times without success, defeated always by Robert Taylor for the Democratic nomination. He once owned valuable land but over the years gave most of it away as political favors; he even lost the family homestead, which became an orphanage for colored children.

John Sharp Williams—a cousin of his father's—was a Senator from Mississippi who became Speaker of the Senate, a noted orator who once said, "I'd rather be a hound dog baying at the moon on a Mississippi plantation than be a member of the United States Senate." The young man's grandfather, Colonel John Williams, the first Senator from Tennessee, was known for his courtly manners—Dolly Madison called him "the Chesterfield of the Senate." He was defeated for re-election only by Andrew Jackson, whom he had assisted in the Battle of New Orleans. Jackson was a great enemy of another Williams ancestor, General John Sevier, the first Governor of Tennessee, who "ruled" the state before Jackson took over. It is through the Sevier-Xavier line that the Williamses are related to St. Francis Xavier.

When I first met him, I thought Cornelius Coffin Williams a handsome, personable young man. He took me dancing a few times, hiring the best-looking rig in the city and setting out for the finest hotel. After his case in court was settled, he returned to Memphis, but he would come back to Columbus every so often to see me. It was not long before he proposed. As with other beaus, I did not give a definite answer at first.

During the time Cornelius was courting me, I came down with typhoid fever and malaria, both at once. I lost half my hair. The young lawyer who introduced me to Cornelius was so concerned lest I lose all of it that he brought over a special hair tonic, claiming it would save what remained. Thus I owe him both my husband and my hair!

I was delirious for a while and when I came to, I opened my eyes to see a large bouquet of red roses by the bed. I asked Mother, "Where did these come from?"

"You've been getting a bouquet every day," she said, "from that Mr. Williams in Memphis."

His thoughtfulness impressed me, as did the telephone calls every night. Since he was a telephone company employee, they didn't cost him anything, but the roses that still arrived daily did.

Cornelius was the kind of man who never took no for an answer. He showered me with attention and even though I refused his proposal several times, he kept persevering in the tradition of his family motto, *Know Your Opportunity—Seize It.* One day the roses stopped coming. Instead I received a package. In it sparkled a beautiful engagement ring.

My parents were sold on Cornelius. When he asked my hand
185

in marriage, Father said, "But Edwina can't sew. And she can't cook. There's nothing she can do but be a social butterfly."

"Mr. Dakin, I am not looking for a cook," said Cornelius.

Father gave his consent to the marriage.

We planned a large church wedding. Then Cornelius' father fell seriously ill and was not expected to live. I did not hear from Cornelius for a while. I learned his father had died.

I had about given up the idea of marrying him and accepted an invitation to a college house party, intending to go with the sister of the man who asked me. As I was leaving the house, the telephone rang. It was Cornelius. "I'm coming down with the wedding ring," he announced.

We were married very quietly in St. Paul's Church by Father. I didn't invite anyone in the congregation because if I had asked one, I would have had to ask all. For a while they felt insulted, as if they had been deprived of fun, but finally they relented and gave me a beautiful set of flatwear from Tiffany's and I knew I had been forgiven.

We spent our honeymoon in Gulfport, Mississippi, where we were to live because my husband had just been appointed manager of three Southern telephone exchanges. We enjoyed life there, sometimes going out to dance, sometimes playing cards, sometimes chaperoning young couples on moonlight boat parties to Ship Island.

After a year and a half, in 1909, I left Gulfport to go back to Columbus. I was expecting my first baby and wanted to be with my parents, as my mother had been with hers when I was born.

The baby was a beautiful girl and I called her Rose, after Mother. Two years later, in 1911, I had my second child, the boy I named Thomas Lanier Williams.

He was to give much more to the world than either the world or I could give to him.

12.

"A Tragedy of Incomprehension"

THIRTY-SIX years after my first son's birth, I was preparing to attend the premiere of his third play on Broadway.

Just as I was ready to leave St. Louis, I received a postcard from Boston where the play was trying out.

> We are playing to capacity in Boston. The notices were mostly good, some reviewers a bit shocked by play. Really think you should wait for "Summer and Smoke" as this play is hardly your dish. Love—Tom.

Naturally this intrigued me all the more, and wild horses in the form of all the shocked reviewers in the world could not have kept me away. I wrote, telling Tom I would be in New York for the opening.

"Well, if you insist on coming, bring that rose-colored shawl I brought you from Italy for Blanche to wear in the second act—and leave your moralizing at home," he instructed.

The play was *A Streetcar Named Desire* and I thought it Tom's greatest. Sons have such trouble understanding mothers!

Dakin and I traveled to New York and registered at the Barbizon-Plaza Hotel. I had a few hours to spare and wandered into the small library on the first floor where people can sit in comfortable chairs and read in peace. I'm small town and friendly and usually wind up talking to the man or woman next to me, and this time I found myself chatting with a middle-aged woman who seemed to be guarding a secret.

Finally she leaned over and confided, "There's a very exciting play opening tonight on Broadway and I was lucky enough to get a ticket."

"Yes?" I drew her out.

She lowered her voice as if speaking of things illicit. "I understand it's very risqué."

"What's it called?" I asked.

"*A Streetcar Named Desire*," she whispered, as if the very name held the fascination of the forbidden.

"I came here from St. Louis for the opening," I said casually. "My son wrote it."

She gave me a startled look, as if I were an escapee from Bellevue, and edged away. She said not a word more, soon lifted herself from the chair and fled.

Just as she predicted, it was an exciting evening. As the curtain rose, the audience burst into applause at the sight of the set, a section of the French Quarter of New Orleans which Tom knew and loved so well. Then unreeled the story of Blanche DuBois, her sister Stella, and Stella's Polish husband, Stanley Kowalski, and by the time the curtain descended on the final scene there was no doubt Tom had surpassed *Menagerie*.

The play gripped me so deeply I could not rise from my seat; I heard others stand up and leave, but I could not move. Dakin sat beside me and we waited for Tom. He had brought me an orchid before the performance but, as usual, was wandering around somewhere. He found us after the waves of deafening applause receded.

Cornelius would not go with us to New York for the opening but took a trip East a few weeks later to see *Streetcar*. He called Audrey to find out where he could reach Tom, and when she informed him his father was trying to get hold of him, Tom said bitterly, "Tell him I'm lecturing at Harvard this afternoon." This was Tom's way of fighting his father. He did not wish to see him but did not want to tell him so.

Cornelius was not shocked at *Streetcar*. After all, it would take a lot to shock him, for he was veteran of many "A Poker Night," as the play was originally called.

Irene Selznick produced *Streetcar* and I was touched on opening night to receive an orchid and a card:

> For Tennessee's mother:
> I hope you know how
> deeply we all pray for your
> happiness and pride tonight.
> We welcome—
> and we salute you.
> IRENE SELZNICK

Leonard Lyons once wrote that James Kirk Merrick, the little-theatre director, discussing Tom's opening-night nerves, told of a dinner party given at Sardi's by Mrs. Selznick just before the premiere of *Streetcar*. Everyone ordered early so they would reach the theatre in time for the curtain, and all courses were brought in simultaneously.

"I was sure that Tennessee suffered from first-night jitters," said Mr. Merrick, "because I saw him order a steak, pour sauce on it and then I noticed he didn't touch it at all."

Mr. Merrick later mentioned this to Tom and Tom assured him he had not been nervous. Mr. Merrick brought up the uneaten steak.

"I didn't eat the steak," Tom explained, "because the sauce I poured on that fine steak came from the wrong pitcher. It was fudge for Irene's ice cream."

This sounds like Tom, who is sometimes very absent-minded. He will flick cigarette ashes in a vase or anything handy. A friend once said to me in amazement, "Why, Tennessee was even shaking ashes down my collar!"

Mrs. Selznick was another woman important in Tom's life; he has received more kindnesses from women than men, except for his grandfather. The first Christmas after *Streetcar* she sent me a little gold streetcar with DESIRE engraved on it, for my charm bracelet, to keep company with Dakin's honor pin, the first ring I ever received which Father gave me, and the key to New Orleans presented by the mayor. The bracelet itself is a gift from Dr. Hugh Hyatt, a dentist in Memphis who is a friend of Tom's.

Mrs. Selznick was thoughtful enough to write when she returned from England in June, 1948:

> DEAR MRS. WILLIAMS:
>
> Here, belatedly, is the picture of you and Dakin taken opening night which I ordered then and which has just come through.
>
> I got home yesterday from Europe and I wanted to tell you that I saw Tennessee last Wednesday night in London. I thought you would like to know that he was looking remarkably well and seems to have lost that little excess weight he had—he looks shockingly young. He seems to be enjoying his experience in England and I am sure that he is eagerly looking forward to your arrival.
>
> I will be in California, unfortunately, by the time you go through New York. If there is any way at all my office can be of assistance to you, please do not hesitate to call them.
>
> Affectionately,
> IRENE

She was referring, speaking of my "arrival," to attending the London opening of *Menagerie*.

When Tom sent Audrey the script of *Streetcar* in February, 1947, she decided to take it first to Mrs. Selznick, who was looking for a play after *Heartsong*, by Arthur Laurents, died out of town. Mrs. Selznick's former husband was David Selznick, the Hollywood producer, her father was Louis B. Mayer, head of

MGM where Tom had worked so briefly—and, according to their description, so ineptly—and her brother-in-law, William Goetz, was head of Universal-International.

Mrs. Selznick liked the play and decided to produce it. Elia Kazan was chosen to direct it, Jessica Tandy to play Blanche, Kim Hunter, Stella, and Marlon Brando, Stanley. When I first met Marlon, I thought he was well cast as Stanley, but that was a long time ago and I am sure he has changed. Dakin is very proud of a photograph taken with Marlon. I may be prejudiced, but I think Dakin is handsomer.

I read that Irene put in her own money to the extent of $25,000 as the sole general partner and that limited partners included Betsy Cushing (Mrs. John Hay) Whitney, Joan W. Payson, Howard S. Cullman, Clinton E. Wilder, Jr., Robert Lehman, Cary Grant, Howard Reinheimer and Audrey, each of whom invested $5,000, while the late Adele E. Levy, E. Y. Harburg and Irving Schneider were credited with putting in $10,000. The total raised was supposed to be $100,000, "an exceptional sum for a drama," said the report.

But worth it when the reviews came out. The play won the New York Drama Critics' Circle award that year, 17 out of 21 critics voting for it, an exceptionally high majority, with *Mr. Roberts* receiving two votes and *Command Decision* and *Medea* each one. *Time* said the critics' choice of *Streetcar* as the best play made Tom "the leading contender for the title of the nation's most gifted young playwright."

Streetcar was produced in Rome, Brussels, Stockholm, Buenos Aires, Mexico City, Melbourne, among other places. Russia permitted no version, although the play was reviewed in Moscow, described as part of the Broadway plot "to stupefy men and turn them into beasts."

Jean Cocteau adapted it for Paris and a newspaper there reported, "The presentation has created a furor. Latter-day Parisians, it appears, are shocked at this violent fable of New Orleans."

A letter from Lillian Gish told us why. Cocteau had put in

some of his own fancy touches, none of them even hinted at by Tom in the original. At various critical points in the action, the principals were practically blacked out while behind a gauze curtain in the rear of the stage, little pantomimes were acted, including one of near-rape in the street, a sidewalk shooting, and a belly dance by a naked Negro strip-teaser during the scene where Blanche is raped by Stanley. Lillian wrote from the Hotel Matignon, Paris:

DEAR TENNESSEE WILLIAMS:

Have just seen your play "Streetcar" in French and want to report that with the exception of one scene it loses nothing in translation. The cast is excellent, Arletty superb— you were prophetic in naming her Blanche DuBois. Her mad scene chills your blood and makes your heart tender. Vincent is more subtle than Brando but as convincing. Perhaps I liked Kim Hunter better (she seemed perfect to me) but this actress is good. The scenes going upstairs the audience follows as they have a typical New Orleans balcony crossing above front stage and they use it to help your play. The dancing back stage leaves nothing to the imagination. I suppose the French prefer it that way. The scene that disappoints is the one with the young bill collector. They miss the pathos and strain for comedy. To my mind it is staged badly. He does not come into the room at all. She goes to him at the door. But that is a small flaw in an over all fine production. It is a thrilling evening, and one can not get seats. I *almost* had to say I knew you to get two in the balcony. Do come over soon and see for yourself.

LILLIAN GISH

NOVEMBER FIFTH, 1949

Streetcar won for Tom not only the New York Drama Critics' Circle Award but the Pulitzer Prize, which *Menagerie* lost in 1945 to Mary Chase's *Harvey*. It became the first play ever to win all three theatrical awards, the Pulitzer, Drama Critics and Donaldson. Tom gave the money from the Pulitzer award to the University of Missouri as a scholarship for graduate work in journalism.

When the New York Film Critics voted the movie version of *Streetcar* the best English-language drama of 1951, Cheryl Crawford, who had just produced *The Rose Tattoo* and later produced *Camino Real* and *Sweet Bird of Youth,* sent Tom a newspaper story with the comment:

> DEAR TEN,
> Art and recognition, too?
> What's the world coming to?
> CHERYL

The Pulitzer prize, a special scroll and $500, was sent to Tom in Rome where he was now residing part of the year. He became enchanted with Rome, as he had once been with New Orleans, although he has given up his apartment there. He liked Rome because "to me it is the place where I find the sun not only in the sky, where Italy also keeps it, but in the heart of the people," he said.

He also described Rome as "spelling peace, which is what I want above all. But it spells it without isolation, which I don't want. I want to have peace in the middle of many people and here I find it. And I can work here. That's the thing."

Our home in St. Louis was hardly a haven of peace for Tom, not with the man of wrath dominating it, so I understand how he felt about Rome where he could, as he said, "set himself down for the period of outer oblivion and inner violence" that work demanded.

Tom has described *Streetcar* as a "tragedy of incomprehension," the inability of people to understand one another. Accused of writing about "sordid" characters, he said he did not believe Blanche sordid but "rather noble," that he did not think deeply troubled people were sordid.

"I think pettiness and meanness is sordid," he said. "I would never choose a person of that sort for a main protagonist because they don't interest me."

Another time he declared he thought most people possessed deep troubles. "I've yet to find people I didn't think were deeply troubled," he said. "I think that if most people look at others, they'll see deep trouble under the skin." Sometimes what Tom says about his plays, I feel, is as penetrating as the plays themselves.

Brooks Atkinson agreed with Tom, for he wrote of *Streetcar* that "Blanche's sex preoccupation is merely the most conspicuous symptom of the harrowing disease of disintegration that is consuming her. Sex is not the theme of the play nor the basic element in her character. She is in a panicky flight from the catastrophe of a genteel way of life that no longer can sustain her in an animalized world."

Tom took two years to write *Streetcar*, which he called *The Poker Night* up until the time it went into rehearsal. He started it following another eye operation, this one at St. Luke's Hospital in New York in the spring of 1945, after which he went to Mexico to spend the summer in Chapala. There he began two plays, *The Poker Night* and *Summer and Smoke*. He returned to New York when *You Touched Me!* opened at the Booth Theatre on September 26 but left shortly thereafter to visit me in St. Louis. Then he went again to Mexico via Texas where he and Margo Jones made plans for producing *Summer and Smoke* in Dallas.

Summer and Smoke is the story of Alma Winemiller, the inhibited daughter of a puritanical Southern minister and a childish, petulant wife, who falls in love with the boy next door, John Buchanan, the dissolute son of the local doctor. They spend the time together fighting and growing further apart, instead of closer. She indirectly causes the death of his father, shot by the drunken father of a wayward girl with whom John has become involved. As the play ends, there comes about a reversal in roles. John, now a successful doctor, plans to marry a sweet, simple girl, while Alma, in her despair, embarks on a life of promiscuity as she picks up a traveling salesman.

After a winter in Mexico, Tom rented a cottage on Nantucket in the spring of 1946, intending to spend the summer finishing *Summer and Smoke*. He wrote me from that island.

DEAR MOTHER:

I have been working on two things at once. The Southern writer, Carson McCullers, has been here and I have been helping her dramatize her latest novel, and finishing up my own play at the same time. Both are nearing completion. Carson is leaving the island this week and I am accompanying her as far as Martha's Vineyard where we will visit Katharine Cornell and I may show her part of my play which is being written for her, though it is still very rough. Carson's book, "The Member of the Wedding" is one of the finest American novels. I wrote her of my admiration and out of this correspondence came the visit to the island. It was only after we met here that she decided to dramatize it for the stage and I to help her. I think it is going to make a beautiful play.

I'm sorry I didn't write you sooner about the X-rays. They told me that nothing abnormal was shown in them, which relieved me a great deal. I have been feeling a lot better, probably because of having that anxiety removed.

I decided not to visit the Cabots in Canada as I had so much work to do. I was afraid there would be more society than here and it might interfere. A sad thing happened lately. Miss Elizabeth Curtis, the elderly spinster whom I had stayed with in New York, died quite suddenly just about a week after my last visit there. In spite of her great wealth and social prestige she was a very lonely woman and seemed to get a great pleasure out of entertaining me and my friends while I was there. We took her out to the theatre and dancing and she entertained me at her fashionable clubs and she said it was the most fun she had had in many years, so I guess it was Providence that brought me there.

Menagerie seems to have run its course in New York. A while back Audrey wired me that she had a good and definite offer for the movie rights but I have heard nothing further, since the wire. The road company is now in rehearsal. I may visit New York for a few days to see if the cast is all right. I think the play could have run another year if Laurette and Dowling had stayed on good terms and the show had been properly managed. I wish Dakin had a job in New York so he could take a hand in such matters for me.

An alley cat has adopted this house as her residence and has had three kittens here. All four cats are now running about the place. I tried to keep the three kittens in a box on the back porch but the old mother cat did not consider it good enough for them. So she jumped through the window with them, one at a time, and carried them upstairs and deposited them in the middle of the guest-bed. Every time I put them out she repeated the procedure, but we finally compromised on a pile of old blankets in a corner of the upstairs bedroom.

Last week I gave a reading at a local art gallery. Read a couple of my one-act plays before a large audience, including Thornton Wilder and some other notables. I did not have a sugar coupon so I announced before the reading that the only remuneration I wished was for any extra sugar the audience might have to spare. The next morning several packages were delivered, enough to last for the summer.

Have received a letter from Grandfather, which I hope to answer this week. But please send him this one, too. I hope he is happily situated in Ohio.

> With love,
> Tom

Tom introduced Carson to Audrey, who helped her find a producer, just as he introduced William Inge to Audrey after reading *Come Back, Little Sheba*. Tom first met Mr. Inge when he was the amusements editor of the St. Louis *Star-Times* and interviewed Tom in St. Louis before *Menagerie* opened in Chicago. At that time, he asked Tom if he would read a play on which he was working and Tom was so impressed he encouraged him to keep writing. Mr. Inge dedicated *The Dark at the Top of the Stairs* to Tom.

Six months before *Streetcar* opened on Broadway, Margo Jones presented *Summer and Smoke* at her Dallas Theatre and audiences found it very moving. She and Tom decided to bring it to Broadway, but since *Streetcar* was scheduled for a 1947 production, they postponed the show until the following autumn when it opened at the Music Box Theatre on October 6, 1948.

Tom gave a big party after the opening. I was horrified at his delinquency as host. When the guests started to say goodbye, he was nowhere to be found. I asked, "Where is Tom?"

"Oh, he and Marlon went off on Marlon's motorcycle," someone said.

But Tom's manners are improving. He gave out with a few uncomplimentary remarks about the famous Tallulah when she was appearing in a revival of *Streetcar* (some who saw it at the Coconut Grove Playhouse in Miami said she raced through the part of Blanche as though making a dash for touchdown). In Earl Wilson's column one day I read about a party for Tallulah at the Bernard Goodwins which Mr. Wilson attended with his wife. He found Tallulah with her arm around Tom.

"I heard you two were feuding," said Mr. Wilson.

"He knelt at my feet tonight, dahling," said Tallulah.

"I knelt at her feet twice," said Tom gallantly.

"You should write a play just for Tallulah," suggested Mrs. Wilson.

"Um," said Tom.

13.

"Neither Tom nor I Shed a Tear"

AS *Streetcar* rolled rapidly on its way to fame, I told Tom news I didn't know whether he would consider good or bad.

Mother and Father lived with us for a few years in the house on Arundel Place until Mother died in 1943 at the age of eighty, when Father was eighty-six. At first my parents had not been sure they should sell their little house in Memphis and move to St. Louis, knowing Cornelius, but Mother was so ill they really didn't have a choice. I could not allow her to take care of Father or he to try to take care of her. Cornelius did not object to their living with us because he respected Mother; he was fond of her in his way. When she died, I insisted Father remain with us for he now had no one.

Cornelius retired at sixty-five on a large pension, which meant he would now be in the house with Father during a good part of the day. My husband started to become very unpleasant to this old man although Father was a pretty determined old man and would take contempt from no one. Father began to leave us for visits elsewhere, while still considering St. Louis as headquarters. He would spend part of the year with Tom in Key West where Tom had bought a house, or New York, where Tom rented an apartment, or visit old friends in Clarksdale or at the Hotel Gayoso in Memphis.

But the times he did reside with us became more and more distasteful. As Father entered the door, returning from a walk or from church, Cornelius would declaim in a loud, disrespectful voice, "Here comes the old buzzard." Sometime he would show more respect and refer to Father as "the old parson." Father would pretend not to hear and march straight upstairs, not wanting to be in the same room with Cornelius and tempt his anger further. Father never showed animosity toward anyone, not even my husband when he was rude to him. He knew you could not reason with Cornelius, a man without reason.

One day when Father left for a visit with Tom, Cornelius handed me an ultimatum. "You'll just have to tell the old buzzard he can't come back any more," he said.

The idea of throwing my father out of the house was incredible to me. It was Father's home, too, for by now much of the furniture belonged to my parents, brought from Memphis.

I said to Cornelius, "I cannot allow my father to be put out on the street. You'll have to make up your mind whether you want to go or stay. The choice is yours."

After ordering me out of the house for forty years, it was now his turn to face a decision whether to go or stay.

He decided to go. I asked as settlement ownership share of the house but on that I was adamant. I could have taken a good part of his money but I told him the house was all I wanted and if he would not give me that, I would go to a lawyer who would see I received what was properly due me. Cornelius did give me the house and some shares of International Shoe stock.

My husband had ordered Rose out and Tom out and my father and me. Eventually there was nothing to do but take himself out.

There is always a last straw and my father had been it. Otherwise, I would have let things go on. Cornelius was comfortable in the house, I didn't interfere with his life, and I don't think he really wanted to leave.

I said good-bye and signed a contract for which Dakin, now a full-fledged lawyer, arranged. After graduating from the law school at Washington University in 1942, Dakin served with the Army Air Corps as a fighter controller and judge advocate in India and Burma for twenty-eight months. Discharged as captain, he became instructor of law at St. Louis University, and then went into private practice with Martin, Peper & Martin, a firm in St. Louis, before being recalled into service in 1951. He served in Formosa for fifteen months, following which he became the judge advocate at Scott Air Force Base in Illinois. He married, on October 15, 1955, the former Joyce Croft of Big Spring, Texas, whom he met at Webb Air Force Base in Big Spring, where she was secretary to the commander.

Today Dakin is Assistant United States Attorney for the Eastern District of Illinois and holds a major's commission in the Air Force Reserve, having completed twenty years' total service in his country's armed forces.

I never saw Cornelius again after he left Arundel Place. I was happy to have my freedom—the walls of the house had resounded with wrath for too many years and now there was peace at long last.

I truly tried to understand my husband. I know he grew up without the love of a mother, so important to a child. His mother died when he was five and he was shipped from aunt to aunt, then sent to military academy which he called "a school for bad boys." It certainly was, in his case, for he proved a disciplinary problem, running away from the academy and disobeying other rules so that he spent much time in the guardhouse. He would never let me serve turnips because that was the dish so often pushed underneath the door as part of punishment.

His father, upon receiving a distress call from the Academy or the aunts, would sometimes take Cornelius to Washington where the boy would sit in hotel lobbies while he cast political irons into the fire. His sisters tried to help Cornelius but they only spoiled him, giving in to his whims and tantrums. He became a headstrong, wild young man and his father was pleased when he talked of settling down and marrying me, although he never saw us married for he died just before the ceremony.

When Cornelius left me, he went to Knoxville where Ella was running her gift shop, trying to make ends meet on a meager income. She had written me after Isabel's death, when Cornelius went to Knoxville for the funeral, that he had been "a great comfort and consolation to me, and I hated for him to go." But now even she could not cope with him and he lived by himself at a hotel.

Durant Da Ponte interviewed Cornelius after he left me, quoting him in an article called "Tennessee's Tennessee Williams," part of "Tennessee Studies in Literature" sponsored by the University of Tennessee Studies in the Humanities, 1956. In it Cornelius was described as being "ambivalent" about his son's success. "I don't think he means any harm," Cornelius said, in discussing Tom's creating characters in his plays based on members of his family.

The article winds up with this description of Cornelius:

> A family friend of long standing described him to me as being a person not easy to get along with, possessed of a devil-may-care attitude—an evaluation which may be partially just but which certainly leaves out some obvious positive elements in his character. Cornelius Williams seems to be a basically decent sort of person with some traces of bitterness, perhaps, and a certain irascibility. His parting words to me comprised what he wants to be his epitaph; namely, "He paid his debts; he told the truth, and tried to live by the Golden Rule." After this, what more need be said?

I am saying a bit more.

Cornelius died alone in a hotel room in 1957. I wondered, as he faced the final moment of death, of what he was thinking? He had always been so afraid of dying.

He died after a bad attack of asthma and that, combined with a spree, I'm sure, caused his end. I don't know how Tom learned of the funeral, whether Ella or Dakin called him, or he read about it in the newspaper, but he telephoned me and said, "I know you won't want to go to Knoxville, Mother. I'll meet Dakin there."

Tom was present at his father's funeral. Ella walked into the church on his arm; I know she was pleased he came. Dakin told me, "Neither Tom nor I shed a tear."

Tom once wrote of his feelings about his father:

> His was not a nature that could comply with the accepted social molds and patterns without a restlessness that would have driven him mad without the release of liquor and poker and wild week-ends. He held his liquor well, aside from the damage it did to his nervous system over the years —he was never arrested for drunken driving or public disorder. Actually he lived a rather pathetically regular life all week, arriving punctually for a six o'clock dinner, without a cocktail or a whiskey before or after, at least not in the family's presence: after dinner, flopping onto a sofa with a few groans and listening to the radio, hauling off to bed before midnight and rising at six every morning. There was no charm wasted on the family, to be sure, but I never saw him strike Mother other than verbally, and Mother was a worthy adversary in verbal combat, rarely if ever bested. It was just a wrong marriage, as wrong as a marriage could be, and never should have happened to a dog, let alone two desperate human beings, and their bewildered children.

Tom was quoted in the New York *Post*, May 4, 1958, as saying, "My father was a totally honest man, he was never known to tell a lie in his life or to take an unfair advantage of anybody in business. He had a strong character and a sense of honor. He lived on his own terms which were hard terms for his family but he should not be judged as long as he remains the mystery that he is to us who lived in his shadow. Maybe I hated him once but I certainly don't any more."

Cornelius at times tried in his way to get close to his sons.

202

Tom told me his father visited him once while he was in California during a period when it looked as though Tom might be serious about Margo Jones, who was staging his play *Stairs to the Roof* at the Pasadena Playhouse. Cornelius told Tom he did not approve of Margo as a wife because she drank too much. He warned him, "There have been plenty of drinking men in our family, but remember, Tom, there has never been a drinking woman in the Williams family."

Dakin recalls a piece of advice Cornelius once gave him which, he said, "was the nearest Dad ever came to mentioning 'the facts of life.'" When he was about to be inducted into the Army, his father drove him to Jefferson Barracks. As a veteran of the Spanish-American War, Cornelius advised, "Dakin, watch out for the camp followers!" Dakin later commented to me, with a chuckle, "Dad didn't know that camp followers had gone out of style in favor of B girls in the bars that spring up around military establishments."

Cornelius left quite a bit of money to Rose, Dakin and his sister, everybody but Tom and me. He knew Tom had enough in his own right, and in his will he said he had provided for me by giving me a share of the house and the shoe company stock.

When Cornelius departed for Knoxville permanently, I bought the house in which I now live, on Wydown Boulevard, a wide street with double one-way lanes separated by a vast grassy lane. If you could say the house has any architecture at all, you would call it a combination of Spanish and Colonial. Of yellow brick, wrought-iron touches inside and out carry out the Spanish motif. I added a white wrought-iron bench to the front lawn and a wrought-iron railing to the steps leading up to the front door.

Inside, the lighting fixtures are shaped like candles against the wall, the doorways are arches, not squared, in the Spanish tradition, and the stairway leading to the bedrooms has a wrought-iron bannister. Some of the walls are stuccoed and some of the windows made of what I call "bottle glass," giving a soft effect when light streams through their opaqueness.

The living room has an open fireplace with a large mirror above it, and there are chandeliers in both living and dining rooms. My home is filled with antiques, of which I am fond, gifts from Tom including a silver tea service, and from Dakin who sent from India some delicate art objects including one we thought a replica of the Taj Mahal but which, on closer view, proved made only somewhat in its image.

A solid ebony elephant with ivory tusks sits on the mantel. It belongs to Tom, given him as a boy by three maiden ladies of Nashville. They started to dispose of precious possessions in their house saying they did not want to be "tyrannized by things any longer," and at the same time presented Rose with a hand-carved black wood bear which I also have kept.

The walls of the sun porch hold framed copies of many of Tom's awards, including the one given by the New York Drama Critics' Circle for *Menagerie,* which states it was bestowed because of the play's "sensitive understanding of four troubled human beings." There is also a copy of Tom's first Pulitzer Prize, for *Streetcar,* and the second for *Cat on a Hot Tin Roof,* won in 1955, the year another Mississippi-born writer, the late William Faulkner, received it for his book *A Fable.* This was Faulkner's first Pulitzer, although he had won the Nobel Prize in 1949. Tom said of his second Pulitzer, "I got more of a kick out of winning the Pulitzer this time than before because it was unexpected." I have also framed his other three New York Drama Critics' Circle awards for *Streetcar, Cat* and *The Night of the Iguana.*

The house on Wydown Boulevard was built on a slope that rises steeply in the back yard so that at the very edge of the lawn, the earth goes sharply upwards. The hill is banked with two shades of phlox, light and dark pink, and lilacs and syringa. The edge is bordered by a tall fence covered with vines.

There were cracks in the cellar when I bought the house and I called an engineer to find out how serious they were. He looked them over and said, "Mrs. Williams, your house is sliding right down to the street." He explained that this part of St. Louis was built over a cave and that houses occasionally had to be stabilized by supports. Tom used this situation to good comic advantage in *Period of Adjustment.*

One of my passions is flowers. I used to work in the garden a great deal; one year I planted two hundred tulips, which a rabbit promptly devoured. While digging in the dirt, I picked up an infection in my hand and the doctor ordered me to stop. I love to watch flowers grow but these days select the ones that need the least care. The flowers fight it out among themselves in my garden, the roses, iris, weigela, tulips, jonquils (a great supply), narcissus, lilies of the valley and wild violets. There are also flowering bushes. And a cherry tree. There were two, until one of them died leaving only the poor corpse of a cherry tree. I had nursed it from a seedling and one year it gave enough cherries to make a pie. In the past, I made jellies and marmalade but I doubt if I will any more, for there's little fun making them just for myself.

It is peaceful in St. Louis now that I no longer live on the edge of an emotional precipice. I wouldn't advise anyone to go through what I did if they could possibly get out of it, but I knew no way. In my ears often echo the words of fury I heard so many times: "Take the children and go! Go home. Just get out!" But my parents had so little, I could not throw myself and the three children on their shoulders. We were Cornelius' responsibility.

Summer and Smoke was followed by *The Rose Tattoo* in 1951, for which Tom received the Tony award, and which I thought a splendid and amusing play. It tells the story of Serafina Delle Rose, a passionate Italian widow living on the Gulf Coast, who tries to remain true to her late husband by avoiding men. She meets a lusty truck driver who falls in love with her and forces her to face the fact that her husband, a bootlegger killed by the police, had been carrying on an affair with a woman from a nearby cabaret. As a result of Serafina's acceptance of this reality, she becomes more human toward her daughter and allows herself to love the truck driver.

Then there was *Camino Real,* a fantasy set in Mexico, produced in 1953, which started as a short play, *Ten Blocks on the Camino Real,* in 1948. Its hero is Kilroy, an ex-boxing champion, who wanders into a desolate, nightmare world inhabited by beggars and prostitutes, as well as phantoms of the past including Casanova, Don Quixote and Lord Byron. Kilroy, who is seeking a haven from the world's misery, meets only humiliation and cruelty as he is robbed, beaten by the police, forced to dress like a clown. He has an affair with Esmeralda, a young prostitute, and although he tells her the one woman in his life is his wife whom he deserted when he found he had a heart condition, he starts to fall in love with Esmeralda. The Gypsy, Esmeralda's mother, rejects him and he despairs of life and love, and wishing death, dies. He is resurrected, chosen by Don Quixote as companion to set forth into the Terra Incognita, the only way out of Camino Real, and they leave to the exit line, "the violets in the mountains have broken the rocks!"

I attended the play's premiere on Broadway and thought it moving and profound, but it was panned by the critics who did not believe it quite came off as fantasy. When I asked Tom to autograph my playbill a few days after the opening, he wrote across the cover:

> Bloody but Unbowed
> (or more literally)
> Eggy but unbeaten.

No artist likes to be criticized, for he is always doing what he believes his best. Although Tom, like each one of us, artist or no, is sensitive to criticism, he never seems to resent it openly. I think he feels, within himself, that he has failed when someone does not like what he has written. Clark Mills recalled when Tom first began writing plays in the McBurney cellar in St. Louis in 1935 that "Tom had fanatical and inexhaustible energy in his writing. His persistence was almost grotesque." Tom learned to write a successful play, he said, by writing first perhaps a hundred that were not successful.

After his failure with *Camino,* Tom returned to writing of the South he knew so well, with *Cat on a Hot Tin Roof,* produced in 1955. This play deals primarily with the relationship between Margaret, or Maggie, and her husband, Brick Pollitt, who has become alcoholic and detached since the death of his old college friend Skipper, refusing to have sexual intimacy with his wife. Maggie reveals that one night she and Skipper tried to make love, in order to bring each other closer to Brick, whom they both loved, but that Skipper was impotent. Brick believes Maggie caused Skipper's death by making him face the fact he was a homosexual at heart.

Brick's father, Big Daddy, becomes involved in their struggle, as does Brick's brother and sister-in-law who are competing for the family fortune and seem the victor because they have five "no-neck monsters," with a sixth on the way. In the end, Brick decides to help Maggie turn the lie, that she is finally pregnant, into truth, after a furious fight with his father.

The theme of this play, Tom insists, is not homosexuality but mendacity within a family, and the ability of two people to live together without knowing anything about each other. I liked the strength of *Cat*, Tom's seventh play on Broadway in ten years. I had a feeling Big Daddy was patterned somewhat after Cornelius.

Of *Cat*, Brooks Atkinson said that Tom's craftsmanship was now "so much a part of his writings that he can forget it... Being crystal-clear in his own mind, he speaks directly and vividly to the minds of the theatregoers." He called *Cat* Tom's "conscious attempt to make literature and life coincide as closely as possible."

In one of her columns, Mrs. Roosevelt wrote, "Tennessee Williams is showing us the difficulty of communication between people who spend their lives saying and doing things they do not mean and do not feel ... How difficult it was for [the people in *Cat*] to be honest with each other, probably because it is so difficult to be honest with oneself."

I like to tease Tom occasionally, as I did at a dinner party to which he took me at the Brazilian Embassy, given by the Consul, just after *Cat* came out. As we were eating, a woman near me asked (shades of Amanda!) if I were the model for any of the characters of *Cat*.

"Who do you think I was?" I asked curiously.

"The mother, of course," she said.

"Oh, I'm so disappointed!" I purred. "I was hoping you'd say Maggie the Cat."

Tom looked most uncomfortable at this.

After *Cat* came *Orpheus Descending* in 1957, which the critics did not like—the old *Battle of Angels* dressed up anew. Broadway may not have responded warmly but Russia did. Tom was a smash hit in the Soviet Union.

> MOSCOW, AUG. 29—AP—Mossovet Theatre presented Tennessee Williams' "Orpheus Descending" and made a hit with the first-night audience, Tass said. The Soviet news agency said it was the first time a Williams play had been presented in the Soviet Union.

New York next saw *Garden District* in 1958, comprised of two plays, *Something Unspoken* and *Suddenly Last Summer*. The former touches upon a vague, undefined relationship between an overbearing Southern aristocratic woman and her companion of fifteen years, a fragile widow. There is a hint, although it is never put into words, of a lesbian attachment.

Suddenly Last Summer some critics consider among the most powerful of Tom's plays, as do I. Tom called it "a moral fable of our times." It is the story of an aging Southern matriarch, Violet Venable, who demands that a young doctor perform a lobotomy on her niece, Catharine Holly. She wants to prevent her niece from spreading what she calls a vicious story about the death of her son, a poet who had written one poem a summer for twenty-five summers. The young doctor, before he is willing to perform the brain operation, gives Catharine a drug, the so-called truth serum. Under its influence she tells what happened the previous summer on Cabeza de Lobo, an island in the Mediterranean, where her cousin, Sebastian, took her instead of his companion of past years, his mother, who had suffered a slight stroke. Catharine was horrified to find Sebastian was using her beauty to attract young boys for his own sexual pleasure. These young boys, starving children, turned against him, murdered him, then devoured him. The doctor believes Catharine's story and, we assume, does not perform the lobotomy.

Cannibalism, incidentally, was the basis of a short story Tom wrote earlier, called "Desire and the Black Masseur," which tells of a man who goes to a giant Negro masseur, allows himself to be beaten and maimed, and is finally eaten alive by the masseur.

Sweet Bird of Youth was presented in 1959, and I thought Geraldine Page did a remarkable job, as she also did in the off-Broadway revival of *Summer and Smoke* in 1957. She played the fading movie actress, Alexandra Del Lago, who picks up a young gigolo, Chance Wayne, as he returns to his hometown hoping to renew a romance with his childhood sweetheart, Heavenly Finley. Her father, Boss Finley, had originally persuaded Chance to leave town because he did not think he was substantial enough for his daughter to marry. Chance learns he had infected Heavenly with a venereal disease as a result of which she had an operation which removed her reproductive organs. When ordered to leave town, Chance now refuses to go with the actress, who has been restored to fame in a triumphant comeback in a film she thought a failure. Chance believes he can win Heavenly and, when he keeps persisting, her father and brother, in their rage, have him castrated.

Tom told a reporter he felt the ending too violent and intended to tone it down by substituting the psychological equivalent of emasculation for Chance Wayne's physical emasculation. He never did for Broadway but in the movie version the nature of the violence was changed to a brutal slashing of the hero's face.

There was *Period of Adjustment* in 1960, its full title, *Period of Adjustment: or High Point Over a Cavern: a Serious Comedy.* I liked it better as it was first presented in Miami by amateurs; there seemed a freshness and spontaneity about it missing later in New York. This play, built on one humorous situation after another, revolves around the fate of two couples, one married five years, the other on their honeymoon. Both marriages appear doomed but then the husbands, friends in the Air Force, talk over their problems with each other and decide to try anew with their wives.

Tom was represented last year on Broadway with *The Night of the Iguana,* which started as a one-act play at the Film Festival of Two Worlds at Spoleto, Italy, in 1959. The following year a fuller version was tried out at the Coconut Grove Playhouse in Miami. Broadway saw Tom's fourth draft, about par for most of his plays when finally produced. His latest Broadway play, *The Milk Train Doesn't Stop Here Anymore,* is scheduled for 1963 production.

Hollywood has been very receptive to Tom since its first rapid rejection. Ten of his plays have been made into movies as has his only novel, *The Roman Spring of Mrs. Stone.* I liked the latter except for its depressing ending. It was tragic enough for the ex-actress to take up with the young Italian gigolo, but when she beckoned to a strange, uncouth young man on the street who had been lurking outside her room for weeks, you had the feeling she was asking to be murdered.

Tom has not always been happy with the Hollywood treatment. He did not like the flashback in *Menagerie* showing Gertrude Lawrence as Amanda dancing at a ball as a young girl when, as he put it, "they tried to get a *Gone With the Wind* effect." But he liked *Streetcar,* saying, "They filmed it as I had written it except for one change because of censorship. We couldn't mention the homosexuality as a human problem."

One newspaper report about this film must have pleased Tom. It appeared in the Clarksdale *Register,* the paper that had taken him to task seven years before as a native son who had written a "dirty" play, referring to *Angels.* It recanted, "Mr. Williams' reputation as a playwright has never been stronger now that his *Streetcar Named Desire,* first a stage hit, has been made into a highly successful movie, while at the same time, *The Rose Tattoo* is enjoying a smash season on Broadway."

I don't think Tom liked some of the things Hollywood did

with *Baby Doll,* which aroused the ire of the Catholic Church. When the movie opened in New York in December, 1956, Cardinal Spellman told Catholics they were committing a sin if they saw the picture. I don't believe any group should have jurisdiction over what is right or wrong for stage, movies or books.

Tom told me *Baby Doll* held a scene to which he objected because it was in poor taste, but he wouldn't identify the scene. Perhaps it was the one where not a word was spoken as Eli Wallach pursued Carroll Baker through the broken-down mansion. Or when Karl Malden, as the husband, bored a hole through the bathroom wall so he could watch his child-wife take a bath.

I didn't care for *Baby Doll* even though it was nominated for the Academy Award, the only other movie of Tom's to be nominated besides *Streetcar.* I went to the preview with Audrey and Tom, and when it was over, Audrey asked what I thought of it.

"It was a little unbelievable to me," I said. "I just don't know those kind of people."

I don't think Tom did, either, but he doesn't necessarily have to know people intimately to write about them perceptively. He has written of many things to which I am sure he is stranger.

Baby Doll was based on two one-act plays, *The Long Stay Cut Short,* one of his *American Blues,* and *27 Wagons Full of Cotton,* whose world premiere he attended in New Orleans in January, 1955. The *Times-Picayune* interviewed him at the opening, and I learned from the interview that Tom considered himself "a Bohemian." He told the reporter he believed New Orleans should not become "too reformed," saying, "You don't want it to be like Kansas City, do you?" He estimated almost fifty percent of his work up to that time had been accomplished in New Orleans, including *Streetcar* and part of *Menagerie.*

He was asked if he had read any good books lately and replied, "The last really great book I read was *From Here to Eternity.*" He named his favorite writers as Carson McCullers and Hemingway, and the best playwright, Arthur Miller (he must have meant modern playwright, for he always liked Chekhov and Ibsen). Asked how he got along in Hollywood, he said he did so by being honest, that "honesty throws them completely."

The Rose Tattoo was filmed in Key West, next door to Tom's house. Daniel Mann, the director, thought Key West a sunnier substitute for the play's real setting, a Gulf Coast village between Mobile and New Orleans, and selected a weather-beaten cottage near downtown Key West as the home of the Sicilian widow Serafina, played by Anna Magnani. The house just happened to be Tom's neighbor.

I learned from the newspapers that, while watching a love scene between Marisa Pavan and Ben Cooper, the juvenile leads, Tom fell off a gangplank that rolled out from under him. He not only was dunked but wedged perilously between pilings and a boat surging with the swells. "Rescued, he recuperated with a cool drink," I was informed.

Tom brought Anna Magnani from Italy to make the movie. He had wanted her at first for the play, in which Maureen Stapleton eventually played Serafina, but she had refused because she could not speak English at the time. Tom, who knew Italian, coached her as they sailed to New York. Their boat was the *Andrea Doria*. I am glad Tom wasn't aboard when she made her fateful voyage.

The worst danger to befall him occurred when he crashed into a tree in Italy driving his Jaguar at seventy miles an hour. I went through agony when I read in the newspaper he had been hurt and was hospitalized. I didn't know how seriously he was injured or where to reach him. After that, I think he left most of the driving to Frank Merlo.

Television has offered a number of Tom's plays, including *The Purification,* his only play in free verse, *I Rise in Flame, Cried the Phoenix,* and the one-act plays, *Moony's Kid Don't Cry, The Lady of Larkspur Lotion, The Last of the Solid Gold Watches, Hello from Bertha,* and *This Property Is Condemned.* The latter is a portrait of a young girl who picks up tramps

14.

"I've Done a Lot of Traveling with Tennessee"

WHEN Tom was a little boy he loved to accompany his grandfather on calls to parishioners. Now Tom took his grandfather on what stood for *his* calls of duty.

During Father's last years, he spent a good part of them with Tom, whether he was writing in Key West or arranging for a play in New York, and he was usually involved in one or the other. Wherever he was, he would always find a place for Father.

Once Father arrived without notice in New York and Tom asked Libby Holman Reynolds, who was a friend of his, if she could put Father up on her estate on Long Island. She said she would be delighted and Father stayed at her luxurious home, eating elegantly and playing bridge, which he enjoyed. When he told me on his return where he had been, I said, "Father, that's fine, but when you go to Clarksdale, for heaven's sake don't say you stayed with Libby Reynolds." Father's ministerial friends would have been shocked to think he was a guest in the home of a woman tried for the murder of her husband. The fact she was judged not guilty would have made no difference to them, I'm afraid.

Tom was always telling me not to spare any expense where Father was concerned. He gave up a lot of his valuable time to make sure Father was comfortable; few grandchildren would have taken the trouble Tom did. Although Father, in his way, was quite self-sufficient in his old age. He took his first airplane trip at the age of ninety-two. After that he would travel no other way, charging off to airports all by himself.

The first time he was about to step into a plane, a reporter asked, "Dr. Dakin, aren't you afraid to be taking a trip in a plane at your age?"

"What have I got to lose?" he said.

I felt he became bored if he stayed in St. Louis for very long with only me as company. He far preferred to be with Tom where there were always exciting parties and fascinating people. He was quite reproachful because I refused to go to Hollywood when the late Jerry Wald invited us to attend a very elaborate celebration after the preview of Glass Menagerie.

Father enjoyed a few drinks, particularly Manhattans, as though to make up for the many years he had been too poor to spend money on luxuries. Drinking seems to be one of the curses of this age. When I was a girl we had delightful times without drink but now, everywhere you go, the first thing people do is offer you one cocktail after another. Tom once said drinks made him feel buoyed up. They seem to stabilize him when he feels nervous. He certainly doesn't need drink to loosen his tongue, though. When he wants to converse, he can be very gregarious, although I don't think small talk comes easily to Tom. The art of small talk in a large crowd is a special gift.

My sons, of course, as they grew up saw enough of drinking to float our Navy. I enjoy a glass of wine every now and then but otherwise do not drink. Coffee strong as lye, they tell me, and good food are my weaknesses.

Father also enjoyed food. He had a cast-iron stomach. One reporter, interviewing him, wrote:

> I met Tennessee and his grandfather for lunch at Arnaud's, and despite the fact the old man had had a large breakfast, he ordered a shrimp cocktail, a salad, fried oysters, some wine, and a demi-tasse. He told me he didn't want much to drink because a lady had invited him for egg-nog at 3 P.M.

Father was ninety-four at the time. He would sit calmly in Key West for weeks, waiting for Tom to take him to New York or New Orleans where they would eat at the finest restaurants. Father had never indulged himself, but he allowed Tom to indulge him. I don't think there's ever been an old man as happy as Father.

He felt he had a good life. He was always very optimistic, with a wonderful way of dismissing trouble. I think his deep religious faith helped, although Dakin says his grandfather depended too much on God, that he was always saying, "The Lord will take care of it," but the one who did was Mother.

Father would turn things over in prayer; he thought prayer the strongest force in the world. I don't doubt he believed his prayers responsible for Tom's success. I think prayers are a great help but you can't do everything with prayer—God expects you to work as well.

Father was always on time, too much so. Before his days of flying, he insisted on arriving at the railroad station an hour in advance. He never admitted the existence of daylight saving time.

He would get ready to leave the house and I would object, "But Father, with daylight saving, we have an extra hour. We'll have to wait at the station two hours if we leave now."

"No, Daughter, my train goes at such and such an hour," he would say.

"But Father, that's before daylight saving time went into effect," I would try to explain.

"Mustn't be late," he would say cheerfully, holding the door open for me. I gave up. My early training in obedience still clung, so down we'd go to Union Station to sit for two hours. Otherwise, Father had a bright mind. He just could not fathom the mystery of daylight time.

He had two hobbies, people and reading, and he combined both after he retired. He would visit the hospitals in Memphis and talk or read to the sick who hailed from Mississippi. He was a very intelligent man, interested in all the questions of the day. During the war we had to drop everything to follow the news broadcasts. When his eyesight grew poor, I read to him; in his last years, he had difficulty seeing and hearing.

Here was this dauntless old man of ninety-five, nearly blind and deaf, traveling all over the country with only his cane as support, to visit his grandson Tom, and then traveling more with Tom.

"I've done a lot of traveling with Tennessee since I retired from the ministry twenty years ago," he told a reporter proudly.

Tom and Frank shared the responsibility of caring for Father when he stayed with them. Tom said he always felt relieved to hear two sounds in the morning. One was the buzz of the electric razor he had given Father, because then he knew "Grandfather made it through another night." The other was the radio, which Father would turn on full tilt when he got up. It was hopeless to try to sleep late with Father in the house.

There was always a bed for Father in Tom's Key West home, a one-and-a-half-story Bahama cottage with a large guest room under the sloping roof. It is a white house with rose-colored shutters. In the yard stands a hibiscus bush, and a poinciana tree which looked no bigger than a switch when first planted. A paling fence goes around the house and Tom has built a studio on one side. If he calls any place home today, this is it.

He once wrote of the house, which is furnished with bamboo furniture, that "in the living room I have a six-foot work table, and across the room there is a divan for relaxation or contemplation. All the walls in the workroom are covered with theatrical

218

posters, and at either end of the room are bookshelves—lots of them—to hold manuscripts, side by side with conch shells and other treasures I find along the sea shore. I love to entertain here."

The Key West ménage is made up of Frank, Leoncie, a Bahama maid, two bulldogs and a parrot. Tom occasionally sent news of them all.

3/8/56

DEAR MOTHER:

I'm so sick of the typewriter I'm using a pen, have been working 6 or 8 hours a day and that studio is beginning to get pretty hot. It's warm as midsummer, now, in Key West, and only one room is air-conditioned, but there's a breeze at night. Our faithful old "retainer" Leoncie is back with us, she comes and goes on my bicycle in a snow white, severely starched linen dress, yelling and waving to all the neighbors as she approaches or makes her departure. Our house has become a regular stop for the sight-seeing buses and cars in Key West. They all want to see where "Rose Tattoo" was shot. So Leoncie and Mr. Anderson (old Charlie) are having a lot of public attention. Frank does practically all the cooking, has bought an out-door charcoal grill for chicken, steak, etc. We eat "mighty good."

I am trying out the first draft of a new play very secretly at a tiny theatre in Coral Gables just to size it up for myself. Most of my present work is on this. I'm afraid Paramount will have to wait a while longer for the "Summer & Smoke" film script. I wish they would just let it go, as I am not at all pleased with the terms of the contract and I think I could have gotten much more for it, elsewhere. But Harold Clurman has been signed to direct it, and he is a brilliant director.

I had to cancel flight to St. Thomas due to work here.

I hope to go North by way of New Orleans and St. Louis next month.

Nice letter today from Dakin. He seems to expect to return to St. Louis before next Xmas.

Much love—
TOM

Father always traveled with five bags. If you accepted him, you had to be prepared to take care of the five bags. They went with Father as he made the rounds, each bag destined for use in a different place. They were carefully labeled and he insisted on writing out the labels himself although he could barely see, and on packing the bags without any help. He could tell by the touch just where each article was placed. The first bag held clothes for Key West, the second for the Gayoso Hotel in Memphis, the third for Clarksdale where he visited each spring, the fourth for New York and the fifth for St. Louis. The five bags contained his entire possessions.

One time on a trip from Memphis to Key West, the bags never showed up. Tom called and said Father was miserable, sat in his room bemoaning the fact that he did not have his good suit to wear to church. Father, unlike Tom, was always very particular about his dress. After days of trying to locate the missing bags in Miami, Memphis and New York, I finally had the hunch they might have been sent to St. Louis by mistake. And they were, when I finally traced them and sent them on their way at once so Father could again be well-dressed and happy.

Father was not very tall, nor is Tom, who seems to have taken after my side of the family, while Dakin is tall like his father. But I never think of Tom as not tall; he's tall in every other way but height.

The old man Nonno, in *The Night of the Iguana,* is a partially true picture of Father; I don't think anyone could draw a completely true one. He was an individualist of the first order. Unlike Nonno, Father never wrote poetry, although he composed sermons with a great amount of poetry in them, belying what he said when a reporter asked if he had ever written anything and Father replied, "Only some very poor sermons."

Some are old at twenty; my father was young at ninety. He believed people should not allow themselves to deteriorate mentally, that there were far too many interesting things in life to see and enjoy. He proved you don't need to decline into dotage,

220

for his intellect was as keen at ninety-seven as it ever had been.

He never lost his alert mind or his erect bearing or his ready wit. One newspaper carried the misinformation that Father still possessed his Civil War uniform. Reading this, he said to me, "The only uniform I wore at the time of the Civil War was three-cornered."

As he grew older, Father became increasingly candid. Dakin and I were visiting him and Tom in Key West just after the opening of *The Rose Tattoo,* when one afternoon a very elegant lady, a prominent society leader, came over to ask Tom to a tea to honor one of America's top poets. Dakin and I invited her into the living room, explaining that Tom was still in New York. Father sat at the far end of the room playing cards by himself.

When she learned Tom was away, this lady was gracious enough to invite us to her tea. I walked over to Father and, shouting into his ear, explained that she was asking us to her home to tea that afternoon. Whereupon Father replied briskly, mentioning her name, "Not that *pest!*"

Another time, when his nephew, a self-made millionaire in St. Louis, persuaded Dakin and me to drive Father over to see a new oil portrait of "Cousin Ned," Father caused no end of consternation by admiring, not the portrait, but the frame. "It's a nice frame!" he kept repeating, to the chagrin of his nephew, a man then in his seventies.

Whenever he stayed with me, every Sunday Father would set out to early Communion at the Episcopal Church down the street. Although he could hardly see, he would march across busy Wydown Boulevard waving his cane at cars as if defying anyone to hit him. I don't know how he made it but he managed somehow.

"Nobody dares run me over," he would announce as he stalked out of the house.

I like to live under the shadow of a sanctuary, having grown up under one, and St. Michael's and St. George's, two Episcopal churches that joined together, stand almost directly across from my house. I find it deeply satisfying to look over and see the massive elegance of the church. I belonged to St. George's Church when I first moved to St. Louis; I never sang in its choir even though I had sung in choirs all my life. I did not feel like singing in St. Louis.

Tom and Father enjoyed gay times together. A newspaper clipping a friend sent from the Miami *Herald* once informed me they were both interviewed by David Kraslow, a staff writer, along with Gilbert Maxwell, who has been a close friend of Tom's for many years. Gilbert had just written a book, *The Sleeping Trees,* and presented Tom with an autographed copy. (He also gave me one when I was in Miami for Christmas, 1956, autographed, *For Edwina Dakin Williams, one of the loveliest ladies I have ever known.*)

Reminiscing, Gilbert asked Tom, "Remember the time I was the desk clerk and you the elevator boy in that hotel in New York eight years ago?"

"They changed the name after we left," said Tom. "We only worked there a month but it took the place a lot longer than that to live us down."

"The amazing thing about this guy," Gilbert told the reporter, "is that he has never changed. He's still the same elevator boy I knew."

Another time, Tom and Father returned for a visit to Columbus and the rectory in which Tom spent the first three years of life and which he had not seen since. They posed for a photograph at the fount in St. Paul's Church where Tom was christened. I can hear Father telling Tom, as the newspaper reported, "Right here is where you were christened, and over there is where Bishop Green picked you up and blessed you ... and I hope it is sticking."

Tom whispered to the reporter, Douglas Bateman, that he couldn't quite return that far in memory as to recall the church. "But I do believe this is one of the handsomest churches I have ever seen," Tom said.

Father was always being interviewed about Tom as though

he could reveal some of the secrets of his grandson's life. To one reporter he described Tom's daily routine as follows:

> Tom gets up at 9 o'clock. He has one cup of coffee. That's all. Nothing else.
>
> Then he goes to his study and writes till 2 P.M. Frequently we don't see him during that time. He shuts himself up.
>
> At 2 o'clock out he comes with hardly any clothes on. We get in his car and drive to the beach. He swims around for about 20 minutes and I just sit in the water. Then we lie on the sand for two or three hours.
>
> After that we drive back home and our cook has a delightful dinner waiting for us. It's the only meal Tom eats.

It is almost as natural for Tom to wake up and start writing as it is to brush his teeth, he has said. He describes how he works: "When I get an idea I work on it at white heat until it is finished. It doesn't take me long to do a first draft, but I work over my plays a lot. I do a lot of talking to myself when I write, trying out the sound of dialogue. Neighbors must think I always have a roomful of company."

He composes on the typewriter and without mapping out the plays. "I just do them over and over again until they come out right," he says.

He told a reporter on the Miami *Herald* that sometimes he works only three hours a day, at which the reporter commented, "But what hours!"

Tom finds swimming the best relaxation from tension. "A playwright is especially tense," he once said. "He has to work up the same tenseness as the character in the play."

I don't think it a very healthy diet he has chosen, to start off the day with only a cup of black coffee in the morning and go through until evening on an empty stomach. Tom's diet is Spartan. I realize you can't think when you're too full of food, but there is a happy medium such as a soft-boiled egg or even a glass of fruit juice.

Father was Tom's complete champion. He predicted, "In fifty years my grandson will be more noted as a poet than a playwright. All of his plays have a poetic foundation and he is more interested in developing his characters than he is in the stories." He proudly pointed out that some of Tom's first writings were descriptions of the trip to Europe on which he had taken Tom when he was seventeen.

Tom tried to persuade his grandfather, in turn, to go to Europe with him, wanting to take him when he went abroad early in 1948 to see about foreign productions of *Streetcar*, but fearing that the winter in Paris, where he was staying, would be hard on Father because there was a fuel shortage and very little heat. Instead he suggested that Father accompany Dakin and me to the London premiere of *Menagerie*, but Father refused to go. He was afraid of dying on foreign soil.

Father did not want to go to Europe, then or ever again. But Tom persevered.

5/17/48

DEAR GRANDFATHER:

Your letter made me feel quite sad for you. I hope you are not more than temporarily depressed, for that is not like you. I am not at all pleased with your apparent decision to stay in America. I would so much rather you came over with Mother and Dakin for I don't think there is anyone in the world who enjoys traveling as much as you do. Please think it over, reconsider, and let me *and* Audrey know. Audrey has wonderful connections with travel agencies and she can make all the arrangements for your passage by ship or by air. If you are really afraid of an ocean voyage, then why not let Audrey buy you a round-trip plane ticket which is not more expensive and which only takes about 18 hours. Mother says you are not going because you are "afraid of being buried at sea." Now that is ridiculous! In the first place you would not die. In the second place we would make sure that you were returned to Grand's side in Ohio. So put that silly idea out of your mind and take this holiday which is due you after the long winter in Saint Louis. It will make me, personally, ever so much happier to have you there in London. I don't like the English and I am only going out of duty. It is difficult to tear myself away from Italy which is the nearest to heaven that I have ever been, the people are so friendly, gentle and gracious and the days so tranquil and sunny. I have an old Jeep that I travel around in. Perhaps I shall drive it to London. Margo is flying to Rome. She will join me here on the 26th and we will go North together, either in the Jeep or by train. You and she could have some nice card-games as you did in New Orleans while I am at rehearsals. Perhaps we could all get a nice apartment together. So if you feel you really might enjoy the trip, write Audrey a note or have Mother call her long-distance. The trip will be with my compliments, of course, and Audrey will buy the tickets and make the reservations whichever way you decide.

With much love to all of you,
Tom

Although Father declined the invitation to London, he always went eagerly to Key West.

4/2/50

Dear Daughter,

We've been having a lovely time; we attended a Sunday supper at the Newtons' served in the patio back of their big house. She called it a "mobile-supper." We had dinner with Mrs. Hemingway served in her guest-house and she lives in it renting the big house. It was the most delicious dinner in every way; we ate outdoors by her swimming pool. The setting was most romantic and we were an hour late because of Tom's mistake about the time. The pool was lighted along the edge and shaded by palms overhead. The after dinner coffee was served facing the pool: she is the most gracious hostess. We had dinner several times at the Trade Winds.

We may go to New York a little earlier than we had supposed; of course we will let you know when we get there. We shall be at the Sherry-Netherlands Hotel.

I sent you some time ago, by railroad express, my overcoat. Did you get it? Do not get me any shirts or pyjamas as I can find nearer what I wish in New York. I am looking forward to seeing Carol Dakin, and Roy and Cora, and Jessie Watson. Among others whom I want to see are Mrs. Crutcher, and Mrs. Crouse whom I knew as a girl in Clarksdale.

Trusting you and Dakin are both well, with love to you both, in which Tom and Mr. Merlo join, affectionately,

FATHER

P.S. I attended the most wonderful "to me" Palm Sunday service. Preceding the communion service hundreds of men, women and children went to the altar and received their palm leaf. The choir sang the hymns we are used to, the service ending with a procession. The incense was swung by two boys and the priest robes held out by two small boys. I don't believe Dakin saw anything more beautiful at his church. I am looking forward to a beautiful Easter.

On one of his trips to Key West, Grandfather wrote a letter jointly with Tom.

1/25/52

DEAR DAUGHTER AND MOTHER:

We were delighted to get your letter but still are waiting to hear what disposition is being made of Dakin, and we are glad to know that you are planning to come South. Don't put it off long. The big downstairs room is waiting for you, ready whenever you can get here.

After two most delightful weeks in New York, expecting the snow and ice, Tom and I took the train to New Orleans, and had barely registered at the Monteleone when the owner of the hotel sent a great basket of fruit to us and when we went to pay the bill, discovered that we had been his guest the entire time we were there which was about two weeks. We were interviewed and photographed and got on the radio a couple of times. Soon as the paper was out, Grandfather received a number of calls by phone from old friends from Tenn. and Miss. Chiefly among them, Mrs. Flournoy who later had us over on New Year's Day for Egg-nog and a drive about Audubon Park. Grandfather wishes to add that we had fruit-cake and nuts out of their

226

own garden. Mrs. Flournoy's son is married to a lovely woman and they have a grown daughter, soon to be married. They have a charming home. She enquired a great deal about you.

On New Year's morning, Mr. and Mrs. Binning whom I married in Clarksdale about 30 years ago took me to Early Communion. We flew down from New Orleans to Miami and stayed there about four days while Frank drove the Jaguar down from New York to pick us up. The car had been delayed by the big Atlantic storms but arrived in New York without damage. We are now settled here and everything is going smoothly. We have a middle-aged white woman working for us. She cleans well but cannot cook. Frank is cooking dinner for us, and doing it very well.

We are worried about your fingers. St. Louis is noted for its medical talent and should have cured the condition by this time. As soon as you hear about Dakin let us know.

The weather here has been lovely, warm as summer. We found the house in excellent condition but are still trying to get someone to cut our grass, as we have no gardening implements.

Grandfather wishes me to add that our last few days in New Orleans we were the guests of Mrs. Sheriff who gave us her entire house while she stayed at a hotel. We would have remained longer in New Orleans but didn't want to accept too much. It was a wonderful visit and we plan to stop there again on the way North this Spring.

Grandfather says we have the prospects of a brilliant social season here. Ahem!

That's all, says Grandfather. I am working on a play and a film-script, the latter at the command of Audrey and Kazan and not according to my own wishes. Do come down soon as possible. Let us know when!

Much love,
TOM & GRANDFATHER

P.S. "Summer & Smoke" has transferred to Duchess Theatre in London—has been a hit in England and should make money for Rose's trust fund. "Tattoo" still running in Copenhagen and Norway.

On Tom's next trip abroad six months later, he wrote his grandfather what he was missing in the way of new friends.

7/7/52

DEAR GRANDFATHER:

We are back at the old apartment in Rome, after a very pleasant crossing on the French ship LIBERTÉ, and a week in Paris where we saw Mr. and Mrs. McCullers and some other American friends and spent some of my French money waiting for me there. I went out a good deal with the Italian film star Anna Magnani who is now seriously interested in making a picture of "Rose Tattoo." I saw her again here in Rome and am having a conference with her business manager later today. It is fiercely hot here, but I suppose it is no worse than most of America. Soon as I get my business completed, and some other work done, I think I will transfer to a cooler place in the mountains or on the sea. Frank drove the Jaguar down here from Paris without any trouble and I came by train.

Carson McCullers' dog, a beautiful prize-winning Boxer, is going to have puppies this summer and she has promised me one to take back to America, so we may have a young addition to the family in Key West, next Fall. I do hope that you have gone to the mountains where you will be comfortable and that this letter will be forwarded to you there. I worry about you in the heat of Memphis or Mississippi, as I suspect it may be even hotter than Rome.

Frank promises to write you a long letter full of news. I hope he gets around to it soon. He hates writing letters you know, but when he does he thinks of more news than I. I am always wrapped up in my work.

We'll be coming back late in August I think.

Much love,

TOM

He returned late in August as scheduled but it wasn't until a few months later when he was in Hollywood that his grandfather heard from him again.

I have fallen a little behind in my letters lately as I have been going through the busiest period in recent years, what with casting a play with Kazan and watching over the shooting of "Rose Tattoo." I don't even know precisely how long I've been out here, but I have to fly back tonight as Kazan is casting the new play in New York and I have to pass judgement tomorrow on Barbara Bel Geddes for the female lead. She is a fine actress who has appeared in a number of hits on Broadway but I am not sure she is right for this part so I have to return at once to take a look at her.

Anna Magnani and Burt Lancaster had their first fight on the set yesterday, as she was directing the scene and he didn't like it. So he walked off and there was a long and heated consultation before things could be resumed. Both are temperamental. I wish I could remain here as a referee is needed, but I shall just have to hope and pray that Danny Mann, the director, can keep peace between them long enough to finish the picture. So far the picture looks great. There's about two more weeks of work on it, at least.

Frank and the dog are flying to New York from Key West tomorrow so we'll all arrive there about the same time. I haven't gotten much rest or much sun this year, but so far I'm holding up pretty well under the pressure. The fact that I will have Kazan on the play is reassuring and takes a lot of anxiety off me. I just heard today that the Playwrights Company will be the producers, which is good, since they are much more generous than certain other producers, who are penny-pinchers.

I talked to Dakin and Margo over long-distance a few days ago, he was visiting her in Dallas. He says he is "sweating out" his promotion which is a slang expression for waiting and hoping that he will get it. I hope so, too, and that if he does, he'll stay in the Air-Force till economic conditions in the country are more settled.

If I didn't have to put this play on now I would be in Saint Louis with you. I think about you every day. You must get out of bed as often as you can. I know it takes patience and effort, but we are depending on you to be

ready and able to return to Key West with us when we go
back in the early Spring. That's the nicest time of year
there, you remember.

Much love from
Том

Because of Father's great vitality, it came as a shock to me
when one day, without any warning, he suffered a stroke. He was
taken to Barnes Hospital in St. Louis where it became apparent he would not recover. He died on St. Valentine's Day, 1955,
just two months short of ninety-eight and two years short of a
century.

Tom was in the middle of rehearsing *Cat* but dropped everything to fly to St. Louis. He appeared at the front door bearing
a huge pasteboard box. There were tears in his eyes.

I asked what the box held. "It's a blanket for Grandfather,"
he said.

He had carried with him thousands of Father's favorite flower,
sweet-scented spring violets, with white carnations outlining
a St. Andrew's cross, to be placed on Father's coffin.

I had told the minister that since Father did not know many
people in St. Louis we would hold simple services in the chapel
without music. But Paul Bigelow, who flew down with Tom
because he had been so fond of Father, had telephoned the
minister from New York requesting a special musical arrange-
ment of "Crossing the Bar" be played at the service.

"I often heard Mr. Dakin say he wanted this at his funeral,"
said Paul and so we had music.

Father had been a minister for sixty years, most of them spent
in Mississippi and Tennessee, but he wanted to be buried in
the town where he grew up, next to Mother who was buried
there. So, after the service, I took Father's body by train for
burial in Waynesville, Ohio. Tom sent a blanket of yellow
roses and Father's coffin was surrounded with floral offerings
from Tom's friends who had known Father. The casket was
open and I thought how peaceful and stately Father looked
lying there in his robes.

230

Almost all the towns in which Father served as minister carried an announcement of his death. In Clarksdale the *Parish Register* of St. George's Church ran a notice.

In Memoriam
WALTER EDWIN DAKIN
PRIEST

April 23rd, 1857—Feb. 14th, 1955

Our whole Parish was saddened at the news of Mr. Dakin's death yesterday afternoon when a wire from his beloved daughter brought this message, "Father fell on sleep this morning. We do not grieve for him for he was ready and anxious to enter into that rest that remaineth for the people of God."

He had spent many summers after his retirement at Sewanee and the Associated Alumni of the University of the South summed up his career and concluded: "May God's peace rest upon our friend and son of Sewanee."

Both Tom and Dakin would like to own Father's cross which he wore on the pulpit; it has a large amethyst stone in the middle and amethysts on the two arms. But I am determined not to leave it to either for I remember two sisters who stopped speaking to each other the rest of their lives after one was willed a small silver pitcher that the other coveted, too.

Perhaps Father's cross will wind up at the theological school in Sewanee where Tom gave $1,000 to set up a memorial room in his honor.

15.

"He Hit Me Where It Hurt Most"

TOM has always taken time out from his work and life to help others. The one he helped the most has been his sister Rose.

As soon as he was financially on his feet he said, "Mother, from now on Rose is my responsibility." He paid for her care in the best of private psychiatric hospitals, removing her from the state hospital to which her father had her committed. He set up a trust fund for her so she would always be independent, giving her a percentage of some of his plays. Today Rose is an heiress.

Tom recently bought a home for her in Miami where it is planned she will live with a companion when she leaves the hospital in Westchester County, just outside of New York, where she has been staying during the past few years.

The name Rose, and the flower, has each been significant in

Tom's life. He often uses the rose as symbol in his plays, both the flower and the color. He has the hero say to the heroine in *The Rose Tattoo,* the words, "The rose is the heart of the world like the heart is—the heart of the—body!" Tom's sister and grandmother bore the name Rose, although he called Rose "sister" when he was little. His first play was presented in the Rose Arbor Theatre in Memphis. He knows I have always loved roses.

Tom visited his sister in the hospital as often as possible, as he mentioned in letters.

DEAR MOTHER:

I've seen Rose four times since we went out together and you'll be happy to know that she is remarkably better. Yesterday she had on the new black dress and hat that you sent her and looked very handsome in them. We have been going each Sunday to the lovely Tappan Hill Restaurant, near Sleepy Hollow famous for Ichabod Crane and the Headless Horseman. Rose is taking more interest in things and more pleasure, eating much better, putting on some becoming weight again, and has even started smoking. The last few Sundays she has asked for cigarettes, but she says she doesn't smoke except on these outings. She says that you wouldn't approve! She still complains that her parakeet won't take a bath, but that's about her only complaint, and when I took her to the drugstore yesterday, she only bought candy and a toothbrush, not the usual ten or twelve bars of soap. For her birthday my old friend Jo Healy and I are taking her into New York for some shopping. She wants a winter coat so I think I'll give her one for a birthday present, and take her afterwards to a good restaurant and maybe let her spend the night here with Jo, at a nice hotel.

I took a short hop down to Miami to attend the opening there of the new road company of "Cat." It's an excellent company and is doing good business, and in New York, I'm busy preparing to put on a pair of short plays "Off-Broadway," mostly for fun.

I'm in my new apartment. It's a great improvement on

the old one, it has a charming living-room with double French doors opening onto a little iron-grilled balcony covered with wisteria vines which are still green, a fire-place that works and a nice kitchen. Frank has been cooking the evening meals and I find it much nicer than going out to restaurants every night, as well as more economical.

Hope you're all well.

Much love,
Tom

Rose in her way has accomplished a great deal. I think she is remarkable to arrive at a state of mind where she is content with what you might call a half-life. She never complains, never demands anything. She was not happy at the state hospital, though, where her clothes were sometimes stolen. I would bring her a new dress and when I visited a few months later and asked where it was, she would say, "It just disappeared." Tom gave her a beautiful blond beaver coat one Christmas and she begged, "Please, Mother, you take it. It might just disappear here." But I left it with her. I don't own a fur coat; I went without such luxuries for so long, I don't seem to need them now.

Rose is lucid, yes, but without that awareness of herself or the other person that enables her to make any kind of a deep relationship. Although she is not fully able to take care of herself, she often gets along well in the outside world. Once Tom took her to a large hotel in New York for dinner. He excused himself for a minute and Rose waited for a table at the door of the dining room.

She had just learned to smoke and stood there awkwardly puffing away at a cigarette, clad in an unbecoming hat she bought herself which hid her lovely face, her far-too-long coat flopping around her calves.

The headwaiter looked her over critically and said, "Sorry, madam, there are no tables left."

When Tom came back Rose reported this and said casually, "Oh, well, let's just go over to the Plaza."

234

When Rose talks, she makes sense. She asks about members of the family and occasionally remembers the names of some people I have long forgotten. But the passage of time means nothing to her; she never worries about past or future. "She's the most fortunate member of the family," Tom said once, meaning she did not have to face the battle of life like the rest of us. But one pays an even higher price by withdrawing from life.

Once Rose went on a shopping spree, after she learned Tom had given her a part of one show. She always had expensive taste in clothes and on this day, when taken shopping in New York, she found a suit for $150 which she liked, and then another and another. She ended up with about $1,000 worth of suits, some of which, I believe, the hospital returned. Tom took it very good-humoredly, feeling nothing was too fine for Rose. He would have let her keep all the suits.

Another young woman to whom Tom gave aid and comfort was Diana Barrymore. He helped her overcome alcoholism and to land the part of the young girl in the Chicago company of *Garden District.* Sydney Harris of the Chicago *Daily News,* in reviewing the opening, congratulated Diana on her comeback, saying, "She brilliantly redeems her theatrical past from the embarrassing depths to which it had sunk."

He also described her as "a woman of dignity and as an actress of depth of sensitivity" who more than held her own with "that cunning veteran," Cathleen Nesbit, who played the mother.

Diana's rebirth was called "an exciting thing to behold" by Ann Marsters, writing in the Chicago *American* of April 14, 1959. She visited Diana in her suite at the Croydon Hotel and described a double-frame photograph on Diana's desk. It held on one side a picture of John Barrymore in profile and on the other, an informal, laughing shot of Tom. Books scattered around the room were chiefly of Tom's writings which Diana "devours," reported Miss Marsters.

It was Diana who said of Tom, "What other playwright of

today could hold audiences spellbound with no more than soliloquies? For me that's what the play is, primarily—two soliloquies by Cathleen and me. Tennessee Williams is our modern Shakespeare."

Dakin and Joyce met Diana in Chicago and Dakin suggested she visit St. Louis for a weekend and rest at my home, where there was plenty of room. I wrote, inviting her, and she came and was very appreciative. "You make me feel so at home," she told me. She was a perfect lady while with me. She did not drink or smoke.

Dakin and Diana exchanged books. He read her autobiography, *Too Much, Too Soon,* written with Gerold Frank, and she read his book, *Nails of Protest,* written with Walter Stewart, a critical comparison of modern Catholic and Protestant beliefs. Dakin is now working on his second book, *Burma Conversion,* a description of his conversion to Catholicism. Following in his grandfather's tradition, in addition to full-time work as an attorney, Dakin delivers lectures on religious topics. He also addresses civic groups on international affairs and has developed a program based on Tom's works called "An Evening with Tennessee Williams," for charitable, university and civic organizations. He gives instruction in the Catholic faith at the Catholic Information Center in St. Louis, usually permitted only to priests.

After reading Dakin's book, Diana attended Mass for the first time in twenty years, having felt outside the church, she said, since her first marriage. While she was in St. Louis, Dakin introduced her to a friend of his, Father Jerry Wilkerson, whom Diana allowed to hear her confession, an act which officially restored her to good standing as a Catholic. Thereafter she referred to herself and Dakin as "fellow fish" or "fish-eaters."

Diana wrote Dakin a number of letters in which she was quite frank about her feelings for his brother, although Tom never looked on her as anything but a friend. Just after she was introduced to Dakin in Chicago at Henrici's Restaurant on a Sunday morning after the opening, Diana wrote:

DEAR DAKIN—

The abbreviation (Dake) you so kindly said I could use will come in time—it took quite some weeks before I could call your brother Tom. Sunday was a joyous, glorious day— You were a complete surprise (as was Tom). You emanate warmth, goodness, and love of your fellow man. I have not arrived at the last category yet, but with God's help I will achieve it. I hope you liked me as much as I did you. One thing, the most important thing, that we share is our love of Tom. I don't mean this in a sacrilegious way, but *he is* my savior on earth. Through him I went on the wagon —I had to re-learn Blanche after having played it with my dead husband three years before—I told myself I had to stop drinking if I wanted to really be a *good* Blanche. Well, "Streetcar" won—then came "Cat" last summer and then this last fall the most heartbreaking point in my whole life —when Kazan wouldn't even give me a reading for "Ariadnee." It's too long to tell in a letter—but from the end of September up to the opening in Philadelphia of "Sweet Bird" I thought I had a chance. My hatred for Kazan burns black—if he had not wanted to play Svengali with Miss Page I would have done it—the woman is *me*— as I was—*Finished* at 36—I was! If I had been given a reading it would have been mine—Kazan could have started my life in November—now it will be a few months—it is hard to forgive a man who delays your *true* re-birth. But as in the book of Job Love conquers all. My idolatry of Tom chases the black thoughts away—for awhile—but they come back. So many nights I go to the theatre here and I think of her in New York. She's in the dressing room making up for my part. I also comfort myself that Thank God I'm playing *Williams*—that is the one thing that makes this *waiting bearable.* I will pray for London. We have so much to talk about. Naturally when Tom gets here he will call you—perhaps then we can see when I can come and see you—I do so want to meet your mother. Naturally I have heard much of her—regards and love to your wife. That book of mine is ordered from New York. Please remember as you read it *that woman is dead!*—Tom certainly can't find any connection between me and, as he says, *"that woman"!*—I will read your book the minute it arrives. It will help me I'm sure.

A bientot

Bless you

DIANA

P.S. I enclose two clips to prove my point about Tom. He got me those notices. Because the parts he writes make a *good* actress *great,* and a great actress—well who knows?

After her visit to St. Louis, Diana wrote Dakin the following letter, in which "Sister Woman" refers to Joyce.

DAKIN DEAR—

What a wonderful day and a half. There was only one sad moment when we said goodnight—I wish we could have talked alone—but we will—there is a wistful quality about you—a certain sadness that I understand so well. But you are doubly lucky to have found God and a life-mate. That's quite a woman—strong, compassionate, understanding and what a sense of humor! We had such a nice chat Monday afternoon. You are truly blessed. I have no adjective for Mrs. Williams. The woman I saw was 50 mentally and physically—so full of vitality—and again the sense of humor —the life-saver for all of us. I don't suppose there are very many happy people in this terrible world, but her philosophy is so fine—so accepting of all things—good and bad. How I wish it were possible to get a companion for her. She loves all her possessions so—and the smell of the wet grass outside her window—all those things are so important in late years. I hope it will be possible for you and Sister Woman and Father to assist that fabulous mother. But we have so much to talk about—just us—in the meantime we must keep Tom in our hearts and prayers. I long for him to come home. I'm glad the handsome, laughing face has not been impaired—Thank God!

Write when you have a moment—Love to all—

DIANA

In addition to her newly rekindled religious faith, Diana also placed confidence in the stars and often consulted her astrologer who, at one point, predicted Diana would appear in London as the "Ariadnee" of *Sweet Bird,* a part she so desperately coveted. She wrote Dakin of this.

DEAREST DAKIN—

Number one—Tom is back. Heard through Gilbert Maxwell, our mutual friend, who is lunching with him today. The astrologer was amazing. Everything on myself tallied with what the woman said 3 years ago in New York. Not knowing anything of "Bird," she said I would be going to England possibly November—to do a play by the man who had changed my life (all this before she knew it was Tennessee). Among the highlights of *his* chart—something he wants more than anything in the world in 1964—could that be the Nobel Prize? Probably! The more I think about Tom (and that's most of waking and *sleeping* time) I think it's going to come sooner. Before I met him in January I used to think the *big* one will come within eight years. After I met him I narrowed it to five—and she says 1964. Well, if you believe in the stars as I do—then that's it! I'm deeply sorry I won't see you. For such a short space of time I really feel very close—I may unburden myself to you from time to time—brother—I hope you won't mind. I hope Tom comes to Key West. Then when we close, I plan to go to Cuba and *fish,* fish, fish—and lie in the sun. Do you know I haven't had a vacation since 1940? The time I didn't work during those hazy years could hardly be classed vacation! So now I'm going.

I have a friend of twenty years standing who turned up after the matinee today who lives in the Virgin Islands and he asked me to come there from Cuba. I must read "Ariadnee" for Tom and get this "Bird" bit settled. I have lived with this unsettled thing like a cancer—not pressing too much. Because I felt Tom wouldn't understand the desire to play one part when I was already in one of his plays. The whole "Bird" story must come out—and in Key West I will be able to quietly take him aside—away and alone—and tell him the *full* story. Tell Father Wilkerson I am sending the book as soon as they arrive—should he wonder. Naturally I will call you to say good-bye before I leave Chicago. Pray for Tom—love to Sister Woman and your divine mother—

Much love to you dear fellow fish—
DIANA

Not long after that, Diana died tragically, in January, 1960, of a heart attack brought on by too many sleeping pills. Tom flew to New York to arrange the funeral since no one else seemed interested enough to do so. He ordered a blanket of spring violets as he had done for his grandfather and asked the Reverend Sidney Lanier, of St. Thomas' Episcopal Church on Fifth Avenue, New York, who was a cousin, to conduct services.

Diana had hoped in vain Tom would marry her as once perhaps Hazel Kramer did. Tom told me Hazel visited him after the success of his plays and confessed her marriage was a miserable one. She has since died.

Tom has said to me he never intends to marry. I once remonstrated, "Now you've made a lot of money and it's time for you to get married."

"Mother, that's one thing I'm not going to do," he said. "I have no idea of ever marrying. I couldn't bear to make some woman unhappy. I'd be writing and forget all about her." That I believe, for Tom will go off somewhere when he starts on a play and no one hears from him for months.

Once I chided both my sons because I had no grandchildren. (Dakin has since adopted two baby girls when they were each five days old, Anne Lanier, named for Tom, and Francesca Maria, named for my mother). Tom looked aggrieved when I said this, so I reassured him, "Tom, your plays are my grandchildren."

Tom made no secret of his decision to try psychoanalysis in late 1957, which was the year his father died. Many of his friends, including Irene Selznick, Elia Kazan and Marlon Brando, had been urging him for a long time to consult a psychoanalyst. He told Don Ross in a very detailed interview

240

published in the New York *Herald Tribune*, January 5, 1958, that he had started analysis, saying, "I think if this analysis works, it will open some doors for me."

He was spending fifty minutes a day, five days a week, in the office of a leading New York psychoanalyst. Tom informed Mr. Ross he did not intend becoming a permanent patient but figured he would give it up in a year or so. He had tried to solve his problems without help for years, he explained, but then suddenly decided to try analysis when *Orpheus Descending* drew poor notices and closed after a short run in early 1957. He felt "terribly shocked" at its failure because he had invested so much of himself in it and worked longer at it than any other play (about sixteen years). He believed it possessed lyricism, a feeling of tenderness and an attempt to understand people, and yet the critics did not like it.

He blamed himself, not the critics or public, for its failure and associated the failure, he said, "with the extreme difficulty I had in writing it. 'Orpheus' brought all my problems to a head. I knew I must find help or crack up, so I went to an analyst and poured out all my troubles. I felt the most enormous relief."

Mr. Ross asked whether Tom thought analysis would have a disastrous effect on his writing. Tom replied, "I do not believe this. If I did, I would never have gone into it. I would not hazard or risk my ability to work. I would have preferred to remain confused and troubled. I'm very happy that I had writing as an outlet to my reaction to experience. Otherwise, I would have gone really off my trolley. That's the only thing that saved me."

While in analysis, Tom wrote *Suddenly Last Summer,* one of his most violent plays. He told Mr. Ross that although it was shocking, he felt, in a sense, it was a catharsis, a final fling of violence.

"If I am no longer disturbed myself, I will deal less with disturbed people and with violent material," Tom said. "I don't regret having concerned myself with such people, because I think that most of us are disturbed. But I think I have pretty well explored that aspect of life and that I may be repeating myself as a writer. It would be good if I could write with serenity."

From his early childhood, Tom said, he had been neurotic. He was bothered increasingly by periods of panic during which he feared he would die of a heart attack. He also suffered from claustrophobia and was unable to sit in the middle of a theatre with people crowded around him (I don't think I could either, if my play were being presented a few feet away for the world either to tear apart or praise).

He was afraid to walk down a street unless there were a bar in sight, he admitted, not that he took a drink every block but because he needed the assurance that if panic seized him, he could buy a drink, the only act that would calm him at such moments of distress.

He told Mr. Ross that, after six months in analysis, the spells of fear were less frequent—he had only two, whereas formerly he might have suffered as many as twenty during this period. The claustrophobia, too, had subsided. His apartment in the East Sixties had a very small elevator, big enough for only one passenger, which formerly gave him the feeling of being in an "upended coffin," he said. Now he could step into it without a twinge of the old torment.

At the end of one year with the psychoanalyst, Tom wrote Dakin and me telling how he felt.

DEAR MOTHER AND DAKIN:

I've been shamefully remiss about writing you, because of the terrible pressures of my life, having to meet so many demands on my time and not having the energy to meet them. I'm getting away again, Sunday, to Florida, as I felt myself reaching the point of exhaustion. Dr. —— opposes the move but I think I have to consider my physical state as well as what he thinks is of psychological value, i.e., staying with him in New York. I respect the doctor and feel he's done me some good but his fees are too high and if I continue analysis next Fall, it will probably be with

242

someone younger and less expensive to go to. Or maybe I won't feel the need of continuing it at all.

Rose was better than I'd ever seen her when I went out the Sunday after Easter. She had taken off most of the excess weight and was spending a good deal of time out-doors on the beautiful grounds which are especially nice this time of year. She was in excellent spirits and looking quite pretty again.

They've been doing a series of articles about me, in fact about the whole Williams-Dakin tribe, in the New York "Post." I am saving the articles which contain some very good family pictures and will see that you get a set of them. Of course you could also order a complete set directly from the newspaper, in New York. Liebling says he's saving a set for you, too. They get a little too personal, and very inaccurate about my wealth, saying that I make $400,000 a year and have made a total of five million dollars. Naturally calls started coming in from people wanting to borrow money, even a request from the Key West library for five thousand to build a new room. I have asked the newspaper to print a correction on these figures which they have promised to do.

"Look" magazine is also doing a feature story with pictures. A reporter and photographer followed me to Florida on my last trip down there and took many shots at the successful opening of "Orpheus" in Coconut Grove and pictures in Key West. I don't know why I'm getting all this publicity right now, it isn't my idea of fun.

"Garden District" is going to shut down for the summer: the business recession has hit the theatre pretty bad, even Inge's play is under capacity and off-Broadway is hit even worse. The economic condition of the country has deteriorated more than is commonly suspected, I'm afraid.

I hope you're at last having some sunshine in St. Louis. It's warm and sunny today in New York and I have a little balcony facing south where I can sit out and sun-bathe a bit, if I ever have the time to.

Any possibility of your getting to New York this Spring? I will be in Florida till about May 18th, when I have to come back for a reading, a benefit reading for a friend who had a stroke and is penniless. She and her husband were recently thrown out of Morocco because of the political disturbances going on there.

Love,
Tom

Tom told me he thought the year of psychoanalysis a total loss, that it cost a lot and he got little out of it. "And I don't want to spend the rest of my life lying on a couch," he added.

Another time he wrote to me about the psychoanalyst, "He hit me where it hurt most. He said I wrote cheap melodramas and nothing else."

I think perhaps this is the way some, who do not understand the life of others or their own, may feel about Tom's writing.

Actually, the only psychiatrist in whom I believe is our Lord, Jesus Christ. If you follow His teachings, I don't think you'll go far amiss. My father often said the hardest thing one can be is a Christian; many call themselves Christians who have ruined the very name, committing terrible crimes in the name of Christianity.

Tom's psychoanalyst eventually left New York to take an important position elsewhere and Tom said to me, "I'm alive and he's gone." I do not know if Tom thought perhaps he had died, since his name was no longer in the Manhattan telephone directory, or if he meant just gone from New York.

I was amused to read in one newspaper where Tom was questioning a very calm friend to find out if he were neurotic and the friend answered in the negative to all Tom's inquiries. No, he did not have any bad dreams. No, he never felt tense, always relaxed. No, he had no fears, never worried.

Tom stared at him for a long time with his gentle gray eyes, then said seriously, "Man, you're far gone!"

I like this story. It sounds like Tom, who believes you need a feeling of tension and insecurity to propel you toward any kind of progress. After he first achieved fame he began to be indifferent to people, and cynical. He seemed to have a fear of success, at one time even referring to it as a catastrophe.

He started to suspect people of hypocrisy. He has always been terribly impatient of what he considers inane flattery, although deeply appreciative of true admiration. Once, he said, he decided to have an eye operation mainly because it gave him an excuse to withdraw from the world behind a gauze mask. He found the friends who visited him in the hospital no longer seemed insincere now that he was in pain, their voices once again held the sound of honesty and understanding.

Tom believes it is only in work that an artist can find reality and satisfaction, "for the actual world is less intense than the world of his invention and consequently his life, without recourse to violent disorder, does not seem very substantial," he has said.

Another time he called security "a kind of death." He added, however, that it was never altogether too late to escape it "unless you embrace the Bitch Goddess, as William James called her, with both arms and find in her smothering caresses exactly what the homesick little boy in you always wanted, absolute protection and utter effortlessness."

After his year of analysis, Tom wrote his first full-length comedy, *Period of Adjustment*. All his plays possess a comic spirit, part of their appeal, but this was the first to be based on one humorous situation after another, at the same time offering the profound characterizations for which he is noted.

Tom had fun during the play's tryout in Miami.

DEAR MOTHER:

I have been finishing a new play (a *comedy!*) which I am going to try out at the Coconut Grove Playhouse with an all-Broadway cast. We start rehearsals December 18th and open the 29th and I'm going to direct it myself so this month is going to be pretty lively for me. I do hope you will fly down here for Xmas. And see the opening. Everyone seems to feel it will be a happy event and our cast is wonderful: Barbara Baxley who played the gypsy's daughter in "Camino Real," Cliff Robertson who played the male lead in "Orpheus Descending," and three other first-rate players. I think I'll enjoy directing and perhaps get values

245

out of the play that otherwise wouldn't be gotten. Maybe Dakin and his Joyce could come down, too, if they're not spending Xmas in Texas. Marian and Mrs. Black are longing for you to appear on the local scene and I think we'd all have a nice holiday together. This will be better, in many ways, than my attempting to come up to Saint Louis and get Rose down there. I notice that Rose does better if she leads a quiet, routine life, since she has her dreamworld which appears to be peaceful. So please make plans, and reserve your plane-space now, since there may be a lot of holiday traveling. After the play opens I will still have about two weeks of rest before I go to New York for the start of rehearsals on the Broadway production of "Sweet Bird."

I enjoyed Dakin's visit, he looked fine and has a fine air of maturity and poise about him.

Miss Brinda had another heat-stroke in Key West, it was terribly hot there, but she survived it again. She had the remarkable sense to jump into the bath-tub and stand there under the faucet. I mean lie under it, as she was just about "out." The faucet was dripping and the veterinary says this probably saved her life, as no one was in the house with her at the time. She had a 106 fever, received penicillin to prevent pneumonia and was rubbed with ice till she got back on her bow-legs, and is now as well as usual.—Key West is too hot for her. So was Rome last summer. The poor thing leads a dog's life!

Wire or call me collect soon as you've made your plans about Xmas. I want you to be my guest here.

Much love,

Tom

Tom became involved with several of his movies when *Period of Adjustment* was completed.

4/6/59

Dear Mother:

Marian Vaccaro and I are back in Havana for a week or ten days before I fly to Europe to participate in the filming of "Suddenly Last Summer." I will fly over on April 22nd

246

and remain over till late in May when they start shooting the film of "Orpheus Descending" on Long Island and on location in Mississippi, with Brando and Magnani.

I hope you'll feel well enough to come up for a visit with me this summer: you might enjoy the fresh sea-air of Long Island, in some nice summer hotel. Dakin doesn't think you ought to take trips, he feels that they are a strain on your nerves. But I am not so sure about that. I think you need a little change now and then. What do you think about it?

I'll call you from New York before I fly to Europe this month. Sam Spiegel, the film-producer, has a yacht on the Mediterranean which he has offered me while I am finishing work on the film-script.

Marian and Mrs. Black send you their love.

Much from me, too,
Tom

How are the jonquils in your garden this Spring? And the birds? You haven't written about them yet!

I was amused and touched that, in the midst of his frenetic, fascinating life, Tom would think of the jonquils and birds in my garden.

16.

"Ye Devil's in Ye Hempe"

WHAT will Tom think of my writing a book? He's gone through so much, I guess he can take this.

Tom never complains. If he feels blue, he says nothing, just won't write, unlike some who always insist on sending you all the bad news. That was never Tom.

I worry about his working so hard and reading so much with sight only in one eye, and have told him so. His answer is typically Tom.

"Mother, I think my other eye is all the stronger because I can only see out of the one," he says.

He and I are close even though we are not demonstrative and do not tell each other everything, just as he and Dakin are very close. In one letter he wrote, "Will Dakin come for the opening and party afterwards? I hope so, it would not seem like an opening without him."

I was delighted recently when a friend told me she had seen Tom at his home in Key West and he had praised me all evening, ending by claiming I had been the prettiest girl in Mississippi. He never said anything complimentary like that in my presence. In return compliment, the only feature I don't like about Tom is his mustache which he first grew because he believed it made him look older. If he ever sports a beard, I'll disown him.

Tom usually gives me parties when I attend his openings. Because of Father's death, I missed the premiere of *Cat*. Tom kept phoning, asking when I would come to New York and I kept postponing the visit, still grieving for Father. Finally he said he intended to give a party in my honor before he left the city and warned, "There's so little time, Mother, if you don't come immediately, I'll have to invite everybody by telegram."

He rented the St. Regis Roof for the party. He must have asked everyone in New York in the theatre profession, judging by the number who crowded into those rooms. I didn't realize how many friends he had. I talked all afternoon, mostly about Tom, but then I'm never happier than when I am talking about him. He claims he likes to have me at parties because I chatter away.

"After the first few cocktails, everybody collapses and has nothing to say, but Mother talks merrily on," Tom says.

He and Dakin usually watch over me like hawks, making sure I have only one drink, as though I didn't have the wit to know how much Mother could take!

One woman at this party told me later she was amazed to find me such a center of attention. "Why, at one point, I saw you sitting on the couch with a number of attractive young men at your feet," she said in surprise.

I laughed, recalling the scene. I had felt weary after standing for hours and sank down on a settee for a minute. Two young women were occupying the rest of it. One of them, wearing a big, broad-brimmed hat, said to me sweetly, "You're Mrs. Williams, aren't you?"

"Yes," I said, smiling back.

249

"I'm Marilyn Monroe," she introduced herself and, gesturing to the other young woman, "This is Gloria Vanderbilt."

All at once came a rush of men to the settee. But not to sink at my feet! They wanted to see the pretty face under that wide-brimmed hat. I had been getting the credit for Marilyn and Gloria's admirers, just as years before in Port Gibson, I had received credit for the other young women's gentleman callers.

I have seen less and less of Tom as he has written more and more plays. He does not write many letters now, although I just received one from Tangiers where he is spending a few months working on another play. He invited me over, adding as a postscript that he knows he is "the worst son in the world." Because he has so much writing to do, I don't expect letters.

He has not remembered Mother's Day in several years. The last time he did, he sent a lovely azalea plant. But he never forgets Christmas. Last year he picked out a very handsome bag and two scarves that blended with the bag and with each other, one to go around my neck and the other for the breast pocket of my coat.

Although he rarely sets foot in the house, it is full of him—his old books, a large amount of writing, and some paintings he once did. I have welcomed the visits of Andreas L. Brown, of the faculty of San Diego State College, San Diego, California, who, as the authorized bibliographer of Tom's writings, has the responsibility of locating everything Tom has written that can be found. A significant number of important items have been discovered through Mr. Brown's search in the many places in the country where Tom has lived. Previously, much of the material stored in my home had been kept in old boxes, desk drawers, trunks and suitcases. The manuscripts, drafts and letters of Tom's have now been sorted, indexed and filed by Mr. Brown. His work will no doubt result in the preservation of a good deal of material that might eventually have been lost.

One of many poems which Mr. Brown unearthed is an early one which I particularly like. It refers, I believe, to Tom's grandmother, rather than me.

DEAR SILENT GHOST...

I see you scraping carrots by the stove
Or spicing meats with cinnamon and clove....

Through memory your patient hands are spun
Lifting white curtains to the morning sun

Or beckoning at twilight from the stair....
I feel your rain-washed, lemon scented hair

Cool on my cheeks, heated and flushed from play
In April woods, some far, nostalgic day....

But where, Dear Silent Ghost, are put away
The wise and lovely things you used to say?

Behind the stove or underneath the stair...
In lemon scent or rain-washed April air?

THOMAS LANIER WILLIAMS

Sometimes I think Tom feels I am his severest critic. He told a reporter, "My mother reads every line I write but she doesn't approve of it."

I *do* approve, of all he has written, although I feel he could have omitted a few vulgarities without harming his work as a whole. But he says that is the way people talk and I suppose it is part of the character he is creating. And perhaps this is just a mother speaking.

Tom writes as he has to write—this is the artist. Some of my friends suggest dramatic experiences in their lives as material for Tom, saying, "It would make a marvelous play!"

I tell them, "Tom writes what is in him. You might as well ask Picasso to paint like Rembrandt."

I, above all others except Tom, know what he had to go through to be able to write as he wished and I would never stand in the way of his freedom to do so. I don't think I ever have. I would not presume to criticize anything he has written even though I might not approve of a small part of it.

Though I admit I did feel tempted, when someone said he was working on a play about an aging actress, to protest, "No, Tom—not another aging actress!" Come to think of it, the heroine of his first prize-winning play, *The Magic Tower,* was an ex-actress.

To me, Tom chooses the crystal-clear word to write with deep discernment about people and with great sympathy for them. I don't know another contemporary writer with such compassion. His plays are rich and full and sometimes it is rather exhausting to see one. You feel used up because they are so packed with emotion. I tell my friends as they set off for one of his plays, "Take your smelling salts."

Often you have to see a play two or three times to understand all Tom is saying. I think this is proof of a profound play, to enjoy it the second or third time. I am always amazed by drama critics who rush out after seeing a play only once and then write hurriedly of their first impressions. Tom never writes on the surface; he has not once written a play for entertainment. Rather, he writes for himself, as he has said.

Just after *Streetcar* opened, Robert C. Lewis of *The New York Times* Magazine, who had known Tom in St. Louis, interviewed him. Mr. Lewis asked Tom to explain why he wrote the play.

"Perhaps my unconscious could tell," said Tom. "I can't."

He was quoted in *Vogue,* March, 15, 1951, as saying, "I prefer a play not to be a noose but a net with fairly wide meshes. So many of its instants of revelation are wayward flashes, not part of the plan of an author but struck accidentally off, and perhaps these are closest to being a true celebration of the inebriate god."

He writes to escape madness, he has noted, and to escape security, and perhaps he also writes to escape the threat of death. "We are all desperately afraid of death, much more than we dare admit even to ourselves," he once declared.

Perhaps fear of death is his obsession, he added, "because years ago when I recovered from that long siege of illness my heart was in very bad shape and I was afraid to walk down the street for fear that it would stop beating. The phrase 'drop dead' was something I lived with night and day." Fear of death was also an obsession in the life of Tom's father.

Death is the ultimate violence. "There is a lot of violence in my work, but there is a lot of violence in my life," says Tom.

There was violence, indeed, in the air around him as he grew up, both open and undercurrent.

He has said he could not handle people in routine situations, that he must find characters who "correspond to my own tensions." One time he remarked that "something violent always happens before I can finish the first act. A miner falls down a shaft or a fugitive from justice shoots it out with the FBI. I had never been able to avoid the undeniable fascination of violence until I wrote *The Glass Menagerie*."

Tom is so mild in looks and manner you would never suspect a violent feeling stirs in him. Yet violence is the way we fight fear and Tom has said he always had to contend with the "adversary of fear" which gave him "a certain tendency toward an atmosphere of hysteria and violence in my writing, an atmosphere that has existed in it since the beginning." Tom has been one to evade and avoid actual violence whenever he could.

He believes a writer's "safety" lies in one of two things, either "living in a remote place, particularly on an island in the tropics, or in a fugitive way of life, running like a fox from place to place." He has tried both from time to time and perhaps has achieved a measure of safety this way.

One critic said Tom was "caught in the trauma of his boyhood" and could write better if he were free of it. He accused Tom of "inexorably re-creating the pattern of his trauma, unable to break through to adult reality. . . . That is why the characters he hates or fears or despises always win, while those to whom his sympathy is drawn invariably go down."

My answer is that I feel Tom could not write any better. He is the greatest playwright of our age, as is.

Why did Tom turn into a playwright, rather than a novelist? He has given us the answer. He said that for him there was no other medium that was even relatively satisfactory, that he felt there was a lack of vitality in the written word. He conceived of things "visually in sound and color and movement," he explained. To him, writing was "something more organic than words, something closer to being and action."

"I want to work more and more with a more plastic theatre

253

than the one that I have so far. I have never for one moment doubted that there are people—millions—to say things to. We come to each other, gradually, but with love. It is the short reach of my arms that hinders, not the length and multiplicity of theirs. With love and with honesty, the embrace is inevitable." This is Tom speaking in "The Past, Present and Perhaps," the Introduction for a book of two plays, *Battle of Angels* and *Orpheus Descending*, published by New Directions.

No matter how Tom feels about psychological security, he certainly never feels secure financially. He always believes he is headed straight for the poorhouse, that he will die a pauper. I can't blame him, since he went through such trying times for so many years.

He and I both feel the income tax structure is not very fair to writers who suddenly are successful and must pay a huge tax on a large income. Some allowance should be made for the years of poverty through which many writers struggle when they may not earn a dollar, years such as Tom suffered.

Once I asked, "Where are all those millions you are supposed to have made?"

"They're at Cape Canaveral, shooting up at the moon," he said philosophically.

I feel Tom has shown great courage throughout his life, a courage that brought him through the critical attack of diphtheria and paralysis, a courage that comes out in the power of his plays. Irene Selznick has said of Tom that while he is outwardly a "shy" man, his "almost bland manner" masks an inner intensity.

I think of Tom as a quiet volcano. He doesn't show the seething interior, he just goes to the typewriter and it erupts in the fire of his words.

I think I understand him better than he understands me. Tom may not realize I often pretended to feel gay when I was in anguish. I do not think it fair of parents to take out their feelings on children; I once remember reading in Tom's boyhood diary, "Horrible day—Mother's sick," and I felt ashamed. So perhaps to Tom I appeared silly in the face of tragedy. But I believe it would have been far more grim had I not pretended things weren't as bad as they seemed. All of us are actors to the degree we must be to survive.

Tom possesses the valiant spirit of his Dakin ancestors as well as of the Williamses. The Dakin motto is quite fitting, I feel, to Tom's life—*Stryke Dakyns, Ye Devil's in Ye Hempe.*

Year after year in his plays Tom keeps striking a blow at the devil in all our "hempes," the wind of savage, primitive passion that tangles the ropes of control, keeping us from serene, thoughtful lives. This, I believe, is part of Tom's greatness.

I laughed to read a note in one of Walter Winchell's columns (I hate to think of trying to keep up with news of Tom without Mr. Winchell's help):

> Fame Must Be Wonderful Dept.:
> Tennessee Williams, author of two
> Pulitzer prize plays, has had a new
> pinball machine named after him.

I thought how much Cornelius would have enjoyed that. After all, there is not too much difference between a pinball machine and a poker game.